RESEARCH IN
SOCIAL MOVEMENTS,
CONFLICTS
AND CHANGE

Volume 3 • 1980

RESEARCH IN SOCIAL MOVEMENTS, CONFLICTS AND CHANGE

A Research Annual

Editor: LOUIS KRIESBERG
Department of Sociology
Syracuse University

VOLUME 3 • 1980

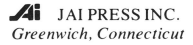 JAI PRESS INC.
Greenwich, Connecticut

CONTENTS

LIST OF CONTRIBUTORS

Howard M. Bahr
Department of Sociology
Brigham Young University

Otomar J. Bartos
Department of Sociology
University of Colorado,
Boulder

Margaret Braungart
Upstate Medical Center
State University of
New York, Buffalo

Richard Braungart
Department of Sociology
Syracuse University

Theodore Caplow
Department of Sociology
University of Virginia

Peter Dreier
Department of Sociology
Tufts University

Dina Goren
Communications Institute
The Hebrew University

Louis Kriesberg
Department of Sociology
Syracuse University

James H. Laue
Center for Metropolitan Studies
University of Missouri

Geoffrey K. Leigh
Department of Sociology
Brigham Young University

John McCarthy
Department of Sociology
The Catholic University of
America

Daniel Monti
Center for Metropolian Studies
University of Missouri

Wing-Cheung Ng
Department of Sociology
University of California, Riverside

Anthony Oberschall
Department of Sociology
Vanderbilt University

Albert Szymanski
Department of Sociology
University of Oregon

James L. Wood
Department of Sociology
San Diego State University

Mayer Zald
Department of Sociology
University of Michigan

INTRODUCTION

This third volume of the series, *Research in Social Movements, Conflicts and Change,* expands the range of topics, theoretical approaches, and research methods included in the first two volumes. The goal, as in the earlier volumes, is to present a diverse set of contributions. This diversity, I hope, will help us all to see links and gain insights that a narrower range would obscure. Given the resulting heterogenity of the contributions, I will not try to subsume all the papers within a grand theory. I will, however, consider two related issues and discuss how the contributions assist our understanding of the issues and our ability to cope with them.

One fundamental issue in the study of conflicts and social movements and even of social change, is the degree to which their sources and course rest on "objective" realistic conditions or have subjective autonomy. The issue, in the case of social conflicts, is sometimes phrased in questioning whether a conflict is "realistic" and has an objective basis or rather arises from displaced hostility or misunderstandings or another interest not reflected in the ostensible matter in contention. Which approach a person takes to conflicts clearly affects the person's prescriptions about ways of pursuing, ending, and managing conflicts.

In the past, an important tradition in the study of social conflicts, movements, and change, stressed the psychological theories of displacement and collective behavioral approaches suggesting loss of personal and social control. But in recent decades, we have seen a shift toward attention to the calculative nature of partisans in conflicts and social movements and in efforts to induce social change. This may reflect a general theoretical shift but it certainly also arises out of social scientists' sympathy for the recent efforts to make changes through conflicts and social movements.

A related issue pertains to the ability to manage conflicts and to direct social change. Sociologists, as well as other social scientists, have often been concerned with controlling conflicts so as to minimize the violence and destruction frequently associated with them. They have also been concerned with the possibility of directing social change to improve the human conditions for oppressed or deprived humans. How one views the basis for conflicts obviously has implications for how one would propose to manage or resolve social conflicts and to direct social change.

I think that the issues of realism and unrealism and of managing conflicts and efforts to induce change provide a useful context to consider the diverse contributions in this volume. I will briefly introduce each paper and suggest ways in which it contributes to our understanding of these issues. This is not the major theme of each paper, but it will provide a vehicle to usefully link them.

McCarthy and Zald examine the important and surprisingly neglected topic of competition and cooperation among organizations within a social movement (cf. Carden, 1978). They draw particularly from the literature on inter-organizational relations and in conjunction with studies of social movement organizations (SMOs), propose 14 hypotheses about relations among SMOs.

This kind of analysis indicates one possible source of unrealistic conflict and social change efforts not based on objective conditions. Perhaps SMO leaders are responding to each other rather than to the presumably primary adversary or to the conditions whose correction is the SMO's goal. Organizational survival and maintenance necessarily are important to SMO leaders. As we shall note in regard to several contributions, we may usefully conceive of these matters as an outcome of the interlocking nature of social conflicts, movements, and changes. Since such efforts cross-cut and encompass each other in many ways, people disagree about which ones are central and which are peripheral. To call a conflict or social change struggle unrealistic, often means that the observer regards another one as more fundamental.

Wood and Ng analyze data from surveys of University of California, Berkely students and their parents, conducted in 1968, and draw upon other studies of student activism during the 1960's. They compare the socialization and the conflict of generation approaches and find that socialization into unconventional families was clearly more significant; it was particularly important at the beginning of the 1960's and the early stages of protest. In addition, situational factors, such as university size, interacted with background.

Studies of participation in social movements and conflicts offer relevant information about the realistic character of those efforts. Is there evidence that the kind of people who participate are displacing feelings? If student activists tend to have been in conflict with their own parents, this might indicate that hostile feelings were displaced or generalized to an external authority or the larger society. The Wood and Ng analysis does not support this interpretation. Rather we see evidence of socialization into different values as a basis for dissensual conflict (Kriesberg, 1973).

Oberschall presents an elegantly simple theory of conflict group formation and of loosely structured collective action. The theory consists of a few elements: the probability of success, the number of demonstrators, and the anticipated net benefit for an individual to join. He elaborates these elements and their relations and suggests, among other deductions, an explanation for the clustering of collective actions in space and time. Oberschall applies his theory to the 1970 protests against the South African tennis team's participation in the Davis Cup semifinals in Nashville, Tennessee.

Oberschall's theory and findings add several important considerations to our understanding of the realistic character of social conflict and movements. From the subjective point of view of the actors, what is calculated as realistic varies with the stage of collective action and the magnitude of the protesting group. (The role of the initial activists is different from that of the later joiners and this relates to the Wood and Ng findings about the increased importance of situational factors in accounting for participation in later stages of the student movements in the 1960's.) Oberschall's findings about the importance of pre-existing networks helps explain who becomes involved in collective action (Leahy and Mazur, 1978); it also affects the mobilization of resources and hence chances of success. The findings indicate that an important component in accounting for participation in collective action is the belief that such action can be effective (Kriesberg, 1973). Underlying conflicts of interest and values bettwen groups will not surface if redressing or reducing grievances seem impossible to the dissatisfied.

Bartos reports on the results of a series of experimental negotiations. He is one of the few sociologists working in this tradition, although it is extensively pursued by social psychologists, psychologists, and some political scientists (Druckman, 1977 and Rubin and Brown, 1975).

Bartos presents a simple theoretical statement from which he deduces several hypotheses. Among the several findings, I note two here: (1) the size of the negotiator's concession is not related to the size of his opponent's concession and (2) the tougher the negotiator, the smaller tends to be his concessions.

These findings suggest that another aspect of unrealistic conflicts is important, at least in such experimental conditions: adversaries tend to act from internal reasons, not responsively to their opponent's actions. It may be that once a conflict is entered, adversaries (particularly naive ones?) pursue it with relatively little attention to the actions of their negotiating partners. Such internally driven actions would generate conflicts which appear to be unrealistic from an observer's perspective since they are not guided by the ostensible external issue in contention. Perhaps as a conflict endures or as the negotiators gain experience and insight they may learn to pay attention to the adversary and adjust themselves accordingly. If so, this suggests that training of negotiators could contribute to conflict management.

In my contribution to this volume I examine six ways in which conflicts are interlocked; they may be (1) connected in a series or nested in each other through time, (2) converging—as the parties nest in wider and wider circles, (3) superimposed one over the other—linking many contentious issues, (4) cross-cutting, (5) internal to one of the contending parties, and (6) concurrent so that one party is engaged in a conflict with a third party—independently of its conflict with the primary adversary. I argue that partisans in a struggle shift their views about which of the many fights in which they are engaged is the primary one. Such shifts are important in helping to understand the rapid escalations and de-escalations which occur in the course of a struggle. The innumerable conflicts among the many governmental and nongovernmental parties in the Middle East are reviewed and their escalations and de-escalations are related to shifts in the set of interlocking fights.

The alternative views of which conflict is primary is one way of thinking about the way in which a struggle may be realistic to some observers or participants and not to others. All the interlocking conflicts exist, but only some of them are major organizing guides for conduct. This also suggests ways in which conflicts may be managed. Partisans or intermediaries may seek to alter the adversaries' view of which conflict is primary. For example, the partisans may come to see that they have a common adversary and hence have important mutual gains as well as differential wins and losses. If the outcomes they envisage include the change of high joint gains and the threat of severe joint losses, trying to win at the expense of the adversary will be less attractive.

Goren considers international conflict from another perspective. She critically examines the democratic model of news media performance in relation to foreign policy formation, exploring the various roles journalists play in this relationship. Goren concludes that news media persons do not assume an autonomous adversary posture. But the news media are not simply manipulated by government leaders. Sometimes they help draw attention to particular events and thus help establish priorities and sometimes they are used by one faction against another within the government establishment. More generally, the news media, by working within the pre-existing consensual framework, reinforce it—for the policy makers, too.

Conflict among large-scale units, such as countries, have special features relating to their degree of differentiation and the shared understandings through which mobilization occurs. Those shared values and beliefs result in ways of viewing adversaries and external issues that are imprecise and rigid. The lack of specificity and precision about a particular adversary and issue in dispute adds an unrealistic component to many conflicts. The pervasiveness of shared national identity is also relevant to the next contribution, by Dreier and Szymanski.

Dreier and Szymanski test Engel's and Lenin's labor aristocracy thesis that a small segment of the working class, because of its privileges, is relatively conservative. They examine a wide variety of data and conclude that the evidence does not support the thesis. For example, they found that workers in imperial-related activities did not earn relatively more than other workers nor do they differ in political opinions (e.g. attitudes about Communism or support for arms spending).

The pervasiveness of nationalism as a primary identification may overwhelm cross-cutting partisan groups such as transnational parties or economic classes. The ability of persons in national authority to mobilize support for policies they think correct is very great. An analyst may regard this ability as a contributor to unrealistic components to a struggle, insofar as the analyst does not regard all members of the country as having the same fundamental interests. On the other hand, the findings might be interpreted as indicating a basis for working class solidarity, within the U.S. society.

Braungart and Braungart analyze the relationship between multinational corporate investments and the characteristics of countries in which the investments are made. They found that U.S.-based foreign investments were particularly related to the gross national product and levels of communication of the recipient country. Non-U.S. based foreign investments are less related to national characteristics, perhaps because of the importance of previous colonial ties. In general, national development indicators are more closely related to multinational corporate expansion into core areas than into peripheral countries.

The expansion of multinational corporations (MNC) is one of the fundamental changes in the modern world. The findings suggest that the patterns of those changes are related to fundamental social forces. The forces are of such magnitude that it is difficult to alter the patterns: gradual modifications that do not radically alter the patterns are conceivable, but large-scale directed change would require altering forces which are not manipulable. Revolutionary leaders may try to introduce fundamental changes, but the implementation of planned change would face almost insurmountable difficulties. At a more local level, analyses of the relative bargaining power of a host government and a MNC can suggest more manipulable variables making directed change by groups of actors possible (Diamond, 1979).

Laue and Monti report about the various kinds of community intervention activities pertinent to school desegregation. In particular, they describe the variety of forms that monitoring has taken as a form of community intervention. Drawing from their experience, they examine in detail the course of monitoring school desegregation in two school districts in the St. Louis area. Their discussion documents one of the emerging ways in which intermediaries intervene in community conflicts in order to facilitate the constructive conduct of community conflicts (Wehr, 1979).

This report reveals the complexity of pursuing even one element of planned social change: monitoring the extent of change. The very monitoring of the change is intertwined with the efforts to bring about change. Laue and Monti provide insights into the ways monitoring can be more effectively conducted. Their analysis suggests that the efforts to plan change and to monitor it cannot be too distant from the underlying social forces affecting a social change.

Barr, Caplow, and Leigh report some of their findings from the replication of the Middletown studies originally done by Robert S. Lynd and Helen Merrell Lynd. Their analysis is based on field work conducted in 1976–78 and which updated the data collected earlier: in 1924–25 and in 1935. In this paper, Barr, Caplow, and Leigh use quantitative indicators of institutional modernization and attitude items which pertain to modernity. They found that Middletown students in 1977 are considerably more modern than were their grandparents in 1924. But what startled the authors was the persistence of widespread non-modern attitudes, e.g. with respect to science, religion, the mass media, and the role of women. On the whole, they were struck by the stability of life in Middletown and they conclude that the rate of social change has slowed considerably since the earlier studies.

It is worth noting that some attitudes seemed particularly unchanged and others were greatly changed. Among the items reported, secularization seemed least altered and openness to ideas the most. This may reflect the relevance of such items to the actual experiences of the people of Middletown. Assessment of religion is particularly difficult and therefore is particularly persistent (Kriesberg, 1970). But acceptance of the propriety of others holding different ideas is a likely consequence of becoming aware of others having different views; pluralism is a safe way of responding to differences of opinions and world views.

The Barr, Caplow, and Leigh findings, like those of Braungart and Braungart and of Laue and Monti, might be interpreted to suggest that social changes are dependent on large-scale and difficult to modify social forces. In Volume 1 of this series, several contributors reported on the effects of the protest and other actions of the 1960's (Carden, 1978; Lang and Lang, 1978; Fendrich and Kraus, 1978; and Oberschall, 1978). They documented some changes when studying the participants in the change efforts. When we consider changes from the perspective of the larger social structure, they seem to be much less. Large-scale changes probably must depend on massive intervention and ones whose direction are compatible with the underlying drift of social forces (Eisenstadt, 1978 and Collins, 1978).

ACKNOWLEDGMENTS

As in earlier volumes, the papers included in this volume were chosen from papers sent to me without being solicited as well as from papers submitted by persons whom I invited to contribute. In either case, I requested other researchers to review the papers to decide whether or not to include them in the volume and for suggestions about possible changes. I have been gratified by the readiness of so many people to help in this editorial task. I have drawn in particular upon colleagues at Syracuse University and upon previous contributors to the series. I wish to acknowledge the help of and to thank: Robert Bogdan, Richard Braungart, Daniel Chirot, James Fendrich, William Gamson, Kurt Lang, Jean Langlie, Chava Nachmias, John Nagle, Anthony Oberschall, and David Snyder.

REFERENCES

Carden, Maren Lockwood
  1978   "The Proliferations of a Social Movement," pp. 179–198, in Louis Kriesberg (Ed.) Research in Social Movements, Conflicts and Change. Greenwich, Ct.: JAI Press.
Collins, Randall
  1979   "Some Principles of Long-Term Social Change: The Territorial Power of States," pp. 1–34 in Louis Kriesberg (Ed.) Research in Social Movements, Conflicts and Change. Vol. 1 Greenwich, Ct.: JAI Press,
Diamond, Larry
  1979   "Power-Dependence Relations in the World System" pp. 233–258 in Louis Kriesberg (Ed.) Research in Social Movements, Conflicts and Change. Vol. 2 Greenwich, Ct.: JAI Press.
Druckman, Daniel (Ed.)
  1977   Negotiations: Social Psychological Perspectives. Beverly Hills, CA.: Sage Publications.
Eisenstadt, S. N.
  1978   "The Social Framework and Conditions of Revolution," pp. 85–104 in Louis Kriesberg (Ed.) Research in Social Movements, Conflicts and Change. Vol. 1 Greenwich, Ct.: JAI Press.
Fendrich, James M. and Ellis S. Krauss
  1978   "Student Activism and Adult Left-Wing Politics: A Causal Model Political Socialization for Black, White, and Japanese Students of the 1960's Generation," pp. 231–290 in Louis Kriesberg (Ed.) Research in Social Movements, Conflicts and Change. Vol. 1. Greenwich, Ct.: JAI Press.
Kriesberg, Louis
  1970   Mothers in Poverty: A Study of Fatherless Families. Chicago, Ill.: Aldine.
Kriesberg, Louis
  1973   The Sociology of Social Conflicts. Englewood Cliffs, N.J.: Prentice-Hall.
Lang, Kurt and Gladys Engel Lang
  1978   "Experiences and Ideology: The Influence of the Sixties on an Intellectual Elite," pp. 197–230 in Louis Kriesberg (Ed.) Research in Social Movements, Conflicts and Change. Vol. 1 Greenwich, Ct.: JAI Press.
Leahy, Peter and Allan Mazur
  1978   "A Comparison of Movements Opposed to Nuclear Power, Flouridation, and Abortion," pp. 143–154 in Louis Kriesberg (Ed.) Research in Social Movements, Conflicts and Change. Vol. 1. Greenwich, Ct.: JAI Press.
Oberschall, Anthony
  1978   "The Decline of the 1960's Social Movements," pp. 257–290 in Louis Kriesberg (Ed.) Research in Social Movements, Conflicts and Change. Vol. 1. Greenwich, Ct.: JAI Press.
Rubin, J. and B. Brown
  1975   The Social Psychology of Bargaining and Negotiation. New York: Academic Press.
Wehr, Paul
  1979   "New Techniques for Resolving Environmental Disputes," pp. 63–82 in Louis Kriesberg (Ed.) Research in Social Movements, Conflicts and Change. Vol. 2. Greenwich, Ct.: JAI Press.

SOCIAL MOVEMENT INDUSTRIES: COMPETITION AND COOPERATION AMONG MOVEMENT ORGANIZATIONS

Mayer N. Zald and John D. McCarthy

Although the literature on social movements is vast, there has been surprisingly little systematic analysis of the interaction of social movement organizations (but see James Q. Wilson, 1973; Zald and Ash, 1966; Gusfield, 1966; Nelson, 1974). Of course, practitioners and the practical theorists have developed strategies for interorganizational relations. Lenin, for instance, knew how to freeze the Mensheviks out in the cold, and his able disciple, Willi Muenzenberger, knew how to create a popular front. Naturally enough, practical theorists have not analyzed the range of possible forms of social movement organization interaction, concentrating instead upon problems of the moment.

If social movements were unified affairs, with one charismatic leader or SMO dominating and holding together the movement, then we could ignore movement organizations, the formal organizations that pursue movement goals, and indus-

Research in Social Movements, Conflicts and Change, Vol. 3, pages 1-20
ISBN: 0-89232-182-2

tries, the congeries of organizations that pursue the goals; at best, such a focus would be marginal, perhaps devoted to understanding factionalism. But it is apparent that social movements are rarely these unified affairs. Whether we study revolutionary movements, broad or narrow social reform movements, or religious movements, we find a variety of SMOs or groups, linked to various segments of supporting constituencies (both institutional and individual), competing amongst themselves for resources and symbolic leadership, sharing facilities and resources at other times, developing stable and many times differentiated functions, occasionally merging into unified *ad hoc* coalitions, and occasionally engaging in all-out war against each other. Organizations associated with a social movement and with its counter-movement may also interact. By definition pursuing antithetical goals, such organizations compete for legitimacy and resources, but, under some circumstances, may also cooperate with one another.

The fundamental task of this paper is to gain analytic purchase on the variety of SMO interorganizational relationships and to begin to specify the conditions under which these various forms of interaction are most likely to occur. In order to accomplish this task, we draw heavily upon a resource mobilization perspective (McCarthy and Zald, 1973, 1977; Oberschall, 1973) on social movements and attempt to combine its insights with the extensive research and analysis which has been done in the study of complex organizations. In the past, social movement analysts and analysts of complex organizations spoke rather different languages. In our attempt to merge these two approaches, we will utilize the concerns and conceptualizations of both. Our earlier work has been informed by the assumption that analysis of SMOs can be informed by the perspectives of organizational theory and research in general. Recent organizational theory and research has focused upon the interrelationships between society, organizational environment, and organizational behavior.

Before we begin to discuss interorganizational interactions, we need to define several terms. First, we define a social movement as a set of opinions and beliefs in a population which represents preferences for changing some elements of the social structure and/or reward distribution of a society. A social movement organization (SMO) is a complex, or formal, organization which identifies its goals with the preferences of a social movement or a countermovement and attempts to implement these goals. A social movement industry (SMI) is made up of all of the SMOs with relatively similar goals (just as an economic industry is all firms offering similar products). A social movement sector (SMS) consists of all SMIs in a society, no matter to which SM they are attached. We have elsewhere (McCarthy and Zald, 1977) discussed competition between the social movement sector and other societal sectors. Here, we focus primarily upon competition and cooperation between organizations *within* the social movement sector, paying attention primarily to intra-industry relations.

Gerlach and Hine (1970) argue that a number of social movements can be characterized exclusively as a web-like structure of informal, unorganized relations of cooperation and communication among local cells. Nevertheless, many SMOs have more coherent organization structures and combine several local units. Our discussion focuses upon organizations which are bureaucratic, as Gamson utilizes that term (1975); that is, organizations which have several levels of membership, lists of members (however faulty), and some kind of written document describing the structure of the organization. Also, we focus upon organizations which pursue goals in more than a local environment; they pursue goals aimed at changing society in general rather than just local conditions.

Even though scholars writing about social movements have paid little attention to interorganizational relations, this has been a lively topic in the study of complex organizations. Dating, possibly, from Levine and White's important paper on exchange relationships among organizations (1961) and Litwak and Hylton's early paper (1962), but including also the emphasis upon organization-environment relations found in the writings of Selznick (1949) and James D. Thompson (1967), in the last decade students of organizations have mapped the forms and determinants of interorganizational relationships (for summaries, see Evans, 1978; and Negandi, 1978). They have explored exchange relations among social welfare agencies, the emergence of federated relations (temporary and permanent), conflict emerging from low domain consensus, the emergence of joint programs, mechanisms used to mediate between clients and organizations, and those used to reduce environmental uncertainties. We draw upon a number of strands of research in this tradition. In particular, we discuss perfect and imperfect competition, ideology and conflict, cooperative relations, and factionalism.

PERFECT AND IMPERFECT COMPETITION

Although organizational analysts have tended, until rather recently (cf. Pfeffer, 1978), to focus upon cooperation instead of competition between organizations, those who have addressed competition have normally utilized the imagery of the market mechanism while at the same time recognizing the social constraints which alter and shape such mechanisms. Let us briefly describe the current consensus about interorganizational competition.

Businesses offering similar products to a large number of potential buyers need not directly interact, but they are able to view the consequences and behavior of others, and are aware of pricing and product decisions through market mechanisms. Pure, or perfect, competitive markets involve homogeneous goods, many sellers (offerers), and many buyers (users). Imperfect competition occurs when there is product differentiation and/or barriers to entry somewhat restricting market access. Where product differentiation is possible, sellers may attempt to divide the market into segments which they "capture," reduce competition, and establish more dependable and organizationally favorable relations. As the number of sellers becomes smaller, we can speak of a movement towards an oligopolistic industry; buyers have limited choices and the number of sellers is small enough so that one or a few may dominate and constrain the choices of others by their influence on buyers, or the sellers may directly interact and concert behavior (establish a cartel).

Organizations (firms) offering relatively similar products may, in some cases, have to deal with a single buyer or supplier (monopsony and monopoly). Such situations create great pressures upon the organizations to concert their behavior. What does such a perspective suggest about SMO competition?

Competition for Resources and Legitimacy

To survive in modern society, SMOs need financial resources if they are to pursue goals in more than a local context. Money is needed for personnel, transportation, office supplies, and the like. Organizations can survive without money when personnel donate their time and money is transferred to them for non-social movement purposes (unemployment insurance payments are widely used for subsistence by SMO organizers). Thus, students can live off their parents, or other organizations may "loan" their personnel and facilities to SMOs for full-time or part-time activity. SCLC, for instance, depended heavily upon the resources of Black church groups in its early days (Oberschall, 1973), and many universities tacitly loaned faculty, chaplains, and students to the anti-Vietnam war movement. But where SMOs employ or wish to employ full-time cadre, even at starvation wages, they will need to regularize or institutionalize the flow of money into the organization. Sometimes, of course, SMOs have windfall resources. Ralph Nader sued GM, which had spied on him and attempted to entrap him in illegal and immoral behavior, leading to a one-half million dollar settlement, which he used for his enterprises (McCarry, 1972). Lenin orchestrated the courting of two sisters, heiresses to a large fortune, who provided an infusion of funds (Wolfe, 1955).

Unless individuals or organizations can be coerced to participate in SMOs (as occurs in armed conflicts where SMOs use coercive techniques to raise manpower and money), SMOs must appeal for support. Consequently, at the most general level, SMOs must compete not only with all other SMOs, but with voluntary organizations of other kinds as well for the time, effort, loyalty, and money which citizens can give or withhold. Here, however, we focus upon the competition between SMOs within SMIs and, peripherally, upon the competition between social movement industries. Competition is for symbolic dominance: Which SMO has the best programs, tactics, and leaders for accomplishing goals? SMOs attempt to convince sympathizers to follow their lead.

Competition for Resources Controlled by Individuals

Organizations within an SMI "ought" to cooperate in goal accomplishment; after all, they seek similar goals. However, because they share to a greater or lesser extent the same adherent pools, both individual and institutional, they are in basic competition for resources from adherents. The intensity of this competition is related importantly to resource availability; the extensity of the demands which SMOs place upon constituents, or those who provide the varied resources to the organization; the social heterogeneity of potential supporters; and the interaction of these three factors.

Hypothesis 1: *Under conditions of the declining availability of marginal resources, direct competition and conflict between SMOs with similar goals can be expected to increase.* Although money is not the only type of resource, it is the most flexible. Obtaining funds from individual constituents (conscience or beneficiary) depends partially upon the availability of marginal dollars. The amount of discretionary resources available is linked to the state of the business cycle, the number of sympathizers, and the ability of organizations to penetrate the pool of sympathizers.

A recent case provides a useful illustration. This is what has been called an "acrimonious dispute" between the NAACP and the NAACP Legal Defense and Educational Fund. The Fund, as the latter is called, separated from the NAACP in 1957, under pressure from the Internal Revenue Service, in order to preserve the tax deductible feature of its financial support. As Brown says, "Few people, however, were aware of that separation. As a result, for the past 22 years the NAACP and the fund (LDF) often were thought of as the same group. Donations intended for one often went to the other, and that was the essence of the dispute . . . (1979, p. A5)." The NAACP has decided to attempt to bar the Fund from using its initials in attempts to raise funds in the future. While there has been some tension between the two organizations over the years, it is noteworthy that the conflict has become increasingly strident at a time when resources for civil rights organizations have been declining.

Hypothesis 2: *Among more inclusive organizations (which demand relatively little from the majority of members), the competition for resources between similar organizations should be less intense than that between more exclusive organizations (which demand heavy commitments from members).* We would expect that multiple memberships would be common in industries with many inclusive organizations, while multiple memberships are frowned upon by exclusive organizations. Exclusive SMOs treat membership as a zero-sum resource. (However, exclusive organizations may use multiple membership as a way of infiltrating other organizations. In this case, multiple memberships result from concerted policy.)

To repeat, SMOs must pursue resources, and, all other things being equal, such competition should be more intense under conditions of resource scarcity. But for some SMOs, even during times when resources are not scarce, it is possible to view constituents of related inclusive organizations as potentially recruitable even while they maintain commitments to other SMOs. Given the extensive literature on voluntary associations generally and social movements in particular, we know that few people affiliate very extensively, but that a small proportion of people are rather widely affiliated. Indeed, a number of studies (Von Eschen, et al., 1971; McFarland, 1977) have shown extensive multiple memberships in the social movement sector. Thus, even though SMOs in the same industry may be competing for the same resources (i.e., the labor and loyalty of the same people), since no organization commands the total loyalty of most of its constituents, this competition is not zero-sum and, consequently, should not be especially rancorous. Once a person gives funds, future solicitations from other SMOs become more likely.

Competition between inclusive organizations in an industry takes the form of slight product differentiation (offering marginally different goals) and, especially, tactical differentiation. Different SMOs may specialize principally in litigation strategies, or lobbying strategies, or protest strategies, or particular targets. Such differentiation provides a rationale for committed constituents to become affiliated with a number of SMOs pursuing similar goals in a number of different ways. This is, we believe, the major form of competition between inclusive SMOs within SMIs in modern America.

Since organizations pursuing similar goals compete for resources, SMOs will form that are based upon differential perceptions and tastes of adherent pools in order to capitalize on such pre-existing differences. As well, when resource availability is expanding, existing organizations can be expected to expand their range of targets and tactics when possible.

Hypothesis 3:   *The range of appeals and the variety of organizations which develop is partly related to the pre-existing heterogeneity of potential supporters. Differentiation of appeal is more important for inclusive than exclusive SMOs.* SMO goals and programs are, of course, importantly determined by the shape of the task, the range of institutional targets, and the means to change targets which stem from a more or less well-articulated ideology. But a heterogeneous potential support base calls forth and permits a range of definitions of the situation.

Though product differentiation may appear sharp to the non-members of more exclusive SMOs, that differentiation is probably less important to growth and resource accumulation than it is for more inclusive organizations. Since ideological transformation is typical of more exclusive SMOs and some evidence exists to suggest that members and non-members are quite similar prior to ideological transformation (Heirich, 1977; Gerlach and Hine, 1970), what pre-existing value heterogeneity there is among potential supporters is probably of less importance for growth than the appropriateness and sophistication of recruitment mechanisms (McCarthy and Hoge, 1978). Consequently, the apparent range and variety of offerings of more exclusive organizations is more related to internal processes than to the pre-existing preferences of potential supporters.

Product differentiation is more important for recruitment among inclusive organizations and especially so among inclusive organizations which do not depend upon face-to-face interaction. For these organizations, product differentiation functions much as it does in the market place. If marginal dollars are in plentiful supply, the possibility of offering slight changes in products in order to capture some of the increased potential market is more likely. These changes may take the form of new organizations, spin-off organizations, or existing organizations expanding their range of related issues, targets, and tactics. In the first two cases, additional organizations are added to the field, thus creating the potential for increased competition for resources on the part of existing organizations. When organizations expand their offerings, they enter into competition for resources with other existing organizations with whom they have not competed in the past. The recent history of the American Civil Liberties Union (ACLU) provides a case in point. Originally an organization devoted exclusively to supporting litigation on first amendment issues, the ACLU expanded its goals during the early 1970s to include ending the war in Vietnam, fighting against the Nixon administration, and for women's rights and abortion. In the process, it gained tens of thousands of new members through its mass mail solicitations and became an organization competing for resources with other existing organizations such as NOW, NARAL, and many anti-war organizations. But these were times of expanding marginal dollars, and little outward conflict occurred between these organizations. Presumably, the expanded appeals brought additional funds into the coffers of the organization. We might expect that the adding of new product lines for an organization such as this one with widespread name recognition would put it, as with firms, in a better competitive position in the social movement sector. Unfortunately, such a diversification strategy proved costly to the ACLU when it took an unpopular first amendment stand to defend the Nazi marchers in Skokie, Illinois. As Mann (1978) persuasively argues, the heterogeneity of the membership which was built by expanding the goals of the organization meant that many new members brought in by these recent appeals could not be expected to support the Skokie decision. The result was a drastic decline in membership renewals for the organization.

Competition for Resources Controlled by Organizations

So far, we have focused upon the competition for support from individual sympathizers—how to transform sympathizers into constituents. But funds are also raised from institutional sources. These funds may be more or less restricted in purposes. Thus, money given to an SMO by a governmental agency for a specific purpose comes under audit. Foundation support may be less restricted— the foundation, for instance, may provide money for a voter registration drive, but in fact not tightly control expenditures. However, since foundations are observed by Congress and their operations controlled by federal statute, they tend to be quite politically sensitive. The least restricted money from institutional sources may well be from church organizations, especially the many "social concern" departments in the Protestant denominations. These groups aggregate a proportion of total givings from the membership and disburse them over a range of organizations and projects. (Such funds are probably more restricted than money provided by individual constituents, since these bodies also operate under accountability procedures.) Elsewhere (McCarthy and Zald, 1977) we have argued that in the United States, resources provided to SMOs by individuals is more insulated from political social control than are those of institutions. The more removed from political control and from membership pressure, the more an institution is free to distribute resources as it wants.

However, remember that competition for funds from individual constituents requires a very different process than attempting to obtain funds from institutional sources; the former requires more public relations skills and styles while the latter requires more program development skills. Lawson (1978) reports that the increase in funds available from institutional sources to the various organizations of the tenants' rights movement in New York City has created both a wider diversity of SMOs and increased levels of competition for the available funds. Where there are limited numbers of institutional funders, competition appears to be zero-sum. Competition becomes conflict as those who cannot gain access to such funds attack the legitimacy of those who can. Most of the SMOs which Lawson describes appear to be inclusive.

Hypothesis 4: *Institutional funding, when publicly known, will increase conflict between more inclusive SMOs.* Whether or not this hypothesis holds for more exclusive SMOs is not clear to us, since it is difficult to untangle the effects of organizational structure, goals, and institutional funding for such organizations.

IDEOLOGY AND CONFLICT

The conflict which occurs between SMOs over legitimacy is normally discussed by analysts under the rubric of the "functions of a radical fringe." As the SMOs of an SMI pursue related goals, some organizations offer a more comprehensive version of the problem and more drastic change as a solution. These organizations are normally called radical. Naturally enough, authorities are likely to prefer to deal with organizations which state less comprehensive versions of change. By virtue of the authorities' recognition of some SMOs as legitimate spokespersons and others as not legitimate, conflict is almost guaranteed between SMOs. This normally takes the form of open attacks by the unlegitimated SMOs upon those who have been accepted, however marginally, by authorities. The rich rhetoric describing fine degrees of cooptation and "selling out" grows out of this process. The legitimated SMOs may gain even more legitimacy from authorities and bystanders counterattacking the unlegitimated SMOs, but this increases the level of inter-SMI conflict. The longstanding conflicts between communist and non-communist trade unions in the United States during the 1940s and 1950s illustrates this process. Under other conditions, no response by the legitimated SMOs reaps the reward of increased legitimacy. This process is described in detail by Killian for the recent civil rights movement (1972).

Hypothesis 5: *Assuming that SMOs are competing for similar audiences, as SMOs within an industry become further apart in their conception of the amount of change and the tactics required, rancorous conflict increases.* So far, we have discussed competition and conflict in which SMOs present verbal claims about themselves and their opponents and competitors. Most often, the appearance of shared goals mutes the direct and more violent attack of one SMO on another, but rancorous and deadly conflict is not unknown between SMOs in the same SMI. In modern America, rancorous conflict occurs in such settings primarily over the legitimacy of representation of constituency or over exclusive membership.

In the U.S., there are two settings in which SMI conflict has occurred: between sect-like SMOs with comprehensive visions of change; and between labor organizations which must, by virtue of the legal and political circumstances under which they operate, require membership exclusivity with regard to other organizations.

It is widely observed that small, sect-like SMOs tend to devote extensive energies toward bitter conflicts with other SMOs which seem to noncombatants only marginally different. For instance, in the late 1960s the Black Muslims and Malcolm X's Organization for Afro-American Unity, engaged in murderous conflict. A major reason for the intensity of such conflict appears to relate to the great sacrifice and commitment required of their members: members are a scarce and valuable resource which have normally required a major SMO investment in socialization.

Hypothesis 6: *The more SMOs with exclusive membership requirements compete for a limited pool of potential members, the greater the potential conflict.* Another situation producing rancorous and deadly conflict occurs, at least in the local context, when organizational survival is at stake. The recent conflict between the United Farm Workers Organization and the Teamsters Union in the fields of California illustrates the intensity that such conflict can reach. Conflict between the AFT and the NEA in many school districts and colleges demonstrates the same process in a milder form.[1] In these cases, organizations depend upon membership enrollment in order to win recognition from authorities. The loser in these battles is not accredited as a bargaining agent and must leave the scene.

Utilizing our resource mobilization logic, then, and viewing the social world from the point of view of a particular SMO, highlights the possibilities of conflict between it and other SMOs offering similar products. But the relative lack of conflict and the extent of cooperation among related SMOs then calls for some explanation. How can we account for cooperation between SMOs which, all other things being equal, our theoretical perspective leads us to believe should be vigorously competing?

COOPERATION: EXCHANGE, THE DIVISION OF LABOR, AND DOMAIN CONSENSUS

In the production of a product or the carrying out of social functions, a set of organizations may develop differentiated but interlinked roles. They then establish exchange relations. Here is where the emphasis upon exchange, domain consensus, and conflict over domain has become relevant to analysts of complex organizations. These relationships vary in their importance to the parties, their stability, and the amount of coordination and mutual adjustment that takes place. To review:

1. *Ad hoc,* small item exchanges may take place in which lower-level personnel of an organization find it advantageous to utilize the services, products, or facilities of another organization.
2. Policy coordination and rules governing interchanges are likely to emerge when two or more organizations are dependent upon each other for an important part of their input or output. These policies and rules are likely to be reviewed by upper-level personnel in organizations. Where the interchange is regular but over changing conditions or issues, interagency committees or liaison groups may emerge to monitor the relations.
3. Cooperative relations occur to the extent that the skills, competencies, tasks, and prices of the partners to the exchange are agreed upon by all parties (this is what is meant by "domain consensus").
4. Where stable relationships have emerged with highly differentiated but interlinked domains, the organizational partners may exchange information and monitor their environments for mutual enhancement.
5. In some cases, cooperating organizations may set up joint organizations or projects. As opposed to coordination, the joint program involves some autonomy of action for the personnel of the joint program; in essence, a new organization is created.

These cooperative relationships occur in both the profit-making and nonprofit sectors. A number of researchers have pursued a description of the role of interlocking boards of directorates in the business sectors, showing their widespread occurrence, their patterned nature, and speculating upon their probable role in coordinating the inter-organizational sector.[2] There have also been studies of joint ventures in the for-profit and non-profit sectors.

Other researchers, such as Domhoff (1976), have explored social relations between the leaders of private sector organizations, again showing widespread contact and extensive communication allowing the development of inter-organizational undertakings about cooperative ventures. Finally, several analysts have argued that private sector organizations have cooperated in the development of certain federal regulatory agencies as a means of reducing competition and of stabilizing industry operation.

Following such leads, there are a number of factors we can isolate which serve to facilitate and shape cooperation among SMOs. We shall discuss several of these: task specialization, social control, interlocking boards of directors, overlapping membership constituencies, and inducements from authorities and elites. Each of these factors may produce either formal or informal cooperation.

Task Specialization

Where an SMI is fairly well established, comprised of several different SMOs, informal domain agreements and exchanges emerge. They emerge usually between those organizations sharing relatively similar conceptions of goals and allowable tactics. First, SMOs may agree upon geographic and functional turf. Basic to domain consensus are economies of expertise and closeness of constituent relationships.[3] On the one hand, legal organizations, lobbying and information groups, and other technical services develop within specific SMIs and consequently have available an expertise which other SMOs in the SMI would find difficult and expensive to duplicate. On the other hand, the highly technical groups rarely develop strong links to constituents.

Hypothesis 7: *Domain agreements are more likely to be reached allowing extended cooperation among SMOs with different but not contradictory task specializations than among those SMOs which pursue goals with similar tactical formulas.* Although SCLC employed lawyers, they largely protected the organization and its leaders from arrest. We know that clear domain agreements existed between CORE and the NAACP during the "Freedom Rides" in the South, where the NAACP strained its resources to provide legal defense for CORE members arrested in local areas (Meier and Rudwick, 1973). We suspect that a similar exchange relationship developed at the height of the Civil Rights movement between the SCLC and both the ACLU and the NAACP Legal Defense Fund. The NAACP was the major legal arm of the movement.

External Social Control

Hypothesis 8: *Social control produces increased cooperation among SMOs when the social control efforts threaten the very existence of a number of SMOs.* Violence, legal restrictions upon operating procedures, and arrests not only commit SMO constituents to their own SMOs (Gerlach and Hine, 1970), but also commit SMOs within the same SMI to one another. This is a pattern which appears in even broader contexts, sometimes even including SMOs from diverse SMIs in momentary cooperative ventures. For instance, the Japanese invasion led to uneasy cooperation between the Nationalists and the Communists in China during World War II. The Berkeley Free Speech Movement (FSM) at the University of California is another example of a coalition which formed as a response to an outside threat. The FSM grew out of an attempt by authorities to restrict off-campus political organizing by on-campus organizations. A wide variety of organizations with sometimes related and sometimes disparate goals coalesced when their base of operations was threatened. Originally, the United Front was formed which eventually became the FSM. The United Front included all three campus Republican groups along with a right-wing conservative society and a wide array of left-wing groups (Draper, 1964).

Social control engenders the same kind of cooperation between SMOs within the same SMI. Political trials regularly have such an effect. The notorious trials of IWW leaders during the 1920s served to develop cooperative relations between organizations which normally worked at arm's length from one another (Dubofsky, 1969). The cooperative defense funds which normally arise in such circumstances serve to informally link SMOs to one another. An unintended effect of such trials when they are badly managed (as in the United States during the 1960s and in pre-revolutionary Russia) is to develop bonds between leaders of diverse SMOs, thereby setting the stage for future cooperative ventures.

Overlapping Constituencies

Boards: Much like modern corporations, many inclusive SMOs in modern society develop boards of directors or advisory councils. These boards serve various purposes, including providing legitimation, providing links with various constituencies, technical and political advice to SMO leaders, and providing links to various elite and institutional funding sources. We are not aware of a systematic evaluation of boards of this type, but a quick look at boards within any SMI shows extensive overlapping membership—or in recent parlance, interlocks. For instance, the leaders of one SMO may be found on the board of directors of similar SMOs. Dignitaries such as Ramsey Clark or Benjamin Spock can be found on a wide variety of boards. It may be possible to describe inter-SMI and SMO relations by inspecting the amount of interlock, much as has been attempted by analysts of the corporate world in modern America. Of course, such interlocks can also be used to infer integration into the larger society by attending to the other positions held by members.[4]

Hypothesis 9: *The more the interlocks, the greater the cooperation among SMOs.* The perspective of the board member who sits on the boards of two similar SMOs ought to incline that individual toward counseling cooperation in the pursuit of goals. Though board members are normally in a formal position of approving the behavior of the SMO, we suspect that these boards, like corporate boards, are often rather less than vigorous. However, the circulation of information in these settings ought to keep each SMO so linked informed of the activities of the closest competitors for resources. Following what we know of similar processes in the corporate sector (Domhoff, 1974), we would not be surprised to find the existence of watering holes (such as Stewart Mott's townhouse across from the Supreme Court in Washington, D.C.), where those who occupy extensive interlocking positions gather socially. It is known, for instance, that leaders of the Civil Rights movement in the South convened at the Highlander Folk Center in Tennessee, and later in Kentucky. These informal groupings should serve to further coordinate the activities of SMOs within an SMI and relations between ideologically-linked SMIs.[5]

Memberships: As we noted above, many citizens belong to a number of voluntary associations, and a subset of them belongs to a number of SMOs. Consequently, any SMO should have some set of its constituents who belong to other related and other apparently unrelated SMOs. We could characterize SMOs by their degree of overlapping constituencies; the inclusive/exclusive dimension includes the end of this continuum as one of its elements.

Hypothesis 10: *The more SMOs have overlapping constituencies, the more they should be constrained toward cooperation.* (However, where we normally refer to the inclusive SMO as a "front group," the cooperation is induced through infiltration.) Overlapping memberships ought to provide communication between affected SMOs, though not as directly as interlocking boards of directors.

Overlapping memberships have different sources and consequences at local and national levels. In local organizations, or chapters of national organizations, clusters of people may belong to a number of similar organizations which pursue similar but discrete goals. The clustering is created through interpersonal networks. Meier and Rudwick (1973) describe the operation of CORE and the NAACP in the South during the height of the Civil Rights movement of the 1960s as one commonly marked by overlapping membership at the local level. In some circumstances, there was almost complete overlapping membership—hence, tactical cooperation was guaranteed.

National organizations with inclusive and non-federated or only partly-federated constituents may find themselves in a situation where many of their constituents hold memberships in similar SMOs created through interchanged membership lists. McFarland (1976) shows, for instance, that approximately 30 percent of the members of Common Cause are also members of the League of Women Voters. There is extensive overlap between the membership of the National Abortion Rights Action League (NARAL), Planned Parenthood, and the National Organization of Women (NOW) (Personal Communication). Some of this overlap appears to occur when the same or similar mailing lists are used in solicitations for membership in parallel SMOs. SMOs loan or rent their lists to one another. SMOs may also contract with a single firm to handle solicitations, and the same pool of lists may be used by more than one SMO. We would expect, for instance, that Richard Viguerie's centrality as a mailing firm for organizations on the right would serve to increase the likelihood of overlapping memberships between similar conservative organizations. The extensity of the overlaps should constrain potential conflict between such organizations. Membership surveys are not at all uncommon among such organizations, so it is reasonable to assume that many leaders are aware of such overlaps. Since such membership is quite unstable (Many organizations with a mail order membership experience less than 50 percent renewals each year), one would expect leaders to be rather careful to show appropriate cooperation, while at the same time retaining images of product differentiation.

Elite and Third Party Constraints

Finally, cooperation between SMOs may be encouraged by authorities and elite institutions. During the days of the Johnson administration, the President held many meetings with "Civil Rights leaders." Though there was extensive conflict between some of these groups at times, some element of cooperation was encouraged as the leaders of SNCC and the more moderate Civil Rights groups maintained ties through the offices of the President. Churches and foundations which support the social movement sector regularly call for cooperation between SMOs pursuing similar goals. Since such funding institutions tend to place great importance on the role of efficiency in goal accomplishment, from their vantage point conflict is counterproductive. When in the business of providing resources, such institutions can back up encouragement with threats and actual sanctions. Dealing with a small number of funding institutions or authorities puts contradictory pressures on SMOs; it heightens conflict because zero-sum situations are created, but it also creates a demand for cooperation.

Hypothesis 11:   *If the funding institution is selecting one among many proposals from different SMOs, conflict is encouraged; if coalition grants are being made, cooperation is encouraged.* SMOs in modern society are linked to one another and to other organizations in a wide variety of ways. These linkages serve to mute the conflict which might be expected from a conception of SMOs as just organizations seeking survival and growth. It is those organizations which are isolated from widespread linkages where we would expect to find more rancorous inter-SMO conflict.

Alliances, Cartels, Federations, and Mergers

Organizations not only cooperate and exchange, they sometimes form supraorganizations—cartels, federations, alliances, and mergers. These forms of organizational behavior have been extensively discussed by organizational analysts. In the merger, two or more formally separate organizations combine into one new organization; the merger can occur by mutual consent or through a hostile takeover. In the federation, units retain their identity but give up certain discretionary rights to the new organization, or, in the dominated alliance, to one of the component units. Federations and alliances differ in their depth and purposes. Indeed, the relatively permanent coordination of policies discussed above can be considered one form of alliance. The formation of alliances, however, is also likely to result from the necessity of dealing with a powerful (monopolistic) resource provider or buyer. Public and private organizations offering similar services and products may need "trade associations" to represent them to the outside world.

Finally, a wide variety of private sector organizations may cooperate in *ad hoc* alliances when an outside threat or a potential outside advantage is perceived. Examples are alliances formed to counter federal taxation and labor policies.

Managerial technocrats might see in the plethora of SMOs in an industry a magnificent opportunity for rationalization by merger. After all, economies of scale would result from the merger of these small, inefficient organizations. And just think how much simpler it would be if the movement spoke with one voice! But an organizational realist, such as James Q. Wilson (1973), would surely point out that the managerial technocrats are both unwise and naive. Naive, because the technocrats assume that efficiency is a prime concern of SMO leaders when it is not, and because they miss the strong drive to organizational maintenance of leaders and their key constituents. Unwise, because they assume that speaking with one voice increases the effectiveness of the movement when, in fact, the effectiveness of a movement, both in mobilizing support and attaining change, may be aided by having many organizations. Moreover, as Gerlach and Hine (1970) demonstrate, there are major advantages to having diversity within an SMI: diversity allows for innovation in tactics and makes it difficult for authorities to target social control efforts.

But ideologically compatible SMOs do form alliances and mergers under special sets of circumstances. SMOs will join together for special events. Marches and mass demonstrations are often run in consortium fashion with several different organizations mobilizing constituencies and interlinked networks. Joint planning and ad hoc liaison committees are used for these occasions. Our conception of ideological leadership and Olson's theory (1965) of the contributions of organizations to the provision of collective goods leads us to believe the following hypothesis.

Hypothesis 12: *The leading or dominant organization in a movement will make contributions greater than its proportional share of resources to carrying out large events for special purposes.* Although coalitions, both formal and informal, are common, mergers between SMOs seem relatively rare. One condition which seems to spur merger is the same one which can also spur bitter conflict, and that is between competing labor SMOs. The United Farm Workers Organization identified with Cesar Chavez, for instance, was formed out of two ethnically distinct SMOs, and the merger of the A.F. of L. and the C.I.O. is well known. The condition of labor representation seems to offer an incentive for both conflict and merger which does not normally exist to the same extent in other SMIs.

As we noted above, monopoly funders may require, as part of their commitment to fund, united action or programs on the part of SMOs, or at least the working out of domain agreements. In this sense, funders may have a technocratic bias that may or may not correspond with organizational effectiveness. Monopoly funders also create formal alliances as did the Ford Foundation in its funding of the Southwest Council of La Raza (Goulden, 1971: p. 270 ff.). This council was designed to fund and direct local boards drawn from existing Mexican-American organizations in a number of states in order to create united action. Similarly, political power-holders may impose an alliance because they want to know to whom they can speak—who represents the movement. On the SMO side, unification comes about because the SMO's leaders realize the elite will pick up on divisions and magnify them, or will not know to whom to listen. A related environmental press toward the formulation of alliances is the need to present a united front in lobbying activities. Lawson's (1978) description of the development of federations of tenant organizations in New York City in recent years seems to represent such a process. The state legislature provided not only the potential for statutes affecting common goals, but also resource flows to various organizations engaging in tenant actions of a diverse nature.

Alliances may often come about as the SMO scents victory; then, coordinated action to achieve goals has a higher priority than organizational maintenance. Besides, at such times organizational maintenance is not under threat, and money and resources tend to be easily mobilized. But at such times no one worries about actual mergers. On the other hand, mergers are often suggested in declining movements; then, mergers may represent the only mechanism for maintaining a viable organization. One other form of alliance: the popular front, represents a coalition of like-minded SMOs against a clear-cut countermovement group.

Hypothesis 13:   *The more clear-cut and vigorous the countermovement, the easier it is to mobilize an alliance.* The need for a unified defense transcends ideological differences. The Southern Conference for Human Welfare represents just such an alliance. Formed in 1938, Krueger (1967) says,

> "The Southern Conference was not a Communist Front (as many had charged), but a popular front, a conglomeration of individuals from organizations as diverse as the Baptist Church and the Communist party united about a minimum program on which all of the constituent factions could agree. That minimum program aimed at repairing the defects of American Capitalism, bring the South up to the economic and social standards of the rest of the country, and finally obtaining elementary justice for American Negroes (p. 181)."

Of course, alliances may stem from common ideological prescription of targets as well.

FACTIONALISM

Both economists and sociologists have a bloodless conception of interorganizational relations, and the sociologists, oddly enough, tend to ignore power imbalances in these relations. The language of domain consensus tends to assume that the partners have shared or at least non-conflicting goals. But organizations may wish death on one another; they may want to absorb the other, take over its domain, squash the competition. As we have noted, the greater the commitment to a zealot's view of the proper state of the world, and the less effective the control of competition, the more one can expect illegitimate, violent, and deadly interorganizational relations. Finally, one other aspect of interorganizational relations deserves mention. *Inter*organizational relations may emerge from *intra*organizational factionalism. Especially in social movements (see Zald and Ash, 1966; and Gamson, 1975), factionalism may lead to splits and the formation of new organizations. A similar process occurs in other organizations when principals (partners, senior executives) split, taking resources and reputations with them.

Factionalism is probably the form of intra-SMO relations which has received the most note historically. Probably as a result of the extensive factionalism within left-wing, sect-like organizations during the 1930s in the United States, the impression was left that exclusive SMOs are more likely to develop factions, leading to the amoeba-like growth of new SMOs. Gamson's (1975) evidence on 53 SMOs suggests that exclusive organizations are no more likely to develop factions than are inclusive organizations. The impression that they do may derive from the fact that bitter conflict tends to occur between newly-formed exclusive SMOs and the parent organization, while bitter conflict is not so likely when inclusive SMOs spin off factions. The impression comes, then, from the after-split behavior of the SMO. Some sub-set of the constituents of an SMO may split off to form a new SMO relating to similar goals for a number of reasons, and under a number of different conditions.

The organization of Afro-American Unity, Malcolm X's organization, represented an off-shoot from the Black Muslims of Elijah Muhammad. The new organization included several members of the Muslims, and was clearly viewed by the Muslims as a competitor for their exclusive members. The bitter conflict which occurred between these two organizations fits older impressions of the process of factionalism.

The Students for a Democratic Society represent a somewhat different case (Sale, 1973). Originally a youth arm of the League for Industrial Democracy, they split off from the parent body when the price of a stable resource flow was non-deviation from the operating tactics and, especially, membership criteria of the LID. Neither organization was exclusive in structure, and, though pursuing somewhat similar goals, the two organizations did not compete for the same constituency or engage in open conflict.

Another case, again quite different, is that of the splitting off from the Sierra Club of the Friends of the Earth (FOE). This organization was created after a faction of the leadership of the Sierra Club lost several debates about tactics. The forming of the new organization was not an occasion for acrimony, however, and the parent organization lent the new organization its mailing list, as FOE attempted to recruit a constituency which backed up its more aggressive lobbying tactics (Wagner, 1972). FOE seems to have drawn its constituency largely from the constituency of the parent organization, and the two SMOs have cooperated in a number of joint activities since. Here, two inclusive organizations, the second a result of factionalism within the parent body, have not engaged in bitter conflict and, in fact, have cooperated rather extensively. FOE has received grants from institutional funders for operational expenses, especially during its early phases.[6]

Hypothesis 14:   *When factionalism and the spinning off of new SMOs occurs, the extent of exclusivity of membership and the extent of integration into a wider array of non-SMO organizations are both related to the extent of after-split conflict.*

CONCLUSIONS

Inter-SMO relations are a central dynamic of any social movement. Whether one reads the history of the making of the Russian revolution or the spread of evangelical Christianity, the pattern of conflict and cooperation leaps to the eye. The resource mobilization perspective's focus upon SMIs led us to ask how interaction within industries parallels the forms and dynamics of organizational interaction found in the literature of economics and the sociology of complex organizations. The parallels are striking.

Only the naive assumption that SMOs all share a common goal and therefore have little interest in conflict and competition has kept scholars from examining such central processes. In addition, since scholars often do case studies of single SMOs (the usual style is to move from a concern with a movement to a study of that movement's[7] dominant organization) industry-wide phenomena are usually treated only in passing.

We have offered a number of hypotheses about the pressures toward cooperation and conflict in an industry, and the forms and permanence of these interactions. Obviously, analysis of these processes is dependent upon a prior description of the structure of an industry. Thus another theoretical task remains: accounting for the differences in industry structure—the number, size, and market locations of SMOs in an industry.

Even with such an analysis, our job would not be finished. Although we think the parallel with economic processes is striking, we should remember that there are differences. In particular, competition for dominance among SMOs is often for symbolic dominance, for defining the terms of social movement action. Social movement leaders are seeking symbolic hegemony. At some point, social movement analysis must join with cultural and linguistic analysis, if it is to fully understand cooperation and conflict in its socially specific forms.

ACKNOWLEDGMENTS

We wish to thank Roberta Ash Garner, William Gamson and Louis Kriesberg for their useful comments upon earlier drafts of this paper.

NOTES

1. Systematic violent conflict between competing SMOs in such contexts, of course, demands special organizational structures. The Teamsters organization, the Black Muslims, and Synanon, for instance, possess squads who specialize in such tactics. Most SMOs do not.

2. See, for instance, Pfeffer (1972) and Allen (1974).

3. Mitchell and Davies (1978), in discussing environmental movement coalitions, argue that newer members of pre-existing coalitions implicitly accept the existing division of labor in joining them. Stallings (1977) argues that the pre-existing structured relations in local communities affects the likelihood and shape of emergent coalitions.

4. See Aveni (1978) on the NAACP and Curtis and Zurcher (1973) on local anti-pornography campaigns for examples of the importance to SMOs of linkages to individuals and organizations both within and beyond particular SMIs.

5. Mitchell and Davies (1978) point to the importance of common headquarters locations in Washington, D.C. as well as sporadic conferences of professional staffs for the cooperative efforts of many national environmental organizations.

6. Later, in fact, FOE split again when some staff members left to form the Environmental Policy Center, designed as a lobbying group without members (Wagner, 1972).

7. Even in Gamson's (1975) otherwise notable study of 53 SMOs, sampling procedures were used that led to ignoring the position of SMOs in an industry—as if we could study the Russian revolution by studying the Mensheviks alone.

REFERENCES

Allen, Michael P. (1974) "The Structure of Interorganizational Elite Cooptation: Interlocking Corporate Directorates," *American Sociological Review,* Vol. 39 (June), 393–406.

Aveni, Adrian F. (1978) "Organizational Linkages and Resources Mobilization: The Significance of Linkage Strength & Breadth," *Sociological Quarterly,* 19 (Spring, 1978), 185–202.

Brown, Warren (1979) "NAACP Votes to Strip Name from Longtime Civil Rights Ally," *The Washington Post,* June 26, 1979, A5.

Curtis, Jr., Russell L. and Louis A. Zurcher (1973) "Stable resources of protest movements: The Multi-organizational Field," *Social Forces,* 52 53–61.

Domhoff, G. William (1974) *The Bohemian Grove and Other Retreats,* Harper & Row, New York.

Draper, Hal (1966) *The New Student Revolt,* New York, Grove Press.

Dubofsky, Melvyn (1969) *We Shall Be All,* Chicago, Quadrangle Books.

Dunne, John Gregory (1967) *Delano,* Farrar, Straus and Giroux, New York.

Evans, William (1978) editor, *Inter-Organizational Relations: Selected Readings.* Philadelphia: University of Pennsylvania Press.

Gamson, William A. (1975) *The Strategy of Social Protest.* Homewood, Illinois: Dorsey Press.

Gerlach, Luther, and Virginia Hine (1970) *People, Power, and Change: Movements of Social Transformation.* Indianapolis: Bobbs-Merrill.

Goulden, Joseph C. (1971) *The Money Givers,* Random House, New York.

Gusfield, Joseph (1966) "Functional Areas of Social Movement Leadership," *Sociological Quarterly* 7, 137–156.

Heard, Jamie (1970) "Friends of the Earth give environmental interests an activist voice," *National Journal,* August 8, 1970, 1712–1718.

Heirich, Max (1977) "Change of Heart: A Test of Some Widely Held Theories about Religious Conversion," *American Journal of Sociology* 83 (Nov. 1977). 653–680.

Killian, Lewis (1972) "The Significance of Extremism in the Black Revolution," *Social Problems* 20 (Summer): 41–48.

Krueger, Thomas A. (1967) *And Promises to Keep: The Southern Conference for Human Welfare, 1938–1948,* Vanderbilt University Press, Nashville.

Lawson, Ronald (1978) "He Who Pays the Piper: The Consequences of their income sources for social movement organizations," paper delivered at the 1978 annual meeting of the American Sociological Association, San Francisco, Ca.

Levine, Sol, and Paul A. White (1961) "Exchange as a Conceptual Framework for the Study of Interorganizational Relationships," *Administrative Science Quarterly*, 15: 583–601.

Litwak, Eugene, and Lydia Hylton (1962) "Interorganizational Analysis: A Hypothesis on Coordinating Agencies," *Administrative Science Quarterly*, 6: 395–420.

McCarry, Charles (1972) *Citizen Nader*, Saturday Review Press, New York.

McCarthy, John D., and Mayer N. Zald (1977) "Resource Mobilization and Social Movements: A *Resource Mobilization and Professionalization*. Morristown, New Jersey: General Learning Press.

McCarthy, John D., and Mayer N. Zald (1977) "Resource Mobilization andSocial Movements: A Partial Theory," *American Journal of Sociology*, 82 (July): 1212–1241.

McCarthy, John D. and Dean R. Hoge (1978) "Mobilizing Believers: Toward a Model of Religious Recruitment," Paper delivered at annual meeting of the American Sociological Association, San Francisco, Ca.

McFarland, Andrew S. (1976) "The Complexity of Democratic Practice within Common Cause," Paper delivered at the 1976 annual meeting of the American Political Science Association, Chicago, Ill.

Mann, Jim (1978) "Hard Times for the ACLU," *The New Republic*, Vol. 178, No. 15, April 15, 1978, 12–15.

Meier, August and Elliott Rudwick (1973) *CORE: A Study in the Civil Rights Movement 1942–1968*, New York, Oxford University Press.

Mitchell, Robert C. and J. Clarence Davies, III (1978) "The United States Environmental Movement and Its Political Context: An Overview," Discussion Paper D-32, Resources for the Future, Washington, D.C. May, 1978.

Negandhi, Anant R. (1969) *Interorganization Theory*. Kent, Ohio: Kent State University Press.

Nelson, Harold (1974) "Social Movement Transformation and Pre-Movement Factor Effect: A Preliminary Inquiry," *The Sociological Quarterly*, Winter (1974), 127–42.

Oberschall, Anthony (1973) *Social Conflict and Social Change*. Englewood Cliffs, New Jersey: Prentice-Hall.

Olson, Mancur (1965) The Logic, *The Logic of Collective Action*. Cambridge, Massachusetts: Harvard University Press.

Pfeffer, Jeffrey (1972) "Size and Composition of Corporate Boards of Directors: the Organization and its Environment," *Administrative Science Quarterly*, 16 (June, 1972), 218–28.

Pfeffer, Jeffrey (1978) *Organizational Design*, AHM Pub. Co., Arlington Heights, Ill.

Sale, Kirkpatrick (1973) *SDS*. New York: Random House.

Selznick, Philip (1949) *TVA and the Grass Roots*, Berkeley: University of California Press.

Stallings, Robert A. (1977) "Social Movements as Emergent Coalition: An Interorganizational Approach," Working Paper No. 14, School of Public Administration, University of Southern California.

Thompson, James D. (1971) *Organizations in Action*. New York: McGraw-Hill, 1967.

VonEschen, Donald, Jerome Kirk, and Maurice Pinard, "The Organizational Sub-Structure of Disorderly Politics," *Social Forces* 1971, 49 (June): 529–543.

Wagner, James R. (1972) "Friends of the Earth Staff members organize new environmental Lobby," *National Journal*, Feb. 5, 1972, 246.

Wilson, James Q. (1973) *Political Organization*. New York: Basic Books.

Wolfe, Bertram (1955) *Three Who Made a Revolution*. Boston: Beacon.

Zald, Mayer N., and Roberta Ash (1966) "Social Movement Organizations: Growth Decline and Change," *Social Forces*, 44 (March): 327–341.

SOCIALIZATION AND STUDENT ACTIVISM:
EXAMINATION OF A RELATIONSHIP

James L. Wood and Wing-Cheung Ng

INTRODUCTION

One of the central conclusions of studies of student political activism of the 1960s was the impact of unconventional family socialization on participation in student activism. It has been stated that "the unconventionality of activists flows out of and is supported by their family traditions."[1] Similarly, "The great majority of these [activist] students are attempting to fulfill and renew the [liberal or radical] political traditions of their families."[2] Also, parents of activists have been seen to socialize their children to be "skeptical about conventional middle-class values, life-styles, and religious orientations . . . in particular . . . sexual repressiveness, materialism, status-striving, and strict methods of child rearing."[3] Finally, "Compared to their own parents, [the parents of these activists] are more likely to instill in their children the special values of self-

Research in Social Movements, Conflicts and Change, Vol. 3, pages 21-43
Copyright © 1980 by JAI Press Inc.
All rights of reproduction in any form reserved.
ISBN: 0-89232-182-2

actualization—independence, sensitivity to feelings, concern for others, free expression of emotion, openness, and spontaneity."[4]

A recent critique has called into question the actual impact of family socialization on participation in such student activism of the 1960s as anti-Vietnam protests, civil rights demonstrations, and struggles for educational reform. Rothman and Lichter (1978) argue that methodological flaws in highly publicized studies of student political activism shed doubt on the major findings of these studies. They point to the existence of small, non-randomly selected samples, a paucity of data analysis, and various questionnaire biases in concept indicators. In addition, it has recently been suggested that part of the relationship between family socialization and student activism could be spurious because activists and their parents "share similar class, ethnic, and religious backgrounds."[5]

In this paper, we intend to determine the actual impact of unconventional family socialization on participation in student activism. We will examine the strength and direction of the relationship between politically left-wing or culturally unconventional family socialization and student activism of the 1960s, with the focus on explaining individual participation in student protests, not on the development of the New Left as a whole. Ultimately, we hope to show that unconventional socialization did influence participation in activism, but that by the late 1960s, the impact of socialization on activism was of lesser magnitude than it had been in the earlier part of the 1960s.

METHODOLOGY

Although this paper draws on data from various investigations of student activism in the United States in the 1960s, it especially analyzes data from three related samples at a central location of activism, the University of California at Berkeley. The three related samples are: (1) a systematic random sample of the University of California, Berkeley campus in 1968 (N= 492); (2) a parental sample with a questionnaire emphasizing social and political characteristics; and (3) a parental sample with a Q-Sort emphasizing childrearing practices. The return rate for the student sample was a very high 89 percent. Its accuracy is indicated by the close correspondence between sample and population. For example, freshman and sophomore men were 13.8 percent of the campus population in 1968 and 14.0 percent of the sample. Also, freshman and sophomore women were 11.2 percent of the population and 13.2 percent of the sample. The other two samples, which were mailed to the students' parents, had response rates of approximately 60 percent of the student sample, which is quite high for mailed instruments. It has been shown that the parental samples were not biased.[6]

In determining the role of socialization in activism, the socialization approach will be compared to alternative explanations of activism. A significant part of the paper will present path analysis data that permit simultaneous examination of the socialization approach and one important competing explanation, the theory of the "conflict of generations." The conflict of generations approach—which points to hostilities between activists and their parents, instead of shared values—has been seen as a critique and refutation of the socialization approach, and evidence for it would support challenges to socialization theory. Path analysis data will also be used to examine the possibility of *improvement* in the relations between the generations, which would be predicted by the socialization approach, but not by the theory of generational conflict.

Besides the approaches included in the path analysis, the role of other factors influencing activism will also be discussed. A review of the literature indicates the following conditions had a roughly similar—or at times greater—impact on activism than unconventional socialization: historical circumstances, particularly the previous civil rights protests of the 1950s and the Vietnam War; conditions of the student status, such as relative deprivation due to lower status in the university and absolute deprivation due to the military drafting of students; situational factors of the university, such as university size and political culture; and societal conditions, such as patterns of control over students and the government's conduct of the Vietnam War. It will be shown that, even though socialization is important to understanding activism, a fuller interpretation must include other variables in addition to unconventional socialization.

With regard to testing the socialization *versus* the conflict of generations approaches, path analysis is a particularly good procedure since it permits examination of the simultaneous impact of multiple independent and intervening variables (or exogamous and endogamous variables) on the common dependent variable, student political activism. Beta weights—standardized regression coefficients—will be used to estimate path coefficients, and are abbreviated as B. The competing theories will be "tested" by examining the strengths of the beta weights measuring relationships in each theory. In general, the higher the beta weights associated with relations in a given theory, the more support for that theory, and vice versa. Similarly, a model with higher beta weights will be considered a better "fit" with the data than a model with lower beta weights. However, the notion of using beta weights to test—i.e., support, reject, or modify—a theory brings up our criteria of substantive and statistical significance for the relations in the path diagrams to follow.

For substantive and statistical significance in all the path diagrams, we have used Kerlinger and Pedhazur's (1973: 318) criterion. They suggest that paths with beta weights under .05 are not meaningful. For comparison to this criterion, we also examined Duncan's (1966) criterion of dropping paths where the beta weights are less than twice their standard error. However, when this was done, theoretically and statistically important variables would have had to be dropped from the models. For example, in our Model II, the multiple correlation coefficient (R^2) is .18907, but was only .10217 when Duncan's criterion was used.

Thus, we employed Kerlinger and Pedhazur's criterion of meaningful and non-meaningful paths, and we suggest that the reader examine the path models in this light.

There are numerous variables with which to examine the socialization approach to activism. However, due to space limitations, it is necessary to be selective about the variables used to test given theories.[7] The focus here is on variables related to left-wing political socialization, in particular variables related to the transmission of radical political consciousness from parents to their children. Also included are variables related to culturally unconventional socialization, in particular the transmission of the value of humanitarianism from parents to their children. In addition, variables will be used that indicate conflict between the generations, as reported by the parents (to avoid possible biases in students' report of conflict—or lack of conflict—with their parents). Finally, the main dependent variable is actual participation by students in political protests—i.e., student political activism.

There are ten variables used in three path diagrams in this study. The variables (with their abbreviations found in the diagrams) are as follows: Mother's Radical Political Consciousness (MRCO); Father's Radical Political Consciousness (FRCO); Mother's Humanitarianism (MHUM); Father's Humanitarianism (FHUM); Student's Radical Political Consciousness (RACO); Mother's Report of Conflict with Child (MCON); Father's Report of Conflict with Child (FCON); Student Political Activism (ACTM); Changing Relations with Child, Reported by Mother (MCRS); and Changing Relations with Child, Reported by Father (FCRS). The concept of radical political consciousness is equated with the term radical political ideology, or radical ideology, in this study.

Since there is an overlap between parents and/or students for some of these concepts (e.g., radical political consciousness applies to students, mothers, and fathers), only the five distinct concepts will be defined and operationalized:

1. *Radical Political Consciousness* refers to the desire to make a change of one or more social systems in order to increase freedom and equality for submerged groups. This is a complex concept, whose dimensions and rationale are further discussed elsewhere.[8] It is indicated by a five-item index which is presented below. In the matrix to follow, Gammas between items in the index are presented to demonstrate the consistency among the items in the index. There is no clear statement in the literature about when to include or exclude items from an index on empirical grounds.[9] Thus, as a "rule of thumb," conceptually relevant items were included in the index when the Gammas between the items were within the range of approximately .20 to .80. Selecting items in this range of association was seen as a way to avoid including items in the index which had "too high" or "too low" an empirical association with each other.[10] This method of selecting items for the index of radical political consciousness is used for students and their mothers and fathers. For convenience, this can be called the "Gamma score method" of selecting items for indices, which is a more straightforward alternative to factor analysis for accomplishing a similar result.

Student's Radical Political Consciousness

A. Five-item index: (1) Agree sweeping economic changes are necessary to solve social problems; (2) Disagree conditions are worsened for Negroes by following advocates of Black Power; (3) Agree that the United States is not sincere in its wishes to negotiate with North Vietnam; (4) Disagree there is a chance for people like me to have any voice in the affairs of the government in Washington; (5) Agree that American society is basically unjust, and that revolutionary changes are needed.

Parents' Radical Political Consciousness

A. Five-item index: (1) Agree sweeping economic changes are necessary to solve social problems; (2) Disagree conditions are worsened for Negroes by following advocates of Black Power; (3) Agree that the United States is not sincere in its wishes to negotiate with North Vietnam; (4) Disagree there is a chance for people like me to have any voice in the affairs of the government in Washington; (5) Agree that American society is basically unjust and that revolutionary changes are needed.

A. Gammas for Students:

	Economic Changes	Black Power	Vietnam	Government	Revolution
Economic Changes	—	−.635	.634	−.326	.801
Black Power	−.635	—	−.640	.182	−.688
Vietnam	.634	−.640	—	−.316	.733
Government	−.326	.182	−.316	—	−.368
Revolution	.801	−.688	.733	−.368	—

2. *Student Political Activism* refers to the engagement by students in non-institutionalized political activities. It is indicated by participation in at least one of three such activities (three political protests): Free Speech Movement of 1964–1965; Student Strike in December, 1966; and Oakland Induction Center Demonstration, Fall, 1967. No Gamma scores are reported between the three events of activism included in the index because various students were not on campus for all three instances of activism. Thus, Gamma scores would be meaningless since only a relatively small number of students had the opportunity to participate in all three instances of activism.

B. Gammas for Mothers:

	Economic Changes	Black Power	Vietnam	Government	Revolution
Economic Changes	—	−.526	.653	−.639	.813
Black Power	−.526	—	−.427	.114	−.429
Vietnam	.653	−.427	—	−.525	.640
Government	−.639	.114	−.525	—	−.746
Revolution	.813	−.429	.640	−.746	—

C. Gammas for Fathers:

	Economic Changes	Black Power	Vietnam	Government	Revolution
Economic Changes	—	−.490	.227	−.311	.657
Black Power	−.490	—	−.561	−.039	−.561
Vietnam	.227	−.561	—	−.354	.116
Government	−.331	−.039	−.354	—	−.317
Revolution	.657	−.561	.116	−.317	—

3. *Humanitarianism* is defined as concern with the plight of others in society. It is indicated by a single item: "It is vital for a growing child to be aware of and concerned about injustice in society."

4. *Parent's Report of Conflict with Child* is defined as struggle between parent and child. It is indicated by a single item: "There was a good deal of conflict between my child and me."

5. *Changing Relations with Child* refers to the improvement or deterioration of relations between parent and child. It is indicated by a single item: "In the last year or so, do you feel that your son or daughter has been growing closer or further away from you?" The categories of response are: improved, worsened, or no change.

The concepts of radical political consciousness and humanitarianism were measured by a Likert scale, with response categories of strongly agree, agree, disagree, and strongly disagree. The concept of student political activism was indicated by asking respondents if they participated, or did not participate, in the three instances of activism noted above. The indicator of parent's report of conflict with child was a Q-Sort, asking if conflict with their child was most descriptive to most undescriptive of their relationship. Finally, the indicator of changing relations with the child asked parents if relations with their child improved, stayed the same, or worsened in the last year or so.

The definitions and indicators of these concepts, including the three Gamma matrices, were reprinted by permission of Lexington Books, D. C. Heath and Company, from James L. Wood, *The Sources of American Student Activism* (Lexington, Massachusetts: Lexington Books, D. C. Heath and Company, 1974), pp. 167–168, 170–171, 175.

THE SOCIALIZATION OF ACTIVISTS

We are particularly concerned with those aspects of socialization that focus on the transmission of political ideology—especially radical political ideology—and the unconventional cultural value of humanitarianism. According to Flacks (1967), Keniston (1968), and the studies that supported them, parents of activists were attached to both radical political values and to cultural values such as humanitarianism.[11] Through the socialization process, parental commitments were seen as transmitted to their children, who then *acted upon* these values in campus protests involving civil rights, the Vietnam War, educational reform, and the like. This theory posits unconventional parental values—both political and cultural—as independent variables, student's radical political consciousness as an intervening variable, and student activism as the dependent variable.

When put into a path diagram, the results are as follows (see Diagram 1):

Diagram I: Impact of Unconventional Socialization on Student's Radical Political Consciousness and Student Activism

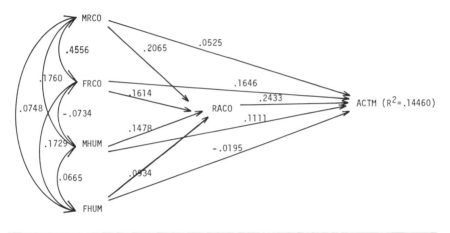

The Variables in Diagram II and their abbreviations are as follows:
Mother's Radical Political Consciousness (MRCO)
Father's Radical Political Consciousness (FRCO)
Mother's Humanitarianism (MHUM)
Father's Humanitarianism (FHUM)
Student's Radical Political Consciousness (RACO)
Student Political Activism (ACTM)

The data indicate an influence of parental socialization on student political activism. Socialization refers to the process of social learning, and thereby points to links between parental ideas or behavior and the ideas or behavior of their children.[12] Socialization can occur when the child's *attitudes* are influenced by parental attitudes or behavior; and it can occur when the child's *behavior* is influenced by parental attitudes or behavior. Various studies have attempted to further specify the particular role of mother versus father in influencing a specific type of attitude or behavior in their children. Keniston (1973: 73, 148, 201), for example, cites data showing a special maternal role in some studies of student activism.

The path diagram indicates some direct links between parental attitudes and student protest behavior. Father's radical ideology has a moderate direct impact on student activism (B = .1646). Mother's humanitarianism has a roughly similar direct impact on student activism (B = .1111). However, two other direct relations between parental attitudes and student activism are considerably weaker or nonexistent. The relation between mother's radical ideology and activism is only B = .0525, and there is a slight negative relation between father's humanitarianism and student activism of B = −.0195.

These direct links between parental attitudes and student protest have a "stimulus-response" character to them; that is, when the direct impact of parental views on student behavior is examined alone, the student's political behavior is seen as broadly responding to parental ideology. However, the student's own ideology is *not* included in the analysis. Yet parental ideas often affect the development of the student's ideology, which in turn can influence a student's political behavior.

Although socialization theory includes direct relations such as those presented, the theory particularly emphasizes *indirect* relations between the variables. Socialization theory often shows how parental attitudes influence the development of *attitudes* in their children, who then *act upon* these attitudes. The latter formulation stresses indirect links between parental attitudes and the student's behavior because the student's own ideology is added as a crucial intervening variable between parental attitudes and student behavior. The approach emphasizing indirect effects is thus a three-stage model of socialization instead of the two-stage model for direct effects.

When the student's own ideology—here, the student's radical political consciousness—is included in the analysis the relations *become stronger*. When the three-stage model between parental ideology, student's ideology, and activism is examined, we find stronger relations than existed when only direct effects of parental ideology on activism were explored. The relation between mother's radical ideology and student's radical ideology is B = .2065, and the relation between student's radical ideology and activism is B = .2433. Similarly, the relation between father's radical ideology and student's radical ideology is B = .1614, and the relation between student's radical ideology and activism remains B = .2433.

In addition, the relation between mother's humanitarianism and student's radical ideology is B = .1478, and the relation between student's ideology and activism is B = .2433. The only three-variable relation of lesser magnitude is between father's humanitarianism and student's radical ideology (B = .0934), although the link between student's ideology and activism is the stronger B = .2433.

Thus, when we add in the mediating factor of student's political consciousness—as should be done when carefully examining socialization theory—we see at least moderate positive relations between parental political or cultural ideology, student's radical ideology, and activism. In this approach, the impact of parental ideology on the student's consciousness is central. The parents not only influence their children's behavior in a direct fashion. The data also indicate that, for various student protesters of the 1960s, unconventional political or cultural ideology of the parents influenced the emergence of radical systems of thought for these students which, in turn, influenced their participation in the protests of the 1960s.

AN ALTERNATIVE TO THE SOCIALIZATION APPROACH: THE CONFLICT OF GENERATIONS

To further test the socialization hypothesis, data on the conflict of generations will be introduced into the path model. The socialization approach just discussed emphasizes the *continuity* between the generations, with the younger generation incorporating unconventional parental values into their own personality systems and then acting on these values. In contrast, critics such as Lewis Feuer (1969) have argued that activists were really rebelling against parental surrogates during the 1960s. Flacks (1967: 68) was well aware of these contrasting positions when he asserted:

> Most students who are involved in the movement . . . are involved in neither "conversion" from nor "rebellion" against the political perspectives of their fathers. A more supportable view suggests that the great majority . . . are attempting to fulfill and renew the political traditions of their families.

Yet Feuer (1969: 10–11, 162) and others have charged that activists were rebelling against their parents, and have even argued that activists had unresolved Oedipal crises that influenced hostile actions by students against campus administrators, faculty, and other authority figures.

Conflict can be seen in two very different fashions. One is the Feuer-type explanation noted above. The other sees activist students coming into conflict with their parents over values they *share*. In the latter formulation, activists come into conflict with their parents because the activists feel the parents have not lived up to their own political or cultural ideals. Keniston (1967) recognized the likelihood of this type of conflict when he referred to parents' expressed but unimplemented values.

It is possible to examine relations in a path diagram to test the Feuer approach to conflict in families of activists, and the alternative approach just discussed which sees conflict *derived from* the continuity between the generations. Whereas we do not have data on the unresolved Oedipal crises of activists—or on the lack of such unresolved crises—we do have data on conflict within the families of activists that can be used to compare these positions.

If conflict occurred over the students' view that their parents did not live up to their own unconventional political or cultural beliefs, then links should exist between parents' unconventional political and cultural beliefs, student's radical political consciousness, conflict between the generations, and activism. This is the case because parental beliefs are seen as giving rise to student's radical political consciousness, which is the source of activism *as well as* generational conflict. In this formulation, student's radical consciousness is *independently* associated with both activism and the conflict of generations. In contrast, if a Feuer-type explanation were correct, we would expect to find a strong *direct relation* between the conflict of generations and activism.

In Diagram II there are at least moderate relations between mother's and father's radical political consciousness and student's radical political conscious-ness (B's of .2065 and .1614). Also a similar relation exists between mother's humanitarianism and student's radical consciousness (B = .1478), although this is less so for father's humanitarianism (B = .0934). In turn, student's radical political consciousness is clearly associated with the conflict of generations (B = .2016 for maternal conflict and B = .1715 for paternal conflict). Finally, student's radical political consciousness has an impact on activism of B = .1991.

In comparison, the direct impact of the conflict of generations on activism is virtually non-existent for mothers (B = .0215). However, there is a stronger

Diagram II: Unconventional Socialization and Conflict Approaches to Student Activism

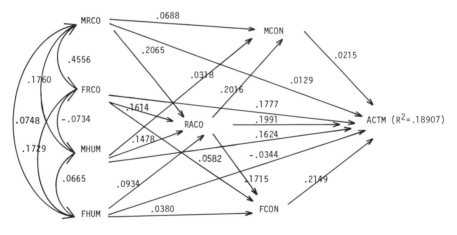

The variables in Diagram II and their abbreviations are as follows:
Mothers Radical Political Consciousness (MRCO)
Father's Radical Political Consciousness (FRCO)
Mother's Humanitarianism (MHUM)
Father's Humanitarianism (FHUM)
Student's Radical Political Consciousness (RACO)
Mother's Report of Conflict with Child (MCON)
Father's Report of Conflict with Child (FCON)
Student Political Activism (ACTM)

relation for fathers (B = .2149). The latter finding is the only support for a Feuer-type approach to activism. As such, the better "fit" appears to be the more complex model that depicts conflict arising from parents failing to adhere to their own ideals. This conflict over parental ideals is quite compatible with the socialization approach to activism because the conflict arises from the *adequate socialization* of students to unconventional views.[13]

ACTIVISM AND IMPROVING RELATIONS BETWEEN THE GENERATIONS

The final element in the socialization approach to activism examined here is the improvement or deterioration of relations between the generations *due to* student activism. The "conflict of generations" view popularized in the media of the 1960s held that student activism drove families apart. According to this view, families could not tolerate heated debates over the students' participation in uninstitutionalized activities that challenged the authority of the government, draft, school administration, and police. As such, activism was seen to *create* much conflict in families and to worsen family relations.

The socialization approach to activism, however, would predict the opposite conclusion. Student activism can be seen as opening channels of communication between parents and children that were previously closed. Since student activism was uninstitutionalized behavior, parents and children would be likely to discuss why the students decided to engage in this type of activity. This type of discussion, in turn, could be seen as *improving* relations between parents and children, who found they shared many similar unconventional values.

As Diagram III indicates, the improvement in relations between the generations does occur between mothers and their activist children (B = .1286). However, this does not occur for fathers (B = −.0292).

Interestingly enough, another study that took the sex of the children as well as the sex of the parents into account indicated that relations with *both* parents improved as a result of activism.[14] Furthermore, this improvement was especially accentuated for mothers in relation to their daughters and fathers in relation to their sons.

In the present study, the sex of the parent was included in the path diagrams, but not the sex of the student. As such, data on mothers reflect changing relations (improvement, no change, or deterioration) between them and their daughters *or* sons. Similarly, data on fathers reflect changing relations between them and their sons *or* daughters. The upshot of all these findings is that participation in activism appears to improve relations between the generations, although this occurs more often between activists (male or female) and their mothers than between activists and their fathers.

It is plausible—though not proven—that mothers may have greater tolerance for their children's unconventional behavior than do fathers. This would help

Diagram III: Unconventional Socialization and Conflict Approaches to
Activism, Including the Impact of Activism on
Changing Relations between the Generations

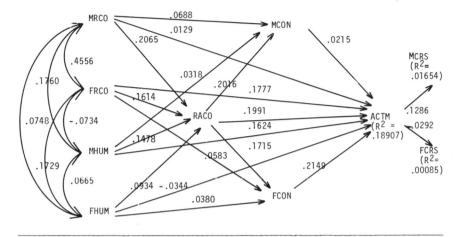

The variables in Diagram I and their abbreviations are as follows:
Mother's Radical Political Consciousness (MRCO)
Father's Radical Political Consciousness (FRCO)
Mother's Humanitarianism (MHUM)
Father's Humanitarianism (FHUM)
Student's Radical Political Consciousness (RACO)
Mother's Report of Conflict with Child (MCON)
Father's Report of Conflict with Child (FCON)
Student Political Activism (ACTM)
Changing Relations with Child, Reported by Mother (MCRS)
Changing Relations with Child, Reported by Father (FCRS)

account for activism improving relations with mothers more so than with fathers.
However, this reasoning is entirely *ex-post-facto* and, to be proven, would have
to be tested in a future investigation. In any case, the improvement in generational relations shown here for mothers, and in the other study for both parents,
lends further support to the socialization approach to activism as compared to the
conflict of generations approach.[15]

SOCIALIZATION AND OTHER CONDITIONS OF STUDENT ACTIVISM

The data above point to an important conclusion about the socialization approach
to student activism: it is a *middle range* theory which explains part of the
variation in activism, but does not account for the entire variation.[16] The
associations presented are of *moderate* magnitude, with various relations around
$B = .20$. Similarly, the multiple correlation coefficients (R^2) for the various

models also indicate moderate variance in the dependent variable explained by the socialization variables. The R^2 for student activism in Models I, II, and III are, respectively, .14460, .18907, and .18907. Thus, a bit less than 20 percent of the variance in activism is explained by the variables in each model. These data thus indicate that unconventional socialization is a contributing, but not necessary or sufficient condition of activism.[17]

The explanation of about 20 percent of the variance in activism is reasonably consistent with other research using similar variables and techniques. In a series of outstanding papers, Richard Braungart has reported findings of similar magnitude. For example, the R^2 in one of his well known models is .288, and most of the corresponding beta weights are between .10 and .30.[18] Also, Keniston (1973), in reporting on many empirical studies of activism, points to various findings within a moderate range. For example, he reports family political variables explaining 15.5 percent and 30 percent of the variance in activism (Keniston, 1973: 172). Similarly, he shows a correlation between parental attitudes and activism of r = .43 (Keniston, 1973: 171). He additionally reports higher correlations between parental attitudes and student activism (e.g., r = .69). But most of the results Keniston reports, which are parallel to our study, are also of a moderate magnitude. As such, various students with an unconventional background— and who even adhered to radical political ideology—were *not* activists.[19] Conversely, many students without an unconventional background *did participate* in New Left activities, especially in the latter part of the 1960s and early 1970s.

The less-than-perfect association between socialization and activism suggests the necessity of examining other factors that influenced participation in activism besides unconventional socialization. Four broad types of factors will be briefly considered that also contributed to the explanation of activism: (1) historical circumstances; (2) conditions of the student status; (3) situational factors of the college or university attended; and (4) societal conditions. Each of these factors operated at least partially independent of the socialization experience; and, as an abbreviated literature review will indicate, each influenced activism in a roughly similar—or at times stronger—fashion than did socialization.

HISTORICAL CIRCUMSTANCES: CIVIL RIGHTS PROTESTS

The civil rights protests in the South during the mid-1950s provided an essential background for student activism of the 1960s. The civil rights movement indicated to students the possibility of challenging the status quo—a possibility that had not been envisioned on a widespread basis since the 1930s. Anti-establishment sentiment among students, though lively in the 1930s, had been relatively dormant through the 1940s and 1950s.[20] Yet, the dramatic challenges to Southern college students requested service at Woolworth's segregated lunch-

counter in Greensboro, North Carolina.[21] When they were arrested after refusing to leave, the attending publicity sparked a distinctive student protest
initiate a "student component," which marked the actual beginning of the student movement of the 1960s. On February 1, 1960, a few well-dressed, black,
Southern college students requested service at Woolworth's segrated lunch
counter in Greensboro, North Carolina.[21] When they were arrested after
refusing to leave, the attending publicity sparked a distinctive student protest
movement against segregation. Within months, students from the North were
flocking to the South to join the Southern students engaged in the movement
(Flacks, 1967; Pinkney, 1968).

The civil rights movement thus had a general and specific impact on student
participation in political activism. It broadly pointed to the strategy of protests to
redress inequality, and it served as a specific vehicle for students to actively
challenge the existing society. However, available evidence indicates that there
was *selective recruitment* to these civil rights protests. In particular, it appears
that those students with unconventional political backgrounds—especially leftist
political backgrounds—were especially likely to participate in student activism
of the early 1960s.

In one of the few systematic studies of activists of the early 1960s, Pinkney
(1968: 47) found that the *modal response* of civil rights activists regarding
political affiliation was *socialist* instead of Democrat or Republican. In addition,
he reports that "an overwhelming majority (67 percent) reject the two conventional parties in the United States," and that various activists made such statements as "Ultimately socialism is necessary" (Pinkney, 1968: 47). Data like
these strongly suggest a left-wing orientation of various early 1960s activists.

Furthermore, Pinkney (1968: 53) indicates that unconventional political and
cultural socialization played a significant role in shaping the activists' views and
actions. He states:

> Often they act out of a sense of deep commitment to certain values which have been instilled
> since early childhood. That is, they have been socialized into feeling strongly about . . . con-
> cepts [such as] freedom, equality, justice, fair play . . .

Thus, it appears—at least in Pinkney's important investigation—that there was a
strong association between unconventional socialization and participation in civil
rights activism of the early 1960s.[22]

HISTORICAL CIRCUMSTANCES: THE VIETNAM WAR

The other crucial historical circumstance affecting participation in activism was
the Vietnam War. While the full details of the impact of the war on activism
cannot be treated here, a few key issues can be addressed.

First and foremost, the development of the New Left movement from the mid-1960s on was intimately connected to the widening war in Vietnam. Beginning in 1965, students could be—and were—drafted into a war that many did not support. This ultimately brought in thousands of new participants in student activism, and literally millions of students participated in some form of protest before the New Left ended in the 1970s.[23]

Early studies of Vietnam protesters—particularly the classic discussions of Flacks (1967) and Keniston (1968)—indicated a close correspondence between unconventional socialization and participation in activism. Most of the quotes that began this paper were taken from these discussions and clearly point to activists being socialized in politically left-wing and/or culturally unconventional homes. Keniston (1968: 123) noted that "many of these young radicals have identified themselves, from a very early age, with some tradition of radical protest against injustice." One radical in this study, for example, "recalls in early childhood attending with an admired relative a meeting of the editorial board of an Old Left journal" (Keniston, 1968: 123). Similarly, as noted, Flacks (1967) reported continuity between the generations of leftist activists and their parents.

These pioneering studies focused on activists who were involved in the movement prior to the late 1960s (e.g., prior to 1968). Similar to the findings reported by Pinkney on early civil rights activists, Flacks' and Keniston's studies point to a close correspondence between unconventional socialization and participation in activism for early anti-Vietnam protesters. In the earlier part of the 1960s, fewer students were involved in the movement, and these early participants tended to come from politically and/or culturally unconventional homes.[24]

The Vietnam War, continually widening its scope, confronted more and more students with the negative prospect of fighting in Vietnam. A base of anti-war sentiment existed as early as 1965, and this base grew much larger throughout the rest of the 1960s and into the early 1970s. With this broadening base of students came a *decreasing* association between socialization and activism. The data we presented on Berkeley, for example, were collected in 1968 and indicated a reduced—although still positive—association between socialization and activism, as compared to the higher associations reported in studies of early- and mid-1960s activists. Our finding of a moderate association between socialization and activism was supported by various studies we cited which were also of the late 1960s or early 1970s. This conclusion is paralleled by still other findings on the broadening *social-economic base* of the New Left movement by the late 1960s—i.e., it was found that students from more heterogeneous social-economic backgrounds were participating in the New Left by the late 1960s than in the early 1960s.[25] Thus, the Vietnam War affected thousands—even millions—of students from various backgrounds by the late 1960s, and the increasing participation of more students from different backgrounds eventually reduced the initially strong relation between unconventional socialization and student activism.[26]

CONDITIONS OF THE STUDENT STATUS

Besides the crucial effect of these historical circumstances on participation in activism, other conditions were also influential. A review of the literature suggests that the special circumstances of students, *qua* students, influenced participation in activism. It has been pointed out that students do not have the social obligations and commitments of adult roles, which permits students to participate in activities that could otherwise seriously threaten jobs, marriages, and other adult relations.[27] This freedom from adult sanctions is seen as broadly conducive of student involvement in illegal demonstrations, marches, and protests, many of which could lead to arrest and imprisonment. This freedom *per se* is not seen as a sufficient—or fully predictive—condition of activism; if it were, students would always be protesting, which is not the case. But when this freedom is combined with strains, as occurred during the Vietnam War, it can encourage activism.

Similarly, relative and absolute deprivations of students have been seen as underlying conditions of activism. It is argued that a student's lower status in the university, as compared to professors or administrators, generates discontents which can influence participation in activism.[28] Some studies suggest that this may be accentuated for students *closer* to the higher level statuses in the university—namely, graduate students and teaching assistants (Dubin and Beisse, 1967; Smelser, 1974: 106–111). However, the status of students, and hence the condition of relative deprivation, is more or less constant.[29] Professors and administrators typically occupy positions of higher authority and prestige than students. As such, relative deprivation would often have to combine with other strains for this kind of deprivation to produce protests.

The 1960s produced these other kinds of strains on students. From 1965 on, students were being drafted to fight in Vietnam. For students who opposed the war, or who were ambiguous about it, getting drafted constituted an extreme, or absolute, deprivation. Even the threat of getting drafted under these circumstances was perceived as an absolute deprivation by many. Thus, by 1968, there was a direct relation between availability for the draft and participation in student activism.[30]

Other aspects of the student status have similarly been seen to influence activism. Flacks (1967) argued that student activists in his sample adhered to values which were inconsistent with adult conceptions of authority. This lack of willingness to accept adult edicts, solely *because* they were issued by adults, is seen as a factor conducive to activism. By the mid-1960s, this position was being specifically applied to such adult decisions as administrators permitting military recruiters on campus. Many protests—such as that over Naval recruiters on the

Berkeley campus in 1966 and assorted protests over recruiting trips to campuses by Dow Chemical, the manufacturer of napalm—were initiated by challenges to adult university authority. Finally, even when students had different interests and motives for participating in protests, many did have similar anti-war goals, which helped expand the student movement to large proportions.

SITUATIONAL FACTORS OF COLLEGE OR UNIVERSITY ATTENDED

Various researches have shown that the size and structure of the university or college which students attended influenced participation in activism. In a thorough investigation, Scott and El-Assal (1969) showed that participation in activism was greater as the size and bureaucratic nature of the university increased.[31] Similarly, a clear left-wing political culture on given campuses has been shown to influence participation in activism (Lipset, 1976: 98). To be sure, this political culture is often developed and sustained by students with unconventional political backgrounds disproportionately attending specific universities, such as the University of Wisconsin at Madison, Columbia University, University of California at Berkeley, and the University of Chicago. This left-wing culture can be drawn upon in times of crisis to produce many active participants in protests, as often occurred during the 1960s.

A part of the student sub-culture involves student social networks, especially associated with living arrangements, as well as with study and recreation activities. It has been shown, for example, that sororities tend to reduce the political activities of the members (Wood, 1969). In contrast, left-leaning "coops" or "communes" apparently encouraged activism.[32] Similarly, apartment-house living, as compared to living at home, in fraternities, or in sororities influenced participation in activism (Lipset, 1965; Wood, 1969). It is possible apartment-house living is associated with graduate student participation in activism; but, in general, apartment dwellers would be more removed from social controls against participation in activism that can exist when living at home, in fraternities or sororities, or even in dormitories.[33]

Encounters with police on campus served as radicalizing experiences for various students (Stark, 1969, 1972). When police came on campuses to "defuse" demonstrations, the effect was often the exact opposite. On various occasions, the presence of police brought into demonstrations liberal or moderate students because of their opposition to the use of force against students in general, and, at times, against them directly (Stark, 1969; Lipset, 1976: 76).

Finally, college campuses are conducive to activism because they concentrate large numbers of students in a relatively small geographic area. When difficulties that affect students arise, rapid communication of the problem—as well as political solutions to it—can quickly diffuse through the student population.[34] This occurred frequently during the 1960s when new escalations of the war were

announced, when campuses were visited by military recruiters, or when police
were brought on campus.

In sum, various aspects of college and university social structure and culture
were conducive to protests of the 1960s. Many of these conditions operated at
least partly independent of family socialization. As such, they are alternative
explanations of activism than unconventional socialization.

Societal Conditions

The most general societal condition influencing—and widening—student activism from the mid-1960s on was the continual escalation of the Vietnam War.[35]
We have previously spelled out various aspects of this central condition of
activism. Only a few points will be added here. On one hand, the conduct of the
war was never "above-board," thus producing cynicism about the actual
motives of the United States in Vietnam.[36] The Vietnam War, in fact, was
never declared an "official" war by the government. Instead, it was euphemisti-
cally called the "Vietnam Era."

On the other hand, the government's policy of drafting students brought
them—especially white middle-class students—"face to face" with a personally
oppressive condition to a greater degree than most had ever previously experienced. This helped radicalize students from conventional homes, as well as give
additional impetus to the radicalism of those socialized in unconventional
homes.[37]

By the early 1970s the U.S. government (or state governments) had: (1)
invaded Cambodia, thereby swelling the ranks of the movement;[38] (2) participated in the shooting of students at Kent State and Jackson State universities,
thereby seriously escalating the level of control over students; and (3) ultimately
withdrew from Vietnam. The use of force against students did increase the
"risk" part of the "risk/reward ratio" for students participating in the anti-war
effort.[39] Whether this type of control would have eventually extinguished the
movement—or pushed it to greater resistance—is a moot point.[40] By 1973,
America's participation in the war was greatly diminished, and by 1975, Saigon
had fallen. The New Left declined significantly when the anti-war goal was
finally accomplished.[41] Yet, prior to this, the movement—and its active participants—had challenged basic governmental policies and social institutions in a
way not seen since the 1930s (Lipset and Ladd, 1971).

CONCLUSIONS

This paper has shown that unconventional family socialization did influence
participation in student activism of the 1960s. This influence was particularly
strong in the early and mid-1960s, but had become moderate by the late 1960s.
The widening scope of the Vietnam War increased the number of active participants in the New Left, which broadened the base of the movement to include

greater numbers of students from politically or culturally conventional family backgrounds, as well as those from unconventional backgrounds.

In addition, various other conditions, such as large campus size and encounters with police during demonstrations on campus, also influenced participation in activism besides unconventional socialization. Many of these other conditions were at least partially independent of family socialization and therefore constituted additional influences on activism. For example, a student with a politically conventional family background who attended a large-sized "multiversity" would be inclined against participation because of family background, but influenced toward participation because of the type of school attended. Thus, by the late 1960s, family socialization moderately contributed to activism, without being a necessary or sufficient condition. The relationship between unconventional family socialization and activism was still positive, but of lesser magnitude, by the late 1960s than it had been earlier. The historical circumstance of Vietnam and the other contributing conditions of activism essentially moderated what was initially a strong relation between family background and a distinctive form of political behavior.

ACKNOWLEDGMENTS

We would like to thank Louis Kriesberg and two anonymous reviewers for their very helpful comments on an earlier draft of this paper. Also we want to thank Robert H. Somers and Jeanne Block for the generous use of their data.

NOTES

1. Flacks (1967, p. 70).
2. Flacks (1967, pp. 66–67).
3. Flacks (1970, p. 347).
4. Keniston (1968, p. 245).
5. Personal communication from Louis Kriesberg.
6. Wood (1974, pp. 43–44).
7. For the examination of additional socialization variables, see Wood (1974).
8. See Wood (1974, Chapter 3; 1975).
9. See Wood (1974, pp. 165–166).
10. Robert H. Somers suggested using the statistic, Gamma, in this connection, in part because it is a symmetrical measure. He also suggested the range of .20 to .80. Only a few Gammas do not fall within this range for students, mothers, and fathers. The items in the indices are all considered "equal"—i.e., there is no weighting of some items as more important than others.
11. For some studies that supported Flacks (1967) and Keniston (1968), see McEvoy and Miller (1969); and Foster and Long (1970).
12. For a classic discussion of political socialization, see Hyman (1959). Also see the many recent studies of political socialization in Wood, Wood, and Ng (1979, pp. 50–53).
13. Other links in the path diagram are not predicted by either model and are generally weak. This weakness lends further support to the theoretical model proposed here.
14. Wood (1974, p. 78).
15. Other weaker approaches to activism include a focus on social alienation, cultural alienation,

permissive childrearing, and reformist ideology. See Wood (1974) for a discussion of these explanations of activism.

16. For a discussion of middle range theories, see Merton (1957, pp. 5–10).

17. Hence, unconventional socialization influences (contributes to) activism, without being a required (necessary) or fully predictive (sufficient) condition of activism.

18. Braungart (1971, p. 121). Also see Braungart (APS Publications, Inc.); and Braungart (1976). For a follow-up study of former civil rights activists, exhibiting similar moderate range coefficients, see Fendrich (1977).

19. Indications of the moderate instead of strong relation between student's radical ideology and participation in activism are the beta weights between these variables of .2433 in Model I, and .1991 in Models II and III.

20. For a discussion of student activism, or the lack of activism, in the 1930s, 1940s, and 1950s, see Lipset (1976, Chapter 5); and Wood (1976).

21. For a discussion of this incident, see Cluster (1979).

22. Also see Horowitz (1962) for a discussion of student activism over issues other than civil rights that similarly points to unconventional backgrounds of early activists at the University of California at Berkeley from 1958–1962.

23. Using data from the Harris Survey, Lipset (1976, p. 45) shows that the following percentages of students were involved in some form of demonstration from 1965 to 1969 to 1970: 29 percent, 40 percent and 60 percent. With a student population in these years of approximately seven million, this means that by 1969 approximately 2.8 million students were involved in some form of demonstration, and that by 1970 approximately 4.2 million students were similarly involved.

24. For a chart showing increasing participation in anti-war demonstrations from 1965 to 1968, see Skolnick (1969, p. 32). For a discussion of the increasing participation in New Left activities in general, see Wood (1974, pp. 1–4).

25. Mankoff and Flacks (1971).

26. Using Harris Survey data, Lipset (1976, p. 93) reports that in May of 1970, *approximately 50 percent* of students whose mother's ideology was Conservative or Far Right had participated in demonstrations against the U.S. invasion of Cambodia, if their school had such protests. Yet a still larger 69 percent participated whose mothers were Liberal, and 80 percent whose mothers were Far Left.

27. For a discussion of the greater freedom from sanctions for students and young people generally, see Kriesberg (1973, p. 124).

28. See Kriesberg (1973, pp. 45–46), and Smelser (1974, pp. 95–111). Smelser explicitly ties in the teaching assistant status with the strains of relative deprivation, which is seen as a condition of protest. For another aspect of relative deprivation, see Kriesberg (1973, p. 78), who shows that relative deprivation can occur when students experience a falling-off of progress, as when administrators decide to deprive students of free speech; this is also seen as a condition of protest. For a general discussion of the impact of relative deprivation on protests, see Gurr (1970).

29. Historical circumstances can, of course, increase or decrease the level of relative deprivation students experience. In the prior footnote (28), Kriesberg (1973, p. 78), for example, discusses a circumstance where relative deprivation is increased for students.

30. See Wood (1974, p. 137). The three categories of draft availability were I-A (immediately available for the draft), II-S (temporary student deferment), and Not Eligible. By 1968, the more available a male student was for induction into the military, the more likely he was to be an activist, at least in data collected at the University of California, Berkeley. To our knowledge, there are not many other such studies relating draft status to participation in activism. However, for an excellent discussion of Americans who went to Canada because of the draft during the Vietnam War, see Kasinsky (1976).

31. The educational research of Astin and Bayer tends to support the conclusion that size of the university or college does influence protests. See, for example, Astin and Bayer (1971).

32. This is a distinct impression of one of the authors of this paper. The role of communes has also been discussed by others such as Richard Flacks.

33. However, dormitories often had sub-groups that encouraged activism. For an interesting discussion of social networks on a particular campus—which were often a-political on this campus in the early 1960s when the study was conducted—see Boltan and Kammeyer (1967).

34. For a discussion of this, see Lipset (1965, p. 6).

35. For an excellent discussion documenting and analyzing this escalation, see Schurmann, Scott, and Zelnick (1966). There was, of course, further escalation after this book was published.

36. For quotes of activists regarding their views of U.S. motives in Vietnam, see Wood (1975).

37. For more discussion on the relation between radical political consciousness and student activism, see Wood (1974, 1975).

38. For the large proportions of many categories of students who participated in protests against the Cambodian invasion, see Lipset (1976, pp. 97–98).

39. For a discussion of the "risk/reward ratio" as it applies to social movement participation, see Oberschall (1973, pp. 161–172). This is part of the "rational calculation" approach to understanding participation in social movements.

40. For a discussion of the complex relations of social control to social movement decline or further development, see Smelser (1963, pp. 364–379).

41. For a discussion of the decline of the New Left, see Wood (1974, pp. 148–150). For an excellent historical account and analysis of the New Left from its beginnings to its end, see Young (1977).

REFERENCES

Astin, A. W., and A. E. Bayer (1971) "Antecedents and Consequences of Disruptive Campus Protests." *Measurement and Evaluation in Guidance* 1(Fall):149–162.

Bolton, Charles D., and C. W. Kammeyer (1967) *The University Student.* New Haven, Conn.: College & University Press.

Braungart, Richard G. (1971) "Family Status, Socialization, and Student Politics: A Multivariate Analysis." *American Journal of Sociology* 77(July):108–130.

———(1976) "College and Noncollege Youth Politics in 1972: An Application of Mannheim's Generation Unit Model." *Journal of Youth and Adolescence* 5:325–347.

———(APS Publications, Inc.) "Path Analysis and Causal Analysis: Variations on a Multivariate Technique of Measuring Student Politics." *Research in Higher Education* 3:87–97.

Cluster, Dick, ed. (1979) *They Should Have Served That Cup of Coffee: 7 Radicals Remember the 60s.* Boston, Mass.: South End Press.

Dubin, Robert, and F. Beisse (1967) "The Assistant: Academic Subaltern." *Administrative Science Quarterly* 11(March):521–547.

Duncan, Otis D. (1966) "Path Analysis: Sociological Examples." *American Journal of Sociology* 72:1–16.

Fendrich, James M. (1977) "Keeping the Faith or Pursuing the Good Life: A Study of the Consequences of Participation in the Civil Rights Movement." *American Sociological Review* 42(February):144–157.

Feuer, Lewis S. (1969) *The Conflict of Generations.* New York: Basic Books.

Flacks, Richard (1967) "The Liberated Generation: An Exploration of the Roots of Student Protest." *Journal of Social Issues* 23(July):52–75.

———(1970) "Social and Cultural Meanings of Student Revolt: Some Informal Comparative Observations." *Social Problems* 17(Winter):340–357.

Foster, J., and D. Long, eds. (1970) *Protest!: Student Activism in America.* New York: Morrow.

Gurr, Ted R. (1970) *Why Men Rebel.* Princeton, N.J.: Princeton University Press.

Horowitz, David (1962) *Student: The Political Activities of the Berkeley Students*. New York: Ballantine.

Hyman, Herbert (1959) *Political Socialization*. Glencoe, Ill.: The Free Press.

Kasinsky, Renee (1976) *Refugees from Militarism: Draft Age Americans in Canada*. New Brunswick, N.J.: Transaction Books.

Keniston, Kenneth (1967) "The Sources of Student Dissent." *Journal of Social Issues* 23(July):108–137.

———(1968) *Young Radicals*. New York: Harcourt, Brace & World.

———(1973) *Radicals and Militants*. Lexington, Mass.: Lexington Books, D. C. Heath.

Kerlinger, Frederick N., and Elazar J. Pedhazur (1973) *Multiple Regression in Behavioral Research*. New York: Holt, Rinehart and Winston.

Kriesberg, Louis (1973) *The Sociology of Social Conflicts*. Englewood Cliffs, N.J.: Prentice-Hall, Inc.

Lipset, Seymour Martin (1965) "University Student Politics," pp. 1–9 in Seymour Martin Lipset and Sheldon S. Wolin (eds.), *The Berkeley Student Revolt*. Garden City, N.Y.: Doubleday Anchor Books.

———(1976) *Rebellion in the University*. Chicago: The University of Chicago Press, Phoenix Edition.

Lipset, Seymour Martin, and E. C. Ladd (1971) "College Generations from the 1930s to the 1960s." *The Public Interest* 25(Fall):99–113.

Mankoff, Milton L., and Richard Flacks (1971) "The Changing Social Base of the American Student Movement." *Annals of the American Academy of Political and Social Science* 395(May):54–67.

McEvoy, James, and A. Miller (eds.) (1969) *Black Power and Student Rebellion*. Belmont, Calif.: Wadsworth Publishing Company.

Merton, Robert K. (1957) *Social Theory and Social Structure*. Revised and Enlarged Edition. London: The Free Press of Glencoe, Collier-Macmillan Limited.

Oberschall, Anthony (1973) *Social Conflict and Social Movements*. Englewood Cliffs, N.J.: Prentice-Hall, Inc.

Pinkney, Alphonso (1968) *The Committed: White Activists in the Civil Rights Movement*. New Haven, Conn.: College & University Press.

Rothman, Stanley, and S. Robert Lichter (1978) "The Case of the Student Left." *Social Research* (Autumn):535–609.

Schurmann, Franz, P. D. Scott, and R. Zelnick (1966) *The Politics of Escalation in Vietnam*. Boston, Mass.: Beacon Press.

Scott, Joseph W., and Mohamed El-Assal (1969) "Multiversity, University Size, University Quality and Student Protest: An Empirical Study." *American Sociological Review* 34(October):702–709.

Skolnick, Jerome H. (1969) *The Politics of Protest*. New York: Ballantine Books.

Smelser, Neil J. (1963) *Theory of Collective Behavior*. New York: The Free Press of Glencoe.

Smelser, Neil J. (1974) "Growth, Structural Change, and Conflict in California Public Higher Education, 1950–1970." Pp. 9–141 in Neil J. Smelser and Gabriel Almond (eds.) *Public Higher Education in California*. Berkeley: University of California Press.

Stark, Rodney (1969) "Protest + Police = Riot." Pp. 167–196 in James McEvoy and A. Miller (eds.) *Black Power and Student Rebellion*. Belmont, Calif.: Wadsworth Publishing Company.

———(1972) *Police Riots*. Belmont, Calif.: Wadsworth Publishing Company.

Wood, James L. (1969) "The Role of Radical Political Consciousness in Student Activism: A Preliminary Analysis." Paper presented to the 66th Annual Meeting of the American Sociological Association, San Francisco, California.

———(1974) *The Sources of American Student Activism*. Lexington, Mass.: Lexington Books, D. C. Heath and Company.

————(1975) *New Left Ideology: Its Dimensions and Development.* Sage Professional Paper in American Politics. Beverly Hills, Calif.: Sage Publications, Inc.

————(1976) "Student Political Activism." Chapter 11, pp. 401–433, in David W. Swift (ed.) *American Education: A Sociological View.* Boston, Mass.: Houghton Mifflin Company.

Wood, James L., Patricia A. Wood, and Wing-Cheung Ng (1979) *Political Sociology Bibliography.* Ill.: Vance Bibliographies.

Young, Nigel (1977) *An Infantile Disorder? The Crisis and Decline of the New Left.* Boulder, Colo.: Westview Press.

LOOSELY STRUCTURED COLLECTIVE CONFLICT:
A THEORY AND AN APPLICATION

Anthony Oberschall

THEORY

Loosely Structured Collective Action

In this section, I present a simple theory of conflict group formation and of loosely structured collective action. In the U.S. during the 1960s, much civil strife and social unrest, as well as non-violent collective actions, was loosely structured. This was true for the civil rights and black power movement, the student movement, and the anti-war movement (Oberschall, 1978). Loosely structured collective action refers to collective action that is undertaken by a loose coalition of activists, part-timers, and sympathizers whose boundaries are ill-defined and shifting, who lack a common, central leadership, organization, and clear-cut procedures for deciding upon a common course of action.

If one puts broad social movements and revolutions under the microscope, one will often observe a loose structure. Hundreds of groups and organizations—

Research in Social Movements, Conflicts and Change, Vol. 3, pages 45-68
Copyright © 1980 by JAI Press Inc.
All rights of reproduction in any form reserved.
ISBN: 0-89232-182-2

many of them short-lived, spatially scattered, and lacking direct communication, a single organization and a common leadership—episodically take part in many different kinds of local collective action: they gather signatures for a petition; they stage a sit-in at a local draft board; sponsor meetings and produce speakers in favor of their cause; stage demonstrations against ROTC and military recruiters on campus; counsel and help draft resisters; open coffee houses near military bases, and so on. There is some wider, common structure nonetheless: despite different ideologies, tactics, and commitment to the issues, most adherents to a movement share common targets (the Washington administration and its local agencies), respond to the same symbols (the peace sign), follow the pronouncements of the most prominent national leaders and figures of the movement, and undertake some supra-local, joint collective action, such as the giant anti-war rallies in New York and Washington called by national leaders and coordinating committees (Mobe).

Collective action is often undertaken against the constituted authorities or privileged social strata protected by the authorities. Even if the collective action is legal and non-violent, it does involve some effort and cost (risk of arrest, injury, and perhaps even death) to participants. There is no assurance that collective action will be successful: the authorities may not be persuaded to change, yield to demands, enter into negotiations, or make unilateral concessions.

The goals of collective action are frequently collective goods, such as terminating the draft, stopping an unpopular war, getting legislation passed or repealed, rescinding increased food prices. Thus, free rider tendencies impede collective action (Olson, 1965).

The organizations and activists who seek to get collective action underway lack the resources to provide selective incentives to participants—at least tangible, material incentives such as lobbies and associations provide their members. Nor do they have the power to compel participation by coercive means. They may have to induce voluntary participation through moral and ideological appeals, and create a sense of fellowship and community (Fireman and Gamson, 1979).

The theory assumes a rational view of human action. People weigh the benefits and costs of various courses of action, and choose the alternative with the highest anticipated benefit. I adopt these assumptions not on philosophic or empirical grounds, but rather for pragmatic reasons. They help develop theories and models that yield useful insights. Models of decision-making in a group context, based on benefit and cost of alternative courses of action, help explain some collective behavior episodes that are otherwise puzzling (Brown, 1965). It has sometimes been observed that a hostile and riotous crowd that police are unable to disperse melts away when it rains. Assume that members of the crowd have an unequal stake in the collective event: some are merely curious onlookers, others are deeply dedicated to the cause, most are in-between. The former are willing to pay only a low price for participation, the latter a high price. Each participant stays as long as anticipated benefit exceeds cost for him or her. Assume further that anticipated cost decreases as a function of the number of participants: people think there is safety in numbers. When it starts to rain, the additional cost of getting wet for those who are experiencing only a small excess of benefit over cost before the rain tips net benefits from slightly positive to negative, and they leave to seek shelter. As size diminishes, anticipated costs increase; that, and the additional cost of getting wet, tips net benefits from positive to negative for still other participants. Thus, a reverse bandwagon results, until size is so small that even the remaining diehards will quit. The crowd has melted away as the result of rain.

A riotous crowd thus scattering does not make sense from the point of view of the conventional wisdom which assumes loss of rational faculties and of moral judgement resulting from the influences of demagogic leaders and of contagion during collective behavior (LeBon, 1960). Critics of the rational view of human action have failed to understand what the assumptions of rationality are and what they imply. The rational view does not deny that most behavior, including collective behavior, is embedded in emotions, sentiments, social norms, conventions, and habits, and that the calculations of benefit and cost might be based on faulty and incomplete information, distorted perceptions, and erroneous arithmetic. All these, however, do not undermine the usefulness of the method, because rational choice is a systematic application of the notion that human behavior tends to be adaptive. One reason that the assumptions of rationality are useful—even when one knows that people do not in their minds perform the calculations assumed in the model—is that habit and normative prescriptions are the cumulative and ever-changing end result of millions of trials and errors, during which the rational-adaptive choices led to higher net benefits than other choices. Nevertheless, much behavior does involve self-conscious calculation of alternative courses of action, and the effect of norms and of social sanctions upon choices can be incorporated into the expression for benefit and cost.

In the theory of loosely structured collective action, two questions need clarification: What accounts for the formation and persistence of small local groups of activists and followers? What accounts for these groups' periodic participation in much larger, supra-local collective action?

At the local level, it is useful to distinguish the more permanent activists from the part-time transitory teams they enlist episodically for demonstrations and other collective actions (McCarthy and Zald, 1973). The activists usually bear much of the costs of local organization, publicity, recruitment. Transitory teams contribute mostly to the cost of collective action itself: opportunity cost and the costs associated with arrest and injury. For any participant, assume that the participation decision will be positive if anticipated net benefits from the collective action are greater than zero, as far as he is concerned. Benefits are of two

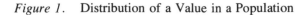

Figure 1. Distribution of a Value in a Population

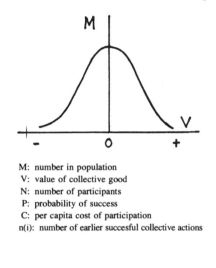

M: number in population
V: value of collective good
N: number of participants
P: probability of success
C: per capita cost of participation
n(i): number of earlier succesful collective actions

kinds: the value V_i of obtaining the collective good itself, and selective incentives S_i. Costs C_i are organization maintenance costs, other opportunity costs,
and costs resulting from collective action.[1]

Assume that the value of the collective good, V, is distributed in the population as shown in Figure 1: there are a small number of individuals who would
benefit a great deal from obtaining the collective good; many individuals are
indifferent; and there are some for whom it is a collective bad. It is from those
with the highest V that the small group of activists is formed. For a small group,
Olson (1965) has argued that it will supply itself with at least a certain amount of
the collective good. Activists will maintain a rudimentary organization and engage intermittently in some opposition activity. When an opportunity arises for
mobilizing a larger following on behalf of an issue or cause, they will step up
their organization and recruitment activities. They know that unless they do so,
no one else will.

How do activists enlist a larger number of part-timers for episodíc collective
action—for instance, a demonstration? Assume that the probability of success P
of the collective action is measured by its public opinion impact, which itself is a
function of the number of demonstrators N, as shown in Figure 2. This function
is assumed S-shaped because a small demonstration is expected to have little
impact up to a certain size, and again large numbers beyond a certain size would
not make much difference either, whereas in the middle range, additional numbers increase visibility and impact. Further assume that for the ith participant, the
decision to join or not join will depend on whether the anticipated net benefits are
greater, equal to, or less than zero; i.e.,

$$\Delta P_i V_i + S_i - C_i \geq 0 \text{ (join)} \tag{1}$$
$$< 0 \text{ (not join)}$$

where $\Delta P_i = P_i - P_{i-1}$. Though the expected value of the collective action is $P_{i-1}V_i$, a person would benefit to this extent regardless of whether he is a free rider or whether he joins. The marginal contribution a person makes to success, $\Delta P_i V_i$, is what enters his decision to join: it is the difference *his* participation makes to P.

Finally, assume that the average cost of participation C in the collective action decreases with increasing number of demonstrators, over the range of N here considered as shown in Figure 3. Such an assumption is reasonable because all three components of cost decrease with number of participants: organization maintenance benefits from economies of scale; opportunity costs decrease because less effort is required per capita with rising numbers; and direct costs decrease as a result of safety in numbers. What then are the dynamics of participation in collective action?

For the activists, who are the first to commit themselves, though ΔP is very small, anticipated V is very large, and the high cost C is offset by the high selective incentives S of participation, which include the personal rewards of participating with like-minded others in a cause, the conviction of doing the right thing, the earned esteem of group members. Given a small N, ΔP will increase for each additional recruit, at first slowly, then more rapidly; V will decrease slowly with each new recruit as those with less dedication to the new cause join;

Figure 2. Success as a Function of Participants

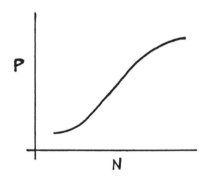

M: number in population
V: value of collective good
N: number of participants
P: probability of success
C: per capita cost of participation
n(i): number of earlier successful collective actions

Figure 3.   Cost as a Function of Participants

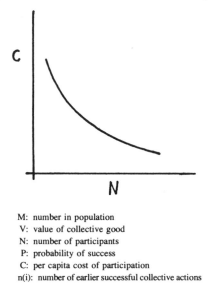

M: number in population
V: value of collective good
N: number of participants
P: probability of success
C: per capita cost of participation
n(i): number of earlier successful collective actions

C will decrease with N (safety in numbers, ability to withstand ridicule and
negative social sanctions, economies of scale); and S also can be expected to
decrease somewhat because the more marginal part-timers get less social incentives. Thus by expression (1), whether more will join will depend on the net
effect of all these functions as they change with N. Under realistic assumptions
for the shape of the functions, inequality (1) stays positive over quite a range of
N. One can end up with a large number of participants until eventually both V
and ΔP become small, and their product very small, and thus net benefits become
zero or negative.

The activists and the authorities try to influence these functions. Activists
propagandize in order to raise the average level of V in the local population; if
they build a cohesive moral community in which new recruits can be readily
absorbed, they increase S for joiners; if they get outside support, C is lowered.
They also try to convince followers that the authorities and targets will give in to
demands (P is high). The authorities, on the other hand, disseminate counter-
propaganda about their resolve to hold firm (P is low), and raise the cost curve C
by placing restrictions on mobilizing activity and by taking intimidating measures against collective action itself (Kriesberg, 1973).

I have no empirical evidence confirming these curves and functions. But we do
know that in many collective behavior episodes of the 1960s, a small band of
activists triggered collective action by recruiting sizable transitory teams. The
process summarized in expression (1) provides a plausible explanation from a

rational choice perspective. It can also explain the demobilization of collective action when applied in reverse. The case of protracted conflict is also amenable to a similar analysis (Oberschall, 1979).

The Diffusion of Collective Action

The second question, to which I now turn, is what mechanism makes possible much larger collective action on a supra-local, national scale. Many social movements promoting a cause influence public opinion and political leaders by means of mass rallies, huge petitions, and demonstrations, for which they need enlist many more than their most active members (Oberschall, 1973: 308). For a movement and leaders who do not have access to the usual political channels of interest aggregation, identifying the size of their following by visible means is a necessity if their viewpoints are not to be dismissed. Another purpose of such ''identification'' moves is to demonstrate to one's supporters one's true strength, sustain their hopes, reinforce their commitment to the cause, and provide an occasion for direct communication between top leadership and movement adherents.

It should not be assumed that large events are the result of the aggregation of large numbers of isolated individuals making independent decisions. Block recruitment tends to be the rule rather than the exception (Oberschall, 1973; Olson, 1965). Large events such as the New York teachers' strike of 1969 is the aggregate result of teachers making collective decisions in particular schools: some schools joined the strike, some remained open. Similarly, in the huge anti-war rallies, many local anti-war groups decided to participate as units, and recruited local transitory teams for the larger rally. The existence of intermediate social units in a larger event is not peculiar to social movements. A Presidential primary campaign or election is made up of the state campaigns, and each state campaign is composed of hundreds of smaller campaigns in given localities.

What incentives do local groups have in participating in the larger event? They know that some collective goods (a Civil Rights Act) will have to be obtained at the federal government level, even though local collective goods (the desegregation of a local public facility) can be gotten with local action. Since obtaining local changes is going to be easier if the national legislation is passed, it is in their interest to participate in national action which will maintain the effectiveness of the national leadership. Highly publicized national events will raise V and P in the local population as well, and make recruitment easier locally. Participation in a large, dramatic event also provides selective incentives. But what else helps overcome free rider tendencies?

The process captured in expression (1) can be applied in this situation as well, with local groups playing the role of building blocs that individuals did earlier. In the literal sense, groups do not have a group mind and do not calculate gains and losses as individuals do. But a cohesive group composed of individuals coordinating their actions may be treated as a single entity like a firm or household.

The argument then remains the same. The most dedicated groups (highest on V) will commit themselves to supra-local action even when they anticipate a low turnout. If that is communicated to other somewhat less dedicated groups, they will commit themselves to the national rally; that will increase the expected size of the national demonstration, increase the anticipated probability of success, decrease the per capita cost, and put the next groups on a steeper slope of the probability curve, decrease anticipated costs yet further, and so on, until the product of V and ΔP becomes small, and no more groups join. Newsletters, traveling speakers, publicity in the news media provide the means for communicating these moods and commitments which are needed to set off the collective dynamics according to inequality (1).

These dynamics can also clarify why many collective behavior episodes cluster in space and time: The sit-ins of 1960; the nationwide student strike in the Spring of 1970 following the Cambodia invasion and the Kent State shootings; the black riots following the assassination of Martin Luther King, Jr.; coup d'etats in Asian and Latin American countries in the 1960s; rebellions in Eastern Europe in 1956; and before the age of mass communication, the peasant uprising in 1789 in France and the revolutions of 1848 in Europe. Clustering in space and time can also be observed for skyjackings and some other non-collective actions. No single process can account for the diffusion of such diverse phenomena, though at times the concept of contagion is invoked to explain them. A useful hypothesis is that diffusion occurs partly as a result of a reassessment by potential activists and participants and by authorities of the chances of success (P) and the costs of collective action (C), after the outcomes of similar collective action elsewhere becomes known to them.

This is especially true in situations where the initial precipitating event occurs at some focal point in a system, as Paris was in 1848. Since the French Revolution, the eyes of revolutionary and reactionary groups alike were focused on Paris. Ideologies, organizational forms, collective action tactics, the authorities' reaction to opposition there were being discussed and adopted and monitored for cues about what might occur elsewhere. When the Orleanist regime was easily toppled in Paris, revolutions broke out in Vienna, Berlin, Budapest, and many other cities shortly after the news got there. Within Germany itself, Berlin was a secondary focal point. Prussia was the strongest of the German states. When the King of Prussia made concessions and promised reforms after popular disturbances, the other kings and princes in German states followed his lead, even where large disturbances were not taking place.

The mechanism that might explain diffusion is as follows: local collective action is based on expression (1); the P and C curves, which depend in part on the authorities' reaction, are based on the participants' guesses and estimates. When the outcomes of collective action elsewhere similar to what the local activists were considering becomes known, they and the authorities both revise their estimates. If similar actions were successful, the revised curves would like as in

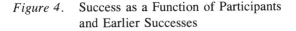

Figure 4. Success as a Function of Participants and Earlier Successes

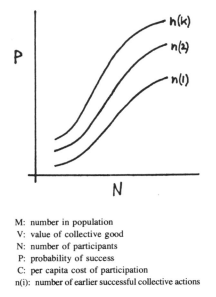

M: number in population
V: value of collective good
N: number of participants
P: probability of success
C: per capita cost of participation
n(i): number of earlier successful collective actions

Figures 4 and 5 where n(k) is the number of other successful collective actions that have taken place in the system. What makes for diffusion then is that with each additional success, a group of activists for whom expression (1) was slightly negative revises estimates of P upward and of C downward so that expression (1) becomes positive for them, and they initiate local collective action. If they, in turn, are successful, and that becomes communicated to other localities where no collective action has yet been undertaken, it will have a stimulating effect by way of further revised P and C curves.

Why do such events often cluster in time and space? Where a focal point exists—i.e. a pace-setter country, or group, or campus—collective action there will have a great impact on the P and C curves of all other social units at the same time. Thus, if collective action at the focal point is successful, many activists groups' estimates of net benefits will change to positive at the same time. Successful collective action at successive peripheral points may also set off diffusion, but probably more slowly.

Beyond this, there is an incentive for activists to act quickly. The P and C curve change can have an impact on collective action only if all concerned—activists, potential followers, opponents—recognize the relevance for local events of similar events unfolding elsewhere. Because spatial and temporal proximity is positively correlated with similarity of all sorts, and most people know that, the likelihood that potential followers and opposing authorities define the

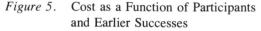

Figure 5. Cost as a Function of Participants
and Earlier Successes

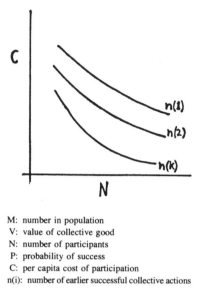

M: number in population
V: value of collective good
N: number of participants
P: probability of success
C: per capita cost of participation
n(i): number of earlier successful collective actions

local situation in terms of the revised P and C function increases with spatial and temporal proximity. Since activists know this, they will act quickly to catch opponents by surprise. Given more time, authorities will take measures to lower P and increase C, such as declaring martial law, or arresting known local activists.

I am not in a position to test systematically the theory of mobilization of loosely structured conflict groups and of the diffusion of collective action described above. Yet the theoretic ideas can be further explicated, and their usefulness and limitations better grasped, by applying them to a real-life conflict. For this purpose, I have chosen the controversies, conflicts and demonstrations on the occasion of the U.S.A.-South Africa Davis Cup matches held at Vanderbilt University in Nashville, Tennessee, on March 17 to 19, 1978.

APPLICATION: THE DAVIS CUP PROTESTS[2]

The Setting
In 1970, Nashville, the capital city of Tennessee, had a metropolitan area population of 700,000, of which about one-fifth was black. As in many Southern cities, public facilities were desegregated in the course of the 1960s civil rights struggle, and at the end of the decade the public school system was integrated after a county-wide busing plan was ordered by Federal Court. Three well-known

black institutions of higher education (Fisk University, Meharry Medical College, and Tennessee State University) provide a sizable black student population and a black middle-class of professors and administrators, augmented by teachers and civil servants.

For decades, Vanderbilt University has been an upper middle-class white university with a southern reputation, and high standing and influence within Nashville on March 17 to 19 at Vanderbilt. This fact was not publicized until the early 1960s, steps were taken to broaden the university's social base, yet the image of Vanderbilt as an elite institution identified with the privileged white upper and upper middle-class has persisted.

In the fall of 1977, the tennis coaches made a persuasive case, based on revenue and prestige, to top administrators for signing a contract with the United States Tennis Association (USTA) for holding the American zone semifinals of the Davis Cup at the university gymnasium. Though South Africa might advance to the semi-finals, this was not anticipated as a problem. Late in 1977, South Africa beat Colombia and thus was scheduled to face the United States team in Nashville on March 17 to 19 at Vanderbilt. This fact was not publicized until the Coalition for Human Rights in South Africa, at a New York news conference in late January, demanded that Vanderbilt University and the USTA cancel the tennis matches.

Though the coalition included a number of black groups and committees, the major organization within it was the NAACP. Its executive director, Benjamin Hooks, announced in a national television interview that unless the matches were cancelled, the NAACP would organize the largest U.S. demonstration since the 1960s on the week-end of the Davis Cup play in Nashville. The USTA and Vanderbilt University (VU), however, declined to cancel the matches. Thus a confrontation became inevitable.

In addition to the coalition and the NAACP, a number of Nashville individuals, groups, and organizations publicly announced their opposition to this event and sought to persuade the USTA and VU to cancel the matches. The following two months saw a steady stream of meetings, press conferences, television interviews, news releases, out-of-town speakers, posters, leaflets, pickets, and marchers (mainly on the Vanderbilt campus), and numerous other incidents as the major actors in the drama appealed to particular constituencies and to the broader public in support of their various positions.

The stakes were high for all concerned. The Davis Cup issue had the potential of polarizing the city along racial lines. Nashville knew that the Davis Cup controversy would attract national and even some international attention, and wished to maintain the image of a progressive city. For the USTA to withdraw from the matches would eliminate the U.S. from Davis Cup competition for two years, according to rules the USTA had vigorously sponsored. Given the publicity surrounding Steve Biko's death, the NAACP decided that the Davis Cup would be a favorable occasion for arousing U.S. public opinion against the inhumanity of the South African apartheid system. The NAACP also aspired to strengthen its leadership position among U.S. blacks by utilizing an issue that was bound to increase in importance in the coming decade. Finally, Vanderbilt University and its top officers wished to protect their liberal, progressive image without jeopardizing the largest fund-raising drive among alumni and business corporations in the history of the university. Financial backers of the university would be upset if it yielded to organized black pressure on the Davis Cup issue.

Despite appearances, the opposition to the Davis Cup was better served by being staged in Nashville than by its cancellation or by a shift to a small, remote community. Nashville has a large NAACP branch of some 1,000 members and three black student bodies that could supply a local mass base for protest. Cancellation might mean momentary victory without, however, the attending access to virtually free publicity and public education about South African matters. Thus, the controversy had the properties of a mixed-motive game, with elements of both conflict and cooperation in the sense that the NAACP was well-served by the matches being held in Nashville, and Vanderbilt University and the city of Nashville would project a tolerant, liberal image, at least to much of the public, if they allowed maximum scope for non-violent, orderly, constitutionally protected opposition.

The Controversy

The boycott of South African team sports and opposition to apartheid are not issues that have an immediate impact on the daily life of Nashville people, whether black or white. They are issues of principle and conscience. Therefore, both sides in the controversy reached out to their constituencies and to public opinion at large by means of moral appeals and philosophic arguments.

The argument of opponents of the Davis Cup matches was that the South African system of apartheid is the most oppressive and inhuman form of domination in the world today, and that only a total isolation of South Africa from the outside world will topple the white regime or create sufficient pressure for change. Thus, any event, activity, or transaction with South Africa that provides relief from increased isolation and mounting outside pressure serves to strengthen and perpetuate the apartheid system.

Two major lines of argument were defended by those who favored keeping the Davis Cup matches. The first, stressed by the USTA, was simply that a tennis match is a sports event and should not be politicized. A second argument for holding the Davis Cup at Vanderbilt was put forward by Chancellor Heard and by university officials. Heard insisted that staging the Davis Cup at Vanderbilt did not mean that he himself, or Vanderbilt as an institution, sympathized or supported in any way the apartheid policies of South Africa. Heard nevertheless maintained that the Davis Cup was covered by the principle of the "open forum" under which Vanderbilt had provided an opportunity for controversial nonconformist and radical groups to present their views before the university community in the context of free and open intellectual debate. The open forum policy had covered speakers ranging from George Wallace to Stokely Carmichael, from the Ku Klux Klan to the Communist Party. The chancellor maintained that artistic and athletic events were also covered by the open forum principle. This line of argument found considerable favor with the Vanderbilt student body, as well as with faculty and alumni, but did not carry much weight with the opposition groups and blacks.

The Events

In February and March, a loosely-structured opposition movement was slowly taking shape, even though it lacked common leadership and a common purpose, aside from opposition to the South African racial policies. The component groups did not agree on the choice of protest targets and tactics, and sometimes worked at cross-purposes to each other. On their part, Vanderbilt University officials, local authorities, and the police were also making extensive preparations for the Davis Cup weekend. In a series of meetings, the leaders of the protest groups, VU administration officials and the Nashville police negotiated the details of the opposition activities that would take place during the Davis Cup weekend. By and large, both sides adhered to the scenario that was thus created.

The first event of the protest demonstration was an afternoon rally on Friday, March 17, by 1,200 students drawn mainly from the three black Nashville colleges. The students gathered in a parking lot adjacent to the gym where the cup matches were going to start at 6 p.m. The rally was followed by two spirited picket lines at the gym entrances, conducted under the watchful eyes of the visible, massed, but restrained police. Though the demonstration was by and large orderly, some protesters intimidated spectators, verbally abused them, and occasionally physically jostled them as they entered the gym. Police officials and protest leaders and marshals managed to defuse all situations in which an angry protester might physically clash with a spectator or policeman. On Saturday, the NAACP-sponsored three-mile march of 1,400 people started at noon from the Legislative Plaza and ended, incident free, at Centennial Park, located three blocks from the VU gym. Joined by another 200 people in the park, the NAACP marchers listened to a series of speeches by national and local black leaders and notables. Most of them went home at the end of the speeches at 3 p.m. A group of about 200 marchers, composed of militants and radicals and some students, broke away from the NAACP Centennial Park rally to join the picket lines already formed at the gym. The tensest moment of the entire week-end occurred when they arrived at the gym site and some of the radicals sought to provoke an attack on the gym. But the organizers, marshals, and police managed to contain the situation. Spectators leaving the march were subject to even more harrassment than on Friday night, yet only one arrest was made.

Sunday, the last day of the matches, proved to be an anti-climax, with curious onlookers and police outnumbering pickets at the gym. Despite the massive show of force by police and the mostly peaceful nature of the protests, spectator attendance was much below seating capacity and below even the financial break-even point for the sponsors.[3]

Application of the Theory

In the theory, the role of a small number of activists was stressed. It is they who bear the costs of creating and maintaining an organization, of developing a plan of action, and of attracting a larger following of transitory teams to participate in collective action. According to the theory, the strategy for attracting transitory teams consists of raising the awareness of an issue and creating commitment to a cause (V); providing selective incentives (S); keeping costs of participation low (C); and convincing people that the collective action will be effective (P) and their participation will contribute to its success (ΔP).

Raising awareness of an issue is usually done by means of an information and propaganda campaign. In the Davis Cup controversy, the protest organizations had three advantages: 1. No group campaigned in support of the apartheid system; 2. Because of Steve Biko's death, the public's attention had for some time been drawn to white minority rule in South Africa; 3. Vanderbilt University's public commitment to the open forum principle ensured that, at least on the Vanderbilt campus, picketing, meetings, speakouts, and fund raising against apartheid would be permitted maximum scope.

Two factors inhibited translating concern over apartheid into active opposition to the Davis Cup matches: 1. Belief in the validity of the open forum principle (a poll of students at Vanderbilt indicated that about 85 percent of the undergraduates supported it); 2. Vanderbilt University was being attacked by outside groups and could therefore count on institutional loyalty from its members at a time of crisis.

Creating selective incentives for participation on moral issues is a function of the social and political milieu. If an issue arises that would profit from liberal collective action in a liberal milieu, it can be expected to be supported by opinion leaders and leading circles. Participation in collective action will then affirm and enhance one's position in a group. There thus exist strong, positive, selective incentives for participation. On the other hand, minority liberal action in an indifferent or conservative milieu will lead to embarrassment, criticism, and isolation from peers, all of them negative selective incentives. The noninvolvement of Vanderbilt students and the participation of students on the black campuses was in part due to the entirely different climate of opinion on the black campuses, where student leaders and influentials came to support protest action and thus set in motion an upward spiral of positive incentives.

The cost of participation is low when the costs of organization maintenance, planning, and recruitment have been borne by others. If the collective action is of short duration, does not conflict with other important activities, and involves only low risk to personal safety, collective action costs for transitory teams will be low. In the Davis Cup controversy, activists sought their participation only for a few hours on one week-end.

Finally, convincing people that collective action will be effective and that their participation will make a difference in success depends upon the visibility of collective action and the number of participants. Extensive media coverage for whatever was going to be happening during the Davis Cup week-end was assured ever since the NAACP announcement of massive demonstrations. Elements favorable for collective action were thus present so long as someone initiated the mobilization process.

The Activists

Two small, new-left groups pre-existed the Davis Cup controversy. On the Vanderbilt campus, the Progressive Action Coalition (PAC) was headed by John Pike, with a dozen followers. Living in a house not far from the campus, another informal group of six to eight young adults—led by former Vanderbilt campus radical David Huet-Vaughn and his wife, Yolanda, a medical student at Meharry—formed the Tennessee Coalition Against Apartheid (TCAA). TCAA supported the liberation movements in South Africa and the international sports boycott. After TCAA entered the Davis Cup controversy, attendance at weekly meetings was about 20 individuals.

TCAA worked jointly with PAC; they both saw the Davis Cup controversy as an opportunity for building a broader radical base in Nashville by getting people involved in the anti-apartheid movement and the Davis Cup protests. When USTA and VU did not back out of the matches, TCAA decided to organize nonviolent protest rallies and demonstrations all three days at the site of the matches. Among other goals, the protest was meant to dissuade spectators from attending the matches. Aside from conducting an information campaign, TCAA hoped to stimulate and coordinate the opposition activities of other groups and organizations. It met with little initial success among church groups and trade unions, and decided instead to concentrate on Nashville campuses. A Student Coordinating Committee (SCC) was created and included members from the black and white universities.

TCAA and PAC, sometimes with the help of other individuals and groups, sometimes on their own, and with no more than about half a dozen of their most active members working 30 to 50 hours a week during the last month before the matches, managed to work out the basic plan of the three days of protests and negotiate arrangements with Vanderbilt University officials and the Nashville authorities down to the last details. These included securing parade permits, permission to use a university parking lot adjacent to the VU gymnasium (the tennis match site) for protest rallies, closing off streets to traffic, erecting a speaker's platform with a sound system, recognition of TCAA marshals as a buffer between demonstrators and the police (as well as anticipated counter-demonstrators), the details of the picket lines, and many other matters that provided a predictable and orderly structure to the protest demonstration. To the end, however, TCAA did not know how many people would participate in the protests it had planned.

TCAA and PAC had little success in directly mobilizing transitory teams. TCAA sent out a national call to anti-apartheid and radical groups throughout the country. Because it was plugged into this radical network, by Saturday, March 18, as many as 200 out-of-town radicals had shown up from as far away as Boston and Wisconsin. But at Vanderbilt University, the largest and most active protest group, with about 50 students, was based in the Divinity School and called itself Students Protesting Apartheid (SPA). SPA was already a constituted and operating group at the time TCAA became active, and affiliated itself with TCAA. The only part of Vanderbilt University where there was a majority sentiment against the Davis Cup matches was the Divinity School. Its faculty sent a statement to the Chancellor and President early in February urging withdrawal of university sponsorship of the matches, and co-sponsored the first antiapartheid and anti-Davis Cup speaker on the campus before an enthusiastic audience of about 200, mostly graduate students and faculty. This event received television coverage on all three Nashville channels.

The Black Universities

Through the SCC, the TCAA had been trying to reach the students on the three black campuses (TSU, Fisk, and Meharry), but the blacks' commitment to the TCAA-sponsored protests was late in coming and remained ambivalent. The big event of the weekend, as far as the news media and public opinion were concerned, was the Saturday NAACP march and park rally. These would clearly be black-dominated collective events. TCAA was mostly white and to some extent identified with VU. Among activist black students, there was considerable anti-VU and anti-white sentiment, and also a feeling that the South African issue belonged to them. On the other hand, since mid-February the NAACP had been moderating its initial call for a huge turnout. It sought to avoid a confrontation with VU by making no plans for marching on the VU campus itself or for joining up with the TCAA picket line after its own rally in Centennial Park. The national leadership of the NAACP de-escalated its collective action to a single three-hour protest against apartheid rather than against Vanderbilt University and the Davis Cup matches. This largely symbolic event would be held at a site some distance from the university. From the point of view of many black students and even some NAACP members, the NAACP action was too limited and cautious.

By the time opinion leaders and activists on the black campuses fully realized the limited character of the NAACP protest, there was little time left for organizing collective action from scratch. It proved expedient to follow the script already prepared by TCAA.

Mobilization on the black campuses, though late, was rapid, but not without difficulties. At Fisk, the head of student government, the editor of the student paper, and the head of the Political Science Club had talked about planning some collective action with the other black colleges on the Davis Cup weekend even before the TCAA had reached them with their plan. Since TCAA had parade permits, a full protest scenario, and possessed handbills and other materials it would supply to the black campuses, the Fisk group decided to join the TCAA action.

Meanwhile, another small group of NAACP-affiliated Fisk students was starting to mobilize Fisk students on behalf of the Saturday NAACP march. They received assistance from a few professional organizers sent to Nashville by the national office to assist the local branch in their operations. Because the NAACP was afraid the students would dissipate their energies on Friday afternoon and evening, it urged them to stay away from the TCAA-SCC protest plans. the NAACP may also have feared that cooperating with radicals entailed unnecessary risks, though TCAA had publicly reiterated the nonviolent character of its opposition actions. the NAACP and TCAA rivalry for black student support on black campuses created some confusion and divided loyalties. At Fisk, the issue wasn't resolved until a mass meeting of students voted to support both groups' protest actions.

Because of the week-long spring holiday that started two weeks before the Davis Cup at all area colleges, the Fisk student body wasn't mobilized by activists until the final week in a post-spring-vacation blitz. Activists contacted the leading members of various student groups, athletes, key people in fraternities and sororities, choir groups, the Jubilee Singers, the large Business and Economic Club, the Georgia and Alabama Clubs, and every important group and clique. Numerous meetings were held; posters were put up; handbills were pushed under dormitory doors; Julian Bond, an influential black leader with a strong following among black youth, was brought in by the NAACP the day before the Davis Cup started and delivered a rousing speech at Fisk. Fisk's administration was supportive: several deans marched with the Fisk students, as did the campus security chief. TCAA, the NAACP, and Fisk security personnel provided training for student marshals. All these activities and meetings created a sense of increasing and large-scale participation and commitment at Fisk.

On the TSU campus, much the same mobilization process took place as at Fisk, with the head of student government, the "big men" on campus, and leading students in the sororities and fraternities activating channels of influence to existing groups to get a hugh student turnout on Friday afternoon. TSU mobilization lasted barely a week and was very effective. TSU, as Fisk, ended up with several hundred black students at the Friday afternoon gym rally. They came carrying signs and chanting slogans, under their own leadership and command structure, with their marshals and campus security personnel. At the peak of the rally, between 1,000 and 1,200 people had collected, about 80 percent black. After 4:30 p.m., in small groups, the majority of black students drifted back to their campuses, with rally leaders unable to counteract the effects of cold,

snow, and boredom. The remaining 400 or so more committed activists, organizers, and marshals then formed picket lines at the two gym entrances.

Organization of the NAACP March

NAACP has some 600,000 members nationwide, large local branches in the
Southeast region, and a 1,000-member local branch in Nashville itself. It also
had the backing of the Coalition for Human Rights in South Africa. Therefore,
their proclaimed goal of mounting the largest demonstration since the 1960s
during the Davis Cup matches was a real possibility. Until the very end, the plans
of police and university officials were based on the assumption that thousands of
demonstrators might sweep into town, bringing in their wake radical groups not
committed to peaceful tactics, and white counter-demonstrators bent on disrupt-
ing the NAACP march.

For reasons that are not entirely clear, the top leadership of the NAACP had
decided sometime in February to scale down the size of the demonstration and to
de-emphasize a direct confrontation with Vanderbilt over cancellation of the
matches. It was also clear, however, that a small turnout would be embarrassing
to the NAACP national leadership, because it would undermine its claim of
representing the views of the U.S. blacks on South Africa and publicly expose
weaknesses within the organization itself.

Be that as it may, with out-of-town participation de-emphasized (in the end,
about ten buses from big cities like Houston, Memphis, New Orleans, Philadelphia, Louisville, and Atlanta brought in about 300 to 400 NAACP members and
sympathizers from outside of Nashville), the local Nashville branch was under
pressure to deliver a respectable number of marchers on Saturday, for which it
received little help from the national office. The South African issue was not one
to which black masses would readily respond. Thus, the local strategy became to
activate the black leadership in as many associations, groups, and communities
as possible, and hope that each group would deliver its most active members.
Since the majority of the black leaders in Nashville are NAACP members and
some sit on its board, there was no problem of reaching the leadership element
itself. A major effort was mounted to pull in the leaders and active members of a
number of neighborhood, community, labor, fraternal, and civic groups. There
was also an effort to mobilize black churches and ministers and their most active
members, and the three black college campuses (as I have already described)
were the target of an active recruitment campaign. However, many fewer black
students participated in the NAACP march then the previous afternoon's march
and rally sponsored by the student organizations themselves. Three local
NAACP organizers did the lion's share of getting the local march organized.

About one in ten marchers were white, though no effort was made to recruit
them. They were largely VU students and faculty, TCAA members, and the
out-of-town radicals who also participated in the TCAA picket lines. NAACP
marshals were recruited from among industrial workers with whom one of the

NAACP organizers had personal ties, but the march was heavily weighted in the direction of adult, middle-class, Nashville blacks.

Participation in a Loosely Structured Movement: Activists, Transitory Teams, and Diffusion

There can be no doubt that the Davis Cup protests were loosely structured. The most glaring division was between the NAACP and its Saturday march on the one hand, and three days of picketing organized by the TCAA at the VU gym. Its concrete manifestations were the competition for black students, especially during the last week before the matches, the attempt by the National Office of the NAACP to keep TCAA members out of its march, and the refusal of the NAACP leadership to join the TCAA picket lines, even for a short time as a symbolic gesture. As a matter of fact, Executive Director Hooks strongly urged his audience not to join the gym pickets at the end of the NAACP rally, but to head for home. On their part, some 200 of the out-of-town radicals and militant black students broke away from the NAACP Centennial Park rally shortly after its start to join the gym pickets in a visible, public display of their disagreement with the NAACP leadership.

Aside from this division, the TCAA itself was a precariously constructed edifice.[4] The Nashville based TCAA-PAC-SPA coalition managed to hang together because it was largely composed of white Vanderbilt students or former students, but it had no wide membership base among VU college students or the white population. The black students supplied over 80 percent of the participants at the Friday afternoon rally, and perhaps a little over half at the picket line on Friday and Saturday. They considered the protest largely their own affair, though a measure of unity and common purpose was achieved, especially on the picket line itself. Finally, the TCAA had only a tenuous hold on the out-of-town white radicals that it had summoned, and these radicals themselves were split into half a dozen ideological factions and splinter groups. Without the participation of the black students and the out-of-town radicals, the Friday and Saturday picket line might have been as tame, small, and frail as the Sunday afternoon picket line turned out to be when these two groups did not participate.

Less obvious was the generation gap between the NAACP on the one hand, and the TCAA and some militant black students on the other. Both groups were fundamentally opposed to the apartheid system in South Africa; for both, the Davis Cup match was a symbolic issue around which a more permanent and widely-based opposition might coalesce. Yet their styles of protest differed. The TCAA and black students were more willing to take risks and to confront VU by means of militant tactics that would intimidate spectators, and thus create a financial loss for the university.

Loose movement structure results from the class, racial, generational, geographic, and institutional divisions within the larger society. Activists are best placed for recruiting within a limited social milieu in which they are already occupying key positions. Thus, the rapid and effective mobilization at Fisk and TSU followed the classic pattern of mobilization for collective action through influential and leading campus personalities using existing networks, groups, and associations in a relatively homogeneous social environment (Oberschall, 1973). Moreover, the leadership group received help from without, principally the NAACP and TCAA. In such a milieu, then, aside from the heightened commitment to an issue itself resulting from information campaigns (V), strong selective incentives (S) are created as the mood swings in favor of collective action, and group members conform to majority sentiment and the leadership. As the mood spreads and information about collective action becomes widespread, anticipated costs (C) decrease: one senses that participation will be massive (safety in numbers) and one learns about a concrete, well organized plan of action that entails few risks. Even though one may lose some sense of being urgently needed to make the collective action effective (ΔP may decrease), free-rider tendencies are overshadowed by the magnitude of other terms in inequality (1).

Even so, at the Friday rally, after about three and one-half hours of assembling, marching, and attending the rally in the face of cold temperatures and a poorly planned program, large numbers of black students drifted back to their campuses before the anticipated climax. Interestingly, their action did not create a runaway reverse bandwagon resulting in a total dissolution of the protest crowd. With diminished size, the sense of being personally needed (ΔP) to make the protest a success sharply increased, and among the remaining active elements of the various protest groups (high V), selective incentives (living up to one's public image and earlier public commitment) operated strongly.[5]

With the same model, it is possible to explain the lack of success TCAA-PAC had on the Vanderbilt campus. Here, the open forum principle achieved such wide acceptance within the student body as well as the faculty that support for protests over the Davis Cup remained weak. Many students were visibly ambivalent, leading students and groups remained on the sidelines over the issue, and protest advocates were clearly in a minority position. A sense of futility in trying to get things going in the face of indifference and ambivalence operated on the VU campus (ΔP was very low). Moreover, TCAA and PAC had nothing to offer students by way of selective incentives. PAC operated as a small clique in which new recruits would not be confortable at first.

As far as the NAACP march in concerned, only a few remarks will be made. With its large membership in the Southeastern region within half a day's drive from Nashville, NAACP could count on some out-of-towners who would already be highly concerned about the South African issue (V) or who had a strong sense of organizational loyalty (S). The financial cost of travel for these out-of-towner's was borne by the NAACP itself (C). As far as Nashville blacks were concerned, the total participation demanded was no more than four hours on Saturday afternoon. The security arrangement and massive police protection was by then highly publicized and had previously been worked out to the march organizers' satisfaction, so that the risk involved in participation was low.

The theory of participation put forward does not account for the existence of small groups of activists prior to a controversy. However, the theory, as well as the Davis Cup events, point to the small number of activists with a prior commitment to an issue or to similar radical causes who act as catalysts and bear the cost of collective action disproportionately, even in the face of a low probability of success. The small number of activists in the TCAA and PAC had a prior history of engagement in radical causes, including opposition to South Africa. In terms of numbers, as few as five and perhaps no more than a dozen key individuals engineered the organizational framework and the scenario for collective action. The main resource they invested was their time.[6] Up until the very start of the demonstrations, they did not know how successful the protest would be in attracting transitory teams yet that did not discourage them. Even in the more organized setting of the NAACP, only three local individuals played a key role in making the Saturday march a reality. As for the Fisk campus, one is again struck by the small number of activists who began mobilizing the campus. An application of the theory of participation put forward here assumes the presence of a small number of such activists.

Can these events tell us anything about the theory of diffusion of collective action? TCAA-PAC activists performed a crucial role in lowering mobilization costs for the black student activists when they developed a total protest plan and negotiated its details with the authorities. Such an effect is shown in Figure 5 in the following manner: the TCAA-PAC actions lowered the entire cost curve on the black campus from $n(1)$ toward $n(k)$. On the other hand, black student mobilization had no reciprocal effect on the TCAA-PAC mobilization effort at white campuses, as Figure 4 implies: it did not shift the relationship of P to N from the $n(1)$ curve to a higher curve, such as $n(2)$ or $n(k)$. This was partly due to the late mobilization on black campuses and the lack of communication across the black-white divide so that white college students were totally unaware of the build-up of protest sentiment among the black students. Even the TCAA leadership did not fully realize this, so loose was the overall structure of the movement.

Yet had there been advance information about black student mobilization, I doubt that it would have helped TCAA-PAC recruitment on the Vanderbilt campus. If anything, it would have strengthened the sentiment that opposition to the Davis Cup was a black collective event, with some white radicals espousing a black cause. The theory of diffusion postulates a reciprocal positive feedback (shown in Figure 4). But for it to occur, some sense of shared purpose and community has to exist or be created, and that was missing in the case at hand.

Are the recripocal effects of the TCAA and the NAACP upon each other illuminated by the diffusion theory? The TCAA would have demonstrated against the Davis Cup matches even if the NAACP had not become involved in the issue. By entering the controversy, the NAACP assured national attention and news media coverage not only for its opposition activities, but for that of other protest groups as well. It certainly encouraged more vigorous opposition activity, since local opposition would contribute to the anticipated, climactic NAACP march and would thus fit into a wider, more visible protest movement. In terms of the theory (as shown in Figure 4) the relationship between P and N for local opposition activity moved from n(1) into the direction of n(k).

Another positive effect of the NAACP upon local activity was the lower cost of mobilization. Faced with the prospect of a massive demonstration in the full limelight of the national news media, both the VU administration and the Nashville authorities and police bent over backwards to negotiate a highly structured, nonviolent protest scenario which came close to the maximum demands of TCAA-PAC as far as time, site, duration, and permissible protest tactics were concerned, at a time when the protesters were no more than a small group of activists speaking for no visible constituency. Had the shadow of a huge NAACP demonstration not hung over all the dealings between the authorities and the local protest groups, the authorities may well have been less accommodating. In terms of the theory (expressed in Figure 5), the NAACP action shifted the cost curve for TCAA from n(1) to the lower n(2) and beyond. Thus, even though the NAACP ended up competing with the TCAA for black student support, the net effect was a more vigorous, large-scale information and propaganda campaign aimed at black students which probably increased their knowledge about South Africa and created greater commitment to all manner of protest against it.

What kind of effect did the local Nashville opposition have on the NAACP? The NAACP statements, press releases, and march would have drawn just as much attention in the national news media with or without the TCAA opposition activity. It is difficult to say what impact the greater local media coverage of the controversy had upon NAACP local mobilization as a result of continuing opposition activity in Nashville itself. The greatest dangers for the NAACP were the possibility of strife and disorder occurring on the week-end of the Davis Cup for which they might be blamed, even though they were in no way responsible for them, and the possibility of having too small a number of participants in the march and rally. The presence of the more militant TCAA represented for the NAACP national office a threat, or at least a question mark, on both these counts. Their actions had a greater chance of leading to incidents, and in return for the small number of participants that TCAA might contribute to the march, it would more likely siphon off some of the black students that the NAACP was counting on. This resulted in the calculated dissociation between the national NAACP and the TCAA, while at the local level a measure of tacit coordination and division of labor was actually achieved. The diffusion theory put forward in this paper does not account for the asymmetrical effect of the NAACP and TCAA upon each other, however.

Other limitations of the theory ought to be mentioned. The theory does not explain the organizational forms that emerged from a combination of cooperation and rivalry among the opponents protesting the Davis Cup, and between them, their targets (VU and USTA) and the authorities. The theory furthermore does not account for the existence of small groups of activists who trigger mobilization, nor does it explain why the value of a particular collective good (V) is distributed as it is. Nevertheless, with all these limitations, I hope to have demonstrated that a parsimonious, rational choice model comprising only five variables (P, C, V, S, N) can help organize vast amounts of data and explain a complex set of events.

NOTES

1. Since this was written, Granovetter (1978) has published a formal analysis of collective behavior that bears many similarities to my thinking. We both recognize the importance of variance in values and dispositions (V in Figure 1), and changes in the cost of collective action with number of participants (Figure 3). Whereas Granovetter investigates thresholds and equilibria for number of participants, I am dealing explicitly with collective, goal-directed behavior, and hence emphasize chances of successful outcome (Figure 2) in the decisions of would-be participants. Granovetter deals with the paradoxical case of no collective behavior despite an average positive preference for it in the group. In my model, I purposely analyze only the positive cases where a group of activists initiate collective action and bear disproportionate costs of mobilization (in Figure 1, I assume a normal distribution of V). Both of us recognize the importance of social structure on costs and benefits of joining collective action (cf., my analysis of different outcomes at black colleges and Vanderbilt). Finally, I deal with collective action in which individuals seek to obtain both collective goods (V) and individual goods (S). V and S in my model have to be kept conceptually and substantively distinguished throughout (cf. expression (1)). For Granovetter, this distinction is not crucial. In both cases, however, the achievement of goods, whether collective, individual, or both, depends in part on the number of others also taking action.

2. I was both a close observer and a participant in the controversy. The data and information on which the account is based are varied and numerous: newspaper accounts and other printed sources; research papers written by students in a course I taught while the conflict was in progress; my own observations and interviews with protagonists and key informants. I personally knew, or came to know, most of the Nashville activists, as well as the officials responsible for dealing with the DC protests. Their willingness to talk to me about their role in the controversy was invaluable as a source of information.

3. Aside from the collective actions that occurred during the Davis Cup week-end itself, February and March witnessed a number of less dramatic actions by both supporters and opponents of the Davis Cup matches which for lack of space I cannot here chronicle. The most important omissions were the Lamb and the Lapchik episodes.

Peter Lamb, a non-white South African Vanderbilt University sophomore and tennis star, was named to the South African Davis Cup squad as one of the junior players and the first ever non-white team member. Proponents of the matches saw it as indication of South African willingness to move away from apartheid in good faith. Opponents saw it as a token gesture and publicity stunt quite in keeping with South African manipulation of public opinion when apartheid faces international criticism. Understandably, the nomination created support for the matches on the Vanderbilt campus.

The second episode (actually a series of episodes) resulted from the Nashville activities of Dr. Richard Lapchik, professor of political science at Virginia Wesleyan College, and head of ACCESS, The American Coordinating Committee for Equality in Sport and Society, an anti-apartheid lobby. Lapchik urged top VU administrators to cancel the Davis Cup matches and spoke to campus audiences and Nashville news media about South Africa and the need for a protest and boycott. In between two of his Nashville appearances, two assailants allegedly attacked him and carved a racial slur on his stomach. The news media sensationalized the ensuing controversy about whether the wounds were self-inflicted. In retrospect, according to activists, the Lapchik episodes had a distracting and negative impact upon the protest. News media highlighted the Lipchik assault instead of apartheid. Lipchik wasn't oriented to building a lasting, radical grassroots organization in Nashville. The controversy delayed the activists' mobilization of support for the protests on the black campuses, which turned out to be the key for their success.

4. A TCAA fund raising and testimonial dinner, for paying off debts and recognizing those who did the most work, was held two months after the Davis Cup protests. It proved to be the last occasion before TCAA became defunct.

5. I can testify personally to the importance of these selective incentives for me and my friends in the picket line. There was also a sense of drama, excitement, curiosity, and fellowship that kept us marching, chanting, and joking as we moved back and forth in front of the gym entrance under the watchful eyes of police, even while spectators kept arriving and sought to get around and through us.

6. Only one protest leader paid a high price (opportunity cost) when he did not graduate after failing to make up course work in time. Yet prior to the controversy, this student had a history of incomplete course work, so that there is some doubt whether he would have in any case.

REFERENCES

Brown, Roger (1965) *Social Psychology,* Glencoe, Ill.: Free Press.

Fireman, Burce, and William Gamson (1979) "Utilitarian Logic in the Resource Mobilization Perspective," in Mayer Zald and John McCarthy, eds., *The Dynamics of Social Movements,* Cambridge, Mass.: Winthrop Publishers, Inc.

Granovetter, Mark (1978) "Threshold Models of Collective Behavior," *Am. Jo. of Sociology 83* (No. 6) May, pp. 1420–1443.

Kriesberg, Louis (1979) *The Sociology of Social Conflicts,* Englewood Cliffs, N.J.: Prentice Hall.

Le Bon, Gustave (1960) *The Crowd,* New York, Viking Press.

McCarthy, John and Mayer Zald (1973) *The Trend of Social Movements in America,* Morristown, N.J.: The General Learning Press.

Oberschall, Anthony (1973) *Social Conflict and Social Movements,* Englewood Cliffs, N.J., Prentice Hall.

———(1978) "The Decline of the 1960's Social Movements," in Louis Kriesberg, ed., *Research in Social Movements, Conflict, and Change,* Greenwich, Ct.: JAI Press.

———(1979) "Protracted Conflict," in Mayer Zald and John McCarthy, eds., *The Dynamics of Social Movements,* Cambridge, Mass.: Winthrop Publishers, Inc.

Olson, Mancur, Jr. (1965) *The Logic of Collective Action,* N.Y.: Schocken Books.

PERSONALITY AND STYLE
IN NEGOTIATIONS

Otomar J. Bartos

To cooperate or to fight is a question that is central to problems in many areas. Should a husband take into account his wife's ideas about raising children, even if he disagrees with her, or should he insist on doing what he feels is right? Should the Israelis relinquish some of the land they recently occupied, or should they defend the land they view as holy? How do I get most out of life—by being reasonable, accomodating, and cooperative, or by being firm, belligerent, and tough?

Not surprisingly, the causes and the consequences of cooperation have been studied in many contexts. One of the most promising areas is that of negotiation and bargaining. The general concept of "cooperation" becomes the more specific "concession-making," and the problem becomes whether it pays to make concessions. Most specifically, is it true that our own concessions encourage concessions in the opponent? Or, is it true that a concession will be taken as a sign of weakness and will be taken advantage of?

These questions have been studied extensively both in experimental and real-life negotiations. An excellent summary of the conditions that have been found to

Research in Social Movements, Conflicts and Change, Vol. 3, pages 69-97
Copyright © 1980 by JAI Press Inc.
All rights of reproduction in any form reserved.
ISBN: 0-89232-182-2

reduce conflict is given by Druckman (1971).[1] Our own work (Bartos, 1974) suggested that toughness is a good strategy, that is seems to pay *not* to make too many concessions. But this conclusion is hard to accept since it is contrary to the general belief that it pays to be cooperative. Moreover, our own work did not explain why this conclusion should be true. In this paper, we shall attempt to throw new light on our findings by analyzing new experiments in which data were gathered on the personalities of the negotiators and their negotiating style.

UNINTERPRETED THEORY

We shall state our expectations concerning the process of negotiation and the conditions that influence it in a formal fashion, as a series of causal propositions that can be expressed verbally, algebraically, or graphically. Since these propositions form a system, we shall refer to them as a "theory of negotiation"; since, in this section, we shall not make a serious effort to interpret empirically (to "operationalize") our variables, we shall call the theory which we shall now outline the "uninterpreted" theory.

Theory of the Process

The literature abounds with theories that refer to negotiation, but only a few of them refer to the *process* of negotiation. Among those that do, the most prominent are those of Siegel and Fouraker (1960), Coddington (1968), and Cross (1969). Our own previous work (Bartos, 1974) is another attempt at stating a theory of the process. Since this theory has been formulated so as to be applicable to the type of of experiments to be analyzed in this paper, we shall use it here.

Our theory starts from the assumption that concession-making is the most essential feature of negotiation: it is through concessions that a negotiation can be brought to its successful conclusion, an agreement based on a compromise. Thus, to understand the negotiation process means, above all, to understand why and under what conditions a negotiator will make a concession. While concessions can be made for a variety of "external" reasons—such as new instructions from the home office—when we consider the process of negotiation, we are interested primarily in reasons "internal" to the process itself: what can a negotiator do to induce a concession by his opponent? In particular, how will my opponent react if I make a concession? Will he reciprocate by making one as well, or will he exploit it by refusing to budge?

As soon as we ask this question, we realize that the answer is likely to be "It all depends on . . .". Yet, in order to start constructing a theory, we must express this basic idea first and qualify it later. One of the simplest ways to start is to speak about a negotiator's "demands" (D_t) and to assume that they are related to his opponent's demands (D_{t-1}) in a linear fashion:

$$D_t = {}_aD_{t-1}+b \qquad \text{for t=0, 1, 2, \ldots}$$

(In this paper, we shall assume that we are talking about two opponents and that they speak consecutively, taking turns. Moreover, we shall use the convention of *italicizing* any symbols referring to the *opponent*.) This equation says that the demand the negotiator makes "now" (at time t), D_t, depends in a linear fashion on the demand made by the opponent when he spoke "last" (at time $t-1$), D_{t-1}.

This equation is a simple but complete theory. In order to see how it works, let us consider first what it implies about concession-making. Since we are assuming that it holds for all times t (which means that we assume that the same parameters a and b apply at all times), we can write:

$$D_t = aD_{t-1}+b$$
$$D_{t-2} = aD_{t-3}+b$$

Subtracting the first equation from the second, we get:

$$D_{t-2} - D_t = (aD_{t-3}+b) - (aD_{t-1}+b)$$

This simplifies to:

$$D_{t-2} - D_t = a(D_{t-3} - D_{t-1})$$

It is obvious that by a "concession" we mean the difference between the negotiator's last demand and his present one, $C_t = D_{t-2} - D_t$. Using this definition, we may write the above very simply as:

$$C_t = aC_{t-1}$$

In other words, our basic equation implies that (we are assuming that) *the negotiator's last concession is positively or negatively proportional to his opponent's last concession.*

Our theory can be expanded to tell us something about the entire process of negotiation—at least, how it should look like if our simple theory is correct. To obtain this extension, we simply assume that the above equation holds for *both* negotiators:

$$C_t = aC_{t-1}$$
$$C_{t-1} = aC_{t-2}$$

Noting that the second equation can be substituted into the first, we do so:

$$C_t = a(aC_{t-2}) = aaC_{t-2}$$

If we continued such substitutions, we would discover that the following holds true:

$$C_{t-1} = (aa)^{t/2} C_1 \qquad \text{for } t = 4,6,8,\ldots$$

where C_1 is the negotiator's first concession, one he delivered at time $t=1$. (The above equation holds only for the first-speaking negotiator, assumed to speak at times $t=1,3,5,7,\ldots$)

This conclusion permits us to say a few things about the (ideal) process of negotiation:

1. If the product aa is positive (that is, if the two negotiators are the *same*, either both cooperative or both exploitative), then the changes in concession size are "smooth." Moreover: if aa is less than one, then the negotiator's concession C_t gradually diminishes in size;[2] if aa is larger than one, then C_t gradually increases in size.[3]

2. If the product aa is negative (that is, if the two negotiators are different, one being cooperative and the other exploitative), then the negotiator will oscillate between raising his demand and making a concession.[4]

We now must consider the intuitively obvious fact that negotiators (and humans in general) tend to be cooperative *only under certain conditions*. Technically, this can be taken into account by adding new variables to our theory, variables that can be viewed as additional causes of cooperativeness (concession-making).[5] It is customary in the literature dealing with these types of theories to assume that a change in a variable depends on the "level" of a variable.[6] For our model, this suggests that the concession a negotiator makes (C_t) depends not only on the concession of his opponent (C_{t-1}) but also on his own previous demand (D_{t-1}):

$$C_t = aC_{t-1}+cD_{t-2}+d$$

(As before, we are assuming that the negotiator's concessions are linear with his previous demand—hence, the new parameters c and d.)

But in making this assumption, we are implicitly assuming that concessions will grow smaller as time goes by: as demands D_{t-2} grow smaller, the term cD_{t-2} grows smaller as well, making C_t smaller. This is a stronger assumption than we wish to make—we wish to allow for the possibility that the size of the concessions remains the same throughout the entire negotiation, or may even grow larger. To permit this, we shall assume that the concessions are also linear with time t. This is our last assumption, thus making our final "model" of the negotiation process as follows:

$$C_t = aC_{t-1} + cD_{t-2} + et+f \qquad (1)$$

(The parameter d shown in the last equation is replaced by parameter f. This parameter combines d and a new parameter due to the influence of time t.)

Equation 1 represents our theory of the negotiation process. If we had time, we could show that, once the four parameters (a, c, e, and f) are known, we can use the theory to predict how negotiation will proceed,[7] explain why a concession was made,[8] and counsel a negotiator whether or not he should make a concession.[9] Note again that this theory is "exploratory": since we have not specified the signs of the four parameters, we cannot use it to state specific hypotheses until we have estimated them through empirical research.

Influence of Personality

As is shown in Equation 1, our theory of the negotiation process considers three possible causes of concession-making: the negotiator's own past behavior (his previous demand D_{t-2}), the opponent's past behavior (his previous concession C_{t-1}), and the passage of time (t). But there is no reason why concession-making cannot be influenced by variables that are "external" to the process, such as the personality of the negotiators. As already indicated, we shall expand the theory reported in Bartos (1974) by adding to it some variables that measure personality.

Various clinical measures of personality have been used while studying concession-making.[10] We, too, used a clinical personality inventory in our earlier research, the so-called "California Personality Inventory." But we now feel that such inventories are not suited for our purposes: they usually require that the subject evaluate himself. It seems to us that what is important in negotiation is not how the negotiator sees himself, but rather how *others* see him. Therefore, in this paper, we shall utilize personality measures that involve evaluation by others. In particular, we shall use the theory and measures of personality developed by Bales (1970). In so doing, we shall build a bridge between a large amount of experimental work done in small groups by Bales and our more specialized work in negotiations.

Bales' conception of personality involves three basic dimensions. They are identified only by letters to indicate directions in space: U - D (up and down), P - N (positive and negative), and F - B (front and back). Some insight into this conception is gained if we consider the "pure types" corresponding to these dimensions:

1. The U-type is interested in material success and power: his opposite, the D-type, is primarily characterized by devaluating himself.
2. The P-type is equalitarian, while his opposite, the N-type, is individualistic and isolationist.
3. The F-type is conservative, while the B-type tends to reject conservative views.[11]

Thus the U-D dimension has to do with a search for *power*, the P-N dimension with a search for *equality*, and the F-B dimension with a respect for *tradition*.

In order to discover what Bales' theory suggests about the relationship be-

Table 1.   Expected Relationship Between Concession-making and
Bales' Personality Types

Presumed Indicators of Concession-Making	Bales Interpretation of the Indicator
Accepts authority	DF
Agrees with others	PF
Does not disagree with others	P
Is not dominant	DP
Seems friendly	P
Advocates loyalty and cooperativeness	UF
Is not independently self-sufficient	UPF
Is not individualistic	UP
Does not advocate individualistic isolationism	P
Arouses liking	PB
Is mature	DP
Asks for opinion	P
Is not prejudiced	DPB
Accepts social conformity	PF
Is responsible	DPF
Does not advocate rugged individualism and gratification	DPF
Is tolerant	DP
Does not advocate toughminded assertiveness	DP
Advocates trust in others	DP
Is understanding	DP
Does not advocate withholding cooperation	UF

tween personality and concession-making, we proceeded as follows. We began by going through a long list of personality traits that served as the empirical basis of his three main personality dimensions.[12] From this list, we selected those that, in our opinion, were indicative of cooperativeness and hence of willingness to make concessions. In making these selections, we were primarily guided by the similarity of meanings. For instance, we viewed the trait "agrees with others" as indicative of concession-making, because persons who tend to agree with others come close to adopting their view—and that is what "making a concession" means. The traits that we saw as indicators of concession-making are listed in the first column of Table 1.

The second column of Table 1 lists the personality types that Bales found— through statistical analysis—to be associated with each personality trait listed in the first column. Thus, Table 1 gives us, in its last column, a set of personality types that ought to make concessions readily. All that is needed now is to extract from that last column an information about how likely each of the three basic personality types is to make concessions. We accomplished this by following a procedure used by Bales in similar situations: we counted the total number of times each letter (U, D, P, N, F, B) occurred in the last column, and then we subtracted the frequences belonging to the same dimension:

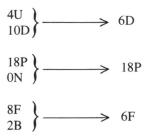

This result suggests that a concession-maker should be, above all, a P-type, but that he also should have tendencies to be a D-type and an F-type. We express this conclusion as the following hypothesis:

> "Concession-making is most likely to be displayed by negotiators who are equilitarian (P-type), self-efacing (D-type), and respectful of tradition (F-type)." (2)

Style of Negotiation

So far, we have discussed two extremes in influences upon concession-making. On one hand, we discussed the variables that change as negotiation progresses: previous demands, opponent's concessions, and time. On the other hand, we took into account the more stable influences, those exercised by the participant's personality or, more accurately, by the way these personalities are perceived. But it is possible to discuss a third aspect of the negotiation process, one that lies somewhere between these two extremes: the style of a given negotiator.

Some negotiators are well informed, others are not; some are clever in the presentation of their argument, others are not; some are tough and make threats easily, others do not; and so forth. Among the aspects of style that seem particularly interesting are the following:[13]

1. toughness
2. fairness
3. knowledge of the subject-matter
4. quality of arguments
5. persuasiveness
6. credibility
7. tactical cleverness
8. readiness to be offended.

Some tentative hypotheses about the relationship between the style of negotiation and concession-making are relatively easy to state. All we need to do is explore the meanings of a given pair of concepts: if they are similar, then we hypothesize a positive relationship. To begin with, we take "toughness" to mean roughly the same as "not making concessions" Hence we hypothesize:

"Tough negotiators are unlikely to make concessions."   (3)

(It should be noted that such "obvious" propositions—technically known as "analytic" or "tautological"—are not the most desirable type of propositions to work with when doing empirical research.[14] The reason why we state them here is that toughness will be measured differently from concession-making. Hence, it is not a foregone conclusion that the two mean the same thing.)

Another hypothesis is equally easy to state, even though it refers to the influence of *opponent's* negotiation style. Generally speaking, we may assume that (almost by definition) a well-made argument is convincing; i.e., induces a concession:

"The more knowledgeable, able to present a good argument, persuasive, and tactically clever is the opponent, the more likely is the negotiator to make concessions."   (4)

PROCEDURE

The theory stated in the preceeding section will be tested on the experiments conducted in the summer of 1978. The negotiators whose behavior and personality we shall study consist of 32 volunteers, all of them students at the University of Colorado. Since the design of the experiments was described in considerable detail in Bartos (1974), we shall discuss here only the main features.

Experimental Design

The participants were asked to take part in experiments simulating two major real-life negotiations: the Israeli-Egypt negotiations, and the Salt II talks. The crux of the design was the so-called "payoff matrix," created to represent fairly realistically the interests of Israel and Egypt.[15]

The dollar amount shown in Table 2, the *payoffs*, represent the amount of money the negotiators would get if a given proposal were accepted. Thus, for example, if proposal 2 were accepted (by both sides), then Israel would be paid $3.00 and Egypt would lose (would owe to the experimenter) $1.00.

Since the interests of the two sides were opposed (when a proposal had a positive payoff for one side, it had a negative payoff for the other), any one of these five proposals would hardly ever be accepted by both sides. But the participants were allowed to agree on a *combination* of two or more proposals, the payoff from a combination being given by the *sum* of the payoffs associated with the proposals in the combination. It can be seen that some combinations have positive payoff for both sides. For example, the combination of the first three proposals has the payoff of $1.00 for both sides.

Several additional features of the design are of interest. First, each role was played by a *team* consisting of two volunteers, and the two members of the team were taking turns representing the team. Second, each team *knew only their own*

Table 2. An Experimental Payoff Matrix

| | Payoff to | |
Proposal	Israel	Egypt
1. Total Israeli withdrawal from West Bank and Gaza strip	−$4	+$7
2. Full recognition of Egypt by Israel	+$3	−$1
3. Creation of joint Israeli-Egypt police to combat terrorism	+$2	−$5
4. Formation of a political and economic alliance between Egypt and Israel	+$7	−$6
5. Creation of an autonomous Palestine state within Jordan	−$8	+$3

payoffs. Third, most of the negotiation was fairly rigidly controlled: After preliminary planning in a separate room, the two teams met to try to reach an agreement. The teams took turns speaking, and each was allowed to make only *three* speeches. If no agreement was reached, the session was recessed and each team retired to their own room for additional planning. Fourth, after *four* such three-speech sessions (i.e., after each team delivered a total of 12 speeches), the teams met for the last time, for the last-ditch effort to reach an agreement. They had 15 minutes to do so. Fifth, a negotiation could end without an agreement either if one of the teams walked out or if, by the end of the 15-minute interval, no agreement was reached. Sixth, each team knew that if an agreement was not reached, both teams would receive zero payoff (no money was earned or lost).

Gathering Data

Our theory of the process, expressed in Equation 1, presupposes that we know what demands and concessions were made by each team. We required the participants to state clearly, at the end of each speech, which proposal or proposals they "endorse" at that time. The experimenter, who was present during the negotiations, created a record of these "endorsements." Since a payoff matrix (such as shown in Table 2) was defined for each experiment, it was possible to associate with each speech a payoff that expressed the implicit demand made at that time. Thus, we had a record of demands D_t (and of opponent demands D_{t-1}, as well as of concessions C_t and C_{t-1}) for each time t.

In order to determine the personality types specified by Bales' theory, the experimenter completed after each experiment the questionnaire shown in Table 3, for each of the four persons acting as experimental negotiators. Each participant also used it to evaluate his team-mate; he did it once, after he had grown to know him well. (Each person participated in four experiments, always with the same team-mate.) The questions shown in Table 3 are those used by Bales (1970). We scored each questionnaire in a manner specified by Bales, obtaining three scores from each questionnaire: one score on the U-D dimension, one on the P-N dimension, and one on the F-B dimension. Since each participant was assessed twice, (once by the experimenter and once by his team-mate), we used

Table 3.   Personality Questionnaire

Please answer as well as you possibly can the following questions about _____.
Your name: _____.

1. Does he (or she) tend to address the group as a whole rather
   than individuals?   Yes _____   No _____
2. Does he seem personnally involved in the experiment?   Yes _____   No _____
3. Does he seem valuable for a logical task?   Yes _____   No _____
4. Does he seem to feel he represents some impersonal higher
   plan for the group?   Yes _____   No _____
5. Does he speak like an autocratic authority?   Yes _____   No _____
6. Does he seem dominating?   Yes _____   No _____
7. Does he seem to demand pleasure and gratification?   Yes _____   No _____
8. Does he seem to think of himself as entertaining?   Yes _____   No _____
9. Does he seem warm and personal?   Yes _____   No _____
10. Does he seem friendly in his behavior?   Yes _____   No _____
11. Is his rate of giving agreement generally high?   Yes _____   No _____
12. Is he generally very strongly work-oriented?   Yes _____   No _____
13. Does he always seem to try to speak objectively?   Yes _____   No _____
14. Does he seem to feel that his personal independence is very
    important?   Yes _____   No _____
15. Does he have a tendency to feel that others are dominating?   Yes _____   No _____
16. Does he tend to see others as too acceptant of authority?   Yes _____   No _____
17. Do you feel liking to him?   Yes _____   No _____
18. Does he seem calm, understanding?   Yes _____   No _____
19. Does he seem submissively good?   Yes _____   No _____
20. Does he seem often to ask for suggestions or for task-
    leadership?   Yes _____   No _____
21. Does he seem to plow persistently ahead with great inertia?   Yes _____   No _____
22. Does he seem resentful?   Yes _____   No _____
23. Does he seem preoccupied with feelings of dislike for others?   Yes _____   No _____
24. Does he show many signs of tension and passive resistance?   Yes _____   No _____
25. Does he seem appealing for understanding?   Yes _____   No _____
26. Does he seem to confine his participation mostly to giving
    information when asked?   Yes _____   No _____

the *means* of these two assessments as indicative of the participant's personality. However, we did *not* average the personalities of the members of the same team, as we might have, had we wished to obtain a single measure for the team. Consequently, when in the forthcoming analysis we refer to the influence of the personality, we are referring to the personality of a single person: that member of the team who delivered a given sequence of three speeches.

The eight aspects of negotiation style (toughness, fairness, knowledge, quality of arguments, persuasiveness, credibility, tactical cleverness, and readiness to take offense) were assessed quite simply: the experimenter evaluated each negotiator on these aspects on a 10-point scale. He was using his own understanding of what these terms meant, and completed these evaluations after each three-speech segment.

Interpreted Theory

Table 4 shows what the variables of our theory were (first column) and how they were interpreted empirically (second column). Since, in most cases, the variables were defined in terms of several "indicators," Table 4 also shows how these were combined into a single whole (last column). In general, each indicator was assigned the weight shown in the last column, and then the weighted indicators were added together. It should be added that resulting "complex" variables, the names of which are listed in the first column, were part of a larger set of data than used for the present purposes. For this reason, some of them have been assigned large subscripts such as X_{55}.

The first three variables represent the three dimensions of Bales' *personality* types. Table 4 shows how each participant's personality was assessed. If, for example, the evaluators (the experimenter or the team-mate) answered "yes" to the first question "Does he (or she) tend to address the group as a whole rather than individuals?", then $+1$ was added to the U-dimension for that participant.

The next set of variables concerns the *negotiating style*. Note that we used the same set of eight indicators to obtain two different styles: toughness and incompetence. We obtained them by factor-analyzing eight style-aspects (indicators): two main factors emerged and yielded the sets of weights listed in the last column of Table 4.[16] These weights were used to create the two "complex" variables. For example, the variable "toughness" (X_{55}) was a weighted sum of its eight indicators:

$$X_{55} = .36 *(\text{toughness}) + .08 *(\text{unfairness}) + \dots$$
$$- .04 *(\text{reluctance to take offense})$$

The starred (*) indicators in Table 4 are those that had factor loading of .50 or more, thus being important in determining the meaning of the variable. For example, a negotiator was rated as having a "tough" style of negotiation if he was seen by the experimenter as tough, unfair, persuasive, and tactically clever. (Table 4 shows factor weights, not factor loadings. Thus, the stars refer to information not shown in Table 4.)

The last four variables shown in Table 4 describe the most crucial aspects of negotiator's *behavior*: the concessions of the two teams and their previous demands. As already mentioned, these measurements were taken from the record kept by the experimenter. If, for example, the spokesman for Israel (in an experiment using Table 2) said that he was advocating proposal 4, we coded this as a demand for $7.00 because this is the payoff Table 2 associates for Israel with proposal 4. And the size of the concession was computed by subtracting the current demand from the last, $C_t = D_{t-2} - D_t$.

We should make some methodological remarks at this point. Our previous work showed that the demands of the negotiators tend to fluctuate considerably from one speech to the next. Although these fluctuations are interesting in their own right,[17] they tend to obscure the main trends we are interested in. For

Table 4. The Variables and Their Empirical Interpretation

Variable	Indicators	Weights
Power orientation (U–P dimension)	"Yes" on questions 1–9 (Table 3) "No" on questions 18–26 (Table 3)	+1 for each question
	"Yes" on questions 18–26 (Table 3) "No" on questions 1–9 (Table 3)	−1 for each question
Equalitarian orientation (P–N dimension)	"Yes" on questions 2, 3, 9–11, 17–19, 25 (Table 3) "No" on questions 5–7, 13–15, 21–23 (Table 3)	+1 for each question
	"Yes" on questions 5–7, 13–15, 21–23 (Table 3) "No" on questions 2–3, 9–11, 17–19, 25 (Table 3)	−1 for each question
Respect for tradition (F–B dimension)	"Yes" on questions 3–5, 11–13, 19–21 (Table 3) "No" on questions 7–9, 15–17, 23–25 (Table 3)	+1 for each question
	"Yes" on questions 7–9, 15–17, 23–25 (Table 3) "No" on questions 3–5, 11–13, 19–21 (Table 3)	−1 for each question
Toughness	*Toughness	.36
	*Unfairness	.08
	Lack of knowledge	.16
	Quality of arguments	−.05
	*Failure to be persuasive	−.07
	Lack of credibility	.00
	*Tactical cleverness	.57
	Reluctance to take offense	−.04
Incompetence	Toughness	.14
	Unfairness	.00
	*Lack of knowledge	.71
	*Quality of arguments	−.22
	*Failure to be persuasive	.11
	Lack of credibility	.00
	Tactical cleverness	−.03
Size of Concession	$\bar{C}_t = \bar{D}_{t-2} - \bar{D}_t$ (means of three consecutive concessions)	1.00
Level of previous demand	$\bar{D}_{t-3}$ (means of three consecutive demands)	1.00
Time	Serial number of the speech, $t = 1, 2, 3, \ldots$	1.00

*Starred indicators have a factor loading of .50 or more, thus specifying the meaning of the variable. (Factor loadings are not shown in Table 4, only so-called factor weights are.)

these reasons, we "collapsed" the three consecutive speeches (delivered between the planning sessions) into one, using them to compute the *mean* demands. Thus, when we speak about the negotiator's demand, we are referring to the "average" (mean) demand he made in his three consecutive speeches; when we speak about a concession, we are referring to the difference between the average demand in the last three speeches and the average demand in the "current" three speeches.

Moreover, the mean demands and concessions we shall use in our statistical analysis are not the dollar payoffs given by the payoff matrices such as shown in Table 2; they are "standardized" payoffs; i.e., numbers that fall mostly between -3 and $+3$. We standardized the payoffs in order to compensate for the differences in the payoff matrices used in the experiments. We standardized them by dividing the demands actually made by our negotiators into eight subsets, one for each role (there being two roles per matrix) and each payoff matrix (there being four different matrices), and by computing the mean and standard deviation for each of the eight subsets. These means $\bar{D}$ and standard deviations s were used to compute standardized payoffs Z:

$$Z = \frac{P - \bar{D}}{s}$$

(where P are the payoffs such as shown in Table 2). These standardized payoffs were comparable because (1) $Z = 0$ indicated a payoff that corresponded to the mean demand of the negotiators and (1) the interval from $Z = -1$ to $Z = +1$ included about 68 percent of the negotiators, no matter what payoff matrix they used or which role they played.

Figure 1 shows graphically what our "interpreted" theory is; i.e., what we expected to find. We used dotted arrows $\cdots\cdots\cdots>$ to indicate the influences that Equation 1 specifies as existing but does not specify their sign. Solid arrows indicate positive influences and the number attached to them refers to the hypothesis they represent. Thus, for example, the arrow

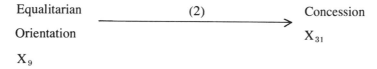

states that equalitarian orientation influences concessions positively in the manner spelled out in hypothesis (2): equalitarians make large concessions. Finally, broken-line arrows refer to negative influences. For example,

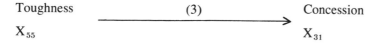

means that toughness influences concessions negatively (tough negotiators make small concessions), and that this is an expression of hypothesis 3.

Figure 1. Interpreted Theory: Expected Influences.

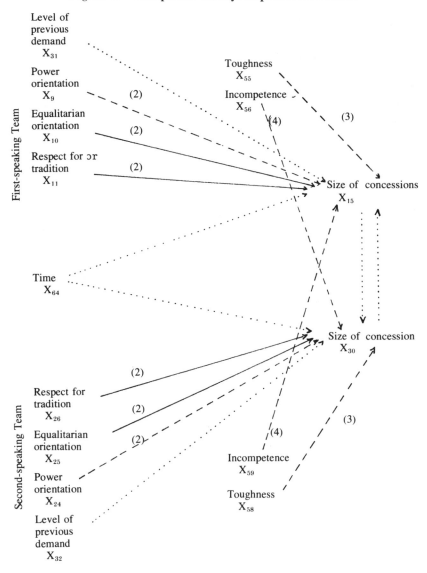

Causal Ordering

There is one aspect of Figure 1 that merits special attention: some variables are listed directly above each other, others are ordered from left to right. In general, these facts convey certain a priori judgments we made, stipulating which variable X_i cannot be a cause of another variable X_j:

1. Variables that are listed directly above each other cannot be causally related.
2. If variable X_j is to the right of variable X_i, then variable X_j cannot be a cause of X_i.

This amounts to the general principle that all variables X_i that are listed to the *left* of variable X_j are *potential causes of* X_i. Whether or not they are its causes in fact will be determined by statistical analysis.

Rule 1, however, has some important exceptions, due to the fact that we are using *mean* demands and concessions. Although Equation 1 shows clearly the opponent's concession C_{t-1} is a potential cause of negotiator's concession C_t (C_{t-1} occuring before C_t), when we averaged the demands and concessions for the three consecutive speeches we have destroyed this one-way flow of influence: we no longer can assume that opponent's (mean) concession occurs entirely before the negotiator's (mean) concession. Similar argument holds for negotiating style since it was ascertained only once for the three consecutive speeches. As a result we must assume that negotiating style, and concession *can* be linked in a loop:

Toughness   Size of concession

X_{55} X_{15}

Toughness   Size of concession

X_{56} X_{30}

(Note that we are not assuming that incompetence of one team influences incompetence of the other.) We shall have to keep these potential loops in mind when we perform our statistical analysis, since they call for a special handling.

VERIFIED THEORY

The causal ordering of Figure 1 can be used as a basis for a series of multiple regression analyses that not only permit us to test the hypotheses we stated earlier but also allow us to discover new influences between our variables. Before we consider the results of such statistical analyses, however, we must say a few words about their nature.

Technical Remark

The causal theory shown in Figure 1 is "block recursive", thus indicating that two types of analysis are needed. The recursive part of our theory is given by variables that are *not* listed directly above each other. For these variables, each endogenous variable X_i (i.e., each variable not listed at the left margin) was

Figure 2.   Empirically Verified Theory: Direct Influences.

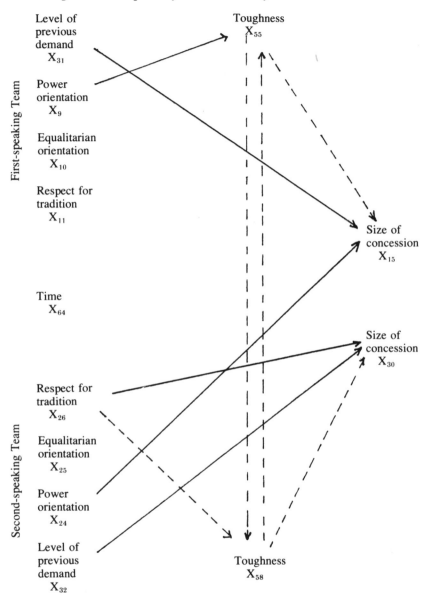

treated as a dependent variable, all of its potential causes X_j (i.e., all variables to the *left* of X_i) as independent variables. Step-wise regression analysis was used, selecting from all the potential causes X_j those that were related to X_i in a statistically significant fashion.[18] The norecursive "blocks" of our theory are the two potential loops we discussed earlier. In order to determine the influences within these loops, we used the so-called "two-step least square" method of estimation.[19] Figure 2 shows the results of both approaches: the arrows represent the causal influences found to be statistically significant.

Before we examine the "empirically verified" theory shown in Figure 2, let us note that to draw conclusions from it may be misleading. For example, there is no arrow between power orientation of the spokesman for team 1 (X_9) and size of his concession (X_{15}), thus suggesting that power orientation has no influence on concession-making. But note that power orientation has *indirect* impact on the size of concession, through toughness:

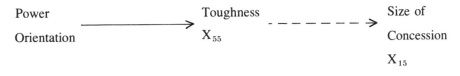

As can be shown, this chain of influences implies that the so-called "total" influence of power orientation and size of concessions exists, and must be negative:[20]

But, until we re-examine our data, we do not know whether this total influence is strong enough to be statistically significant.

This suggests that Figure 2 is insufficient as a representation of our verified theory: we need also a graph showing the *total* influences on the concession-making. We computed these influences and Figure 3 shows the results.[21] Note that several new influences appear in Figure 3: respect for tradition has a total impact on concession-making of team 1 and power orientation exercises total influences of concession-making of team 2.

Test of the Hypotheses

Recall that our model of the negotiation process was described by Equation 1:

$$C_t = aC_{t-1} + cD_{t-2} + et + f$$

Recall also that this model was "exploratory," not asserting anything about the size or sign of the parameters a,c,e, and f. Thus, statistical analysis was used to discover what the values of these parameters are.

Figure 2 reveals, first of all, that parameter a is not statistically significant. Thus we obtain the following conclusion:

"The size of negotiator's concession is *not* influenced significantly by the size of his opponent's concession." (1a)

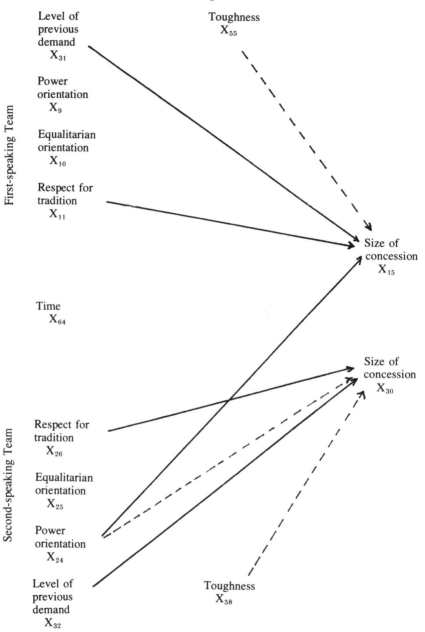

Figure 3.   Empirically Verified Theory: Total Influences on Concession-making.

With respect to parameters c and e, our findings are also clear: for both teams, parameter c is positive, parameter e not significant. The finding that c > 0 can be stated verbally as follows:

"The smaller is negotiator's previous demand, the smaller is his concession likely to be."(1b)

(A positive relationship between X and Y can be expressed either as "The larger is X and the larger is Y" or as "The smaller is X and the smaller is Y.") The finding that e = 0 can be stated as

"Time does *not* exercise direct influence on the size of concession."   (1c)

The next three hypotheses involve variables we have not considered systematically in our previous research, the variables dealing with personality and negotiating style. Recall that hypothesis 2 stated that concession-makers will be self-efacing (D-type), equalitarian (F-type), and traditional (F-type). As Figure 3 shows, two of these three expectations are confirmed, at least in one of the two teams:

"Negotiators respectful of tradition (F-types) and (in team 2) negotiators who are self-effacing (D-types) tend to make large concessions."   (2a)

Conspicuously absent from Figure 3 is the influence we expected to be the strongest: the influence from concern with equality. Our data show that

"Equality orientation has *no* significant impact on concession-making."   (2b)

The next hypothesis stated at the beginning of this paper (hypothesis 3) is fully supported by our data:

"The tougher is the negotiator, the smaller do his concessions tend to be."   (3)

But the last hypothesis (hypothesis 4) is not supported:

"Opponent's competence has *no* significant impact on concession-making."   (4')

Having stated our main findings, let us relate them to our hypotheses as expressed in Figure 1. Of particular interest are the findings that do not meet our expectations: the opponent's concessions are not influenced by the concessions of the negotiator; time does not influence the size of concessions; equality orientation does not influence concession-making; competence has no bearing on opponent's concession-making. Of all these negative findings, the first (that the two teams' concessions are unrelated) is undoubtedly the most important. This being the case, we shall discuss it in a separate section; right now, we shall turn to the remaining three "negative" findings.

The first of these is easily explained: the finding that time does not influence concession-making is an artifact of our theory. Had we not used previous demand (D_{t-1}) as an exogenous variable, we would have found that time does influence concession-making; since we did include it and since time and previous demands are highly correlated (the later it is in a negotiation, the lower is the previous demand), the previous demand in effect *replaces* time. This "disappearance" of time is not complete, since its influence can always be "reconstructed." We illustrated this earlier, when we showed that the equation

$$C_t = aC_{t-1}$$

implies

$$C_{t-1} = (aa)^{t/2}C_1 \qquad \text{for } t = 4,6,8,\ldots$$

Note that in the first equation time does not occur as a variable, that it occurs only as an indexing subscript. In the second equation, however, time occurs explicitly as a variable, as the exponent of the product aa. In general, the fact that time appears as an indexing subscript of the variables in Equation 1 means that it always can be expressed as an explicit variable that influences concession-making C_t.

The second negative finding is that equality-orientation does *not* influence concession-making significantly. This finding is surprising in view of the fact that the hypothesis "equalitarian subjects are cooperative" is strongly supported by Bales' data. Our tentative explanation is that our interpretation of Bales' theory was wrong: a person concerned with maintaining equality will not make concessions indiscriminately, he will *reciprocate* them. Thus, we should have hypothesized that the equality-oriented subjects will have a positive parameter a, since, as Equation 1 shows, such a parameter means that the concessions are reciprocated.

The third finding is that competence has no bearing on concession-making: competent negotiators did *not* induce large concessions in their opponents. We cannot explain this finding except by pointing out that, unlike our proposition dealing with toughness, the proposition dealing with competence was an *ad hoc* hypothesis: we found that "competence" had to be distinguished from "toughness," and thus had to state a hypothesis about its influence. It seemed plausible to assume that competent negotiators will be more effective than incompetent ones.

These are the main "total" failures of our hypotheses. But, in addition, there are two important "partial" failures: power-oriented subjects made smaller concessions than those not concerned with power *only when they belonged to the second-speaking team;* subjects whose opponent was power-oriented made larger concessions than subjects whose opponent was unconcerned with power *only if they belonged to the first-speaking team.* Why this lack of symmetry? We shall return to this question in a moment. But first, let us consider whether our findings can be generalized to real life negotiations.

Is "Lack of Responsiveness" Generalizable?

It is natural to ask of any experimental findings whether they can be generalized to "real life." In our case, this question can be asked most legitimately about our most important "negative" finding: our negotiators were *not* influenced by their opponents' concessions. This finding is important because *some* relationship between opponents' concession-making is postulated not only by our theory, but also by most theories of the negotiation process. Moreover, most of us routinely assume that what we have to say to another person has some impact on what he or she will say in turn. The very idea that people could be talking to each other without listening to what the other person has to say is deeply disturbing. How, then, can we explain our finding?

In a way, this finding of ours is a result of several aspects of our experimental design. First, we prevented our subjects from knowing the payoffs of their opponents: this made it difficult for them to know exactly how large a concession the opponents were making, and thus made it difficult to match them, had they wanted to do so. Second, the fact that our subjects negotiated in teams might have prevented them from making concessions as freely as they might otherwise have done.[22] Third, we asked each team to plan carefully what they will say in their "next three speeches." One could argue that, having planned their speeches, they became inflexible and could not respond readily to the opponents' concessions.

But these features of our design do not necessarily mean that our findings are invalid: they still can be generalized to situations that involve incomplete information, team negotiation, and planning. And most of the real-life *formal* negotiations, such as those between labor and management or between two nations, are of this kind. Thus the only question is whether they can be generalized to informal bargaining as well: can we assume that in everyday "negotiations" people talk but do not listen?

To begin with, we feel quite strongly that everyday negotiations are conducted under conditions of incomplete information: we usually do not know the exact interests of the person with whom we are "negotiating." For example, when I am talking with my wife to determine whether she or I will take our children to school, I do not know exactly how valuable it is to her not to have to make that extra trip, and she does not know that about me, either. Usually, we each have only a rough idea about this value. In our experiments, we attempted to duplicate this: since the payoffs we assigned to the proposals were realistic, any subject who listened to TV or read newspapers had a rough idea of what the payoffs of the opponent were like.

In principle, the fact that our subjects had to negotiate in teams might have made our results less generalizable to everyday discussions between single individuals. Thus, if the findings reported in this paper stood alone, we would hesitate to generalize from them to such conversations. But the fact is that, as reported in Bartos (1974), our findings were similar when our subjects did not act in teams, when negotiation occurred between individuals.

Finally, let us consider the fact that our subjects had to plan their next move, and the conjecture that this might have made them less likely to respond to opponents' concessions. We feel that this fact might account for the lack of relationship between the "simultaneous" concessions, those made during the concurrent three speeches delivered, in alternation, by each team. (Even then we doubt that this was so, since the subjects could have planned their next move in a flexible fashion: "If they do X, we shall do Y." Thus, the fact of planning did not necessarily preclude flexibility and responsiveness.) But it does not explain why we found that the opponents' *previous demands* had no impact on the negotiators' concession-making: after all, these demands always occurred before the planning took place, and thus, in planning their next move, the negotiators could have taken them into account, had they wanted to do so. Moreover, we conducted previously experiments in which no planning took place—still, we did not find a significant relationship between the two sides' concession-making.

We thus conclude that we may generalize our findings to informal negotiations that involve incomplete information. However, we exclude from this generalization negotiations in which information about the opponent's payoffs *is* communicated. Since previous research suggests that under the condition of complete information concessions tend to be reciprocated, *we exclude informal negotiations with complete information from our generalization.* A notable example of such negotiations is a "serious" talk between husband and wife, in which each side tells the other how they "feel" about things. We hypothesize that in such talks, concessions tend to be reciprocated, since, by making clear how they "feel," they have conveyed information about what we call their "payoffs." Still, we feel that most informal discussions do not go that deep, and hence should be viewed as negotiations under incomplete information. And we conclude that our finding can be generalized to most conversations: the participants talk but do not listen.

APPLICATION OF THE THEORY

Having concluded that our findings are generalizable to most negotiations, formal or informal, we wish to examine in some detail what such generalization might mean. But before we do so, we find it desirable to simplify our theory by omitting the style variable of "toughness." We begin by considering the reasons for such a simplification and by stating and discussing this simplified theory.

A Simplified Theory

We shall now discuss a theory that differs from that presented in Figures 2 and 3 in that the intervening variable of "toughness" has been removed from the theory altogether. We have two main reasons for doing this. First, our primary interest (in this paper) is to discover the influences a negotiator's personality exercises upon his concession-making. This being the case, the intervening variable of toughness, while capable of explaining why certain personality influences exist, does not contribute much to our theory. Given the fact that toughness turns out to be the only intervening variable, its omission gives our theory a very simple form: all direct influences are also total influences. It should be noted that, in effect, we are opting for a theory that is identical to that given in Figure 3, except for one thing: since we are omitting toughness, that variable should be ignored. The second reason for omitting "toughness" from our theory is that, at this stage of our analysis, we are not entirely sure whether this variable measures what we think it does.[23]

In order to be able to discuss the relative importance of the various influences of our simplified theory, let us represent them algebraically, showing the exact values of the regression coefficients. We may do so by writing the following two equations:

$$C_t = .73D_{t-1} + .38U + .17F$$

$$C_t = .73D_{t-1} - .16U + .20F \qquad (5)$$

where:

C_t ... mean concession of the first-speaking team
C_t ... mean concession of the second-speaking team
D_{t-1} ... mean previous demand of the first-speaking team
D_{t-1} ... mean previous demand of the second-speaking team
U ... power-orientation of the second-speaking team
F ... respect for tradition of the first-speaking team
F ... respect for tradition of the second-speaking team.

It should be noted that this theory is quite good. In the first place, we obtained considerable predictive power from only three causal variables: the first equation explains 60 percent of variance in C_t, the second 57 percent of variance in C_t. Second, observe that the influence exercised by previous demand is .73 for both teams. Since we obtained the same influence from two different populations, we can put considerable faith in this part of our theory:[24] the negotiators follow basically a very simple formula for determining the size of their concessions: *their present demand was about one-fourth of what they demanded last time.*[25]

This general formula was augmented by each speaker's personality. If the speaker was tradition-oriented, (if he was rated high on the F-dimension of Bales' questionnaire), then he tended to make his concessions somewhat larger than usual; if he was "tradition-free," he intended to make them smaller. We might note that this finding seems consistent with the customary interpretation of traditional orientation. In the writings of sociologists, ranging from Emile Durkheim to David Riesman, we find the notion that tradition-directed persons tend to be cooperative, because traditional (pre-industrial) societies tended to be collectivistic. Moreover, this conclusion is consistent with Gillis and Woods' (1971) finding that subjects who value morality, liberty, charity, responsibility, and established principles of conduct tend to be cooperative. Similar findings have been reported by Bixenstine et al., (1963a,b).

Our findings concerning the influence of power orientation are somewhat harder to explain. To be sure, the findings that power-oriented negotiators tend to make smaller concessions than those not interested in power is consistent with previous research, especially that reported by Gillis and Woods (1971) and Sermat (1968). Still, we found that only the power of the *second*-speaking team had an impact on concession-making. If the spokesman for the second-speaking team was "greedy for power" (rated high on the U-dimension of Bales' questionnaire), then he made smaller concessions and his opponent made larger concessions than "normal"; and, vice versa, if the representative for the second-speaking team was disinterested in power, his concessions were larger and those of his opponent smaller than usual.

Why did the power-orientation of the second-speaking negotiator have an impact on the concession-making of *both* teams? It seems to us that the person who makes the first bid has a distinct advantage over his opponent because he "sets the tone" of the bargaining. If nothing else, the second speaker must react to the opening bid, thus being put in a defensive position. Moreover, if the first-speaking negotiator is also the one who delivers the next-to-last speech, he has another advantage: since his opponent's next speech is going to be the very last speech of the negotiation, the opponent is reduced to either accepting or rejecting the last bid. Thus, in general, *the person who speaks first is in a more powerful position* than the person who speaks second.[26]

This much is rather noncontroversial. But why should this lack of symmetry in speech-making be reflected in the manner our findings show? We hypothesize—and this is a tentative hypothesis—that the power orientation of the second speaker determines whether or not he will accept the circumstances: if he is eager to have power, he will rebel against them and made his concessions small.

In addition to that, we hypothesize that this fact of rebellion—or the absence thereof—will be noted by the opponent, the first-speaking negotiator. If he concludes that this opponent is power-hungry, he also concludes that he himself must make larger concessions than he would normally make. This is why we find that first-speaking negotiators make larger concessions when their opponent is power-oriented than when he is disinterested in power.

Generalization to Everyday Life

When attempting to generalize to everyday life, we should repeat that we see our findings as applicable only to negotiations with *incomplete* information. As we already noted, this means that our theory does not apply to negotiations such as "having a serious talk" with one's husband or wife, if this talk includes revealing how each side "feels" about the matters. In such situations, concessions will be influenced by the other side's concessions.

But that leaves us with a very large number of negotiations that are conducted under the condition of incomplete information. Many of them are formal, such as international negotiations we tried to simulate in our experiments. To these negotiations our findings are applicable. And they suggest, first and foremost, that negotiators tend to follow a basic formula of demanding a constant fraction of their last demand:

$$D_t = aD_{t-2}$$

It is not too difficult to show that this equation implies that

$$D_t = a^{t/2}D_1 \qquad \text{for } t=2,4,6,\dots$$

where D_1 is the negotiator's first demand. This means that, by and large, the changes in a negotiator's demands can be represented graphically by a curve, such as shown in Figure 4.

Finally, we come to negotiations that are not conducted with complete information, nor are they formal. Among these, of greatest interest are "one-shot" negotiations, those that are completed when an action is followed by a reaction, either favorable (acceptance of the demand) or unfavorable (rejection of the demand). We are proposing that everyday conversations may profitably be viewed as such negotiations. We are referring not only to commands such as "Please pass the salt" and assertions such as "Teddy Kennedy would make a fine president," but also to jokes: in all of these cases, the person who listens to the command, assertion, or joke, has to decide whether to accept or reject the message. In the case of a joke, for example, he often must make a conscious decision whether to laugh, or merely chuckle, or say "Oh no!".

For these "one-shot" negotiations, our findings showing the influence of personality are most important. The first generalization is that certain persons will be quite accepting, doing what they are told, agreeing with assertions, and laughing at jokes. They will be those who are tradition-oriented in the sense described in this paper. This conclusion is hardly startling, since the fact that certain persons will be submissive is well documented in literature dealing with small groups. Whatever interest there is lies in the fact that this proposition applies both to formal negotiations and to everyday life.

Our second finding, that the second-speaking negotiators' dominance is important, is of greater interest. Since we have argued that the first-speaking negotiator has an institutional advantage, we generalize it to situations in which persons of *unequal status* are engaged in negotiations. Our findings suggest that a boss will be more "reasonable" (will make smaller demands) if faced by a courageous employee than when faced by a "yes-man."

But we must add an important qualification to this generalization. Our finding

Figure 4. Demands Consistent with $D_t = aD_{t-2}$

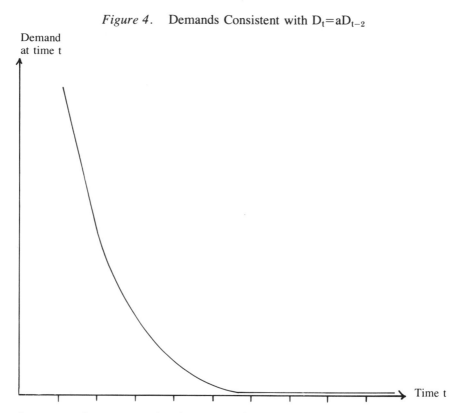

Demand
at time t

Time t

that concessions are unrelated suggests that the courageous employee cannot expect that his verbal behavior (i.e., making only a small concession) will impress his boss. Instead, his boss will be impressed only if he concludes that his employee has a certain *personality*—that he is power-oriented. Thus, at stake is the image the boss has of his employee, and that image may take a while to build. We are thus hypothesizing that any *one* refusal to make a concession (to acceed to an unreasonable demand, to laugh at the boss' jokes) may not have significant impact on the boss, that only the cumulative weight of such refusals will be effective.

Thus, our future data analysis is clear. In the first place, we shall begin by considering data we did not analyze as yet, the *subjects'* evaluation of their opponents (as being tough or soft). If our tentative theory is correct, we should find that the opponents who are power-oriented tend to be perceived as tough. We then should determine how concession making contributes to the emergence of this image about the opponent: when we control for the power-orientation of the opponent, do the opponents who make small concessions tend to be perceived as tough? If we find that they are, then we must further explore our data in order to solve the following riddle: since we (presumably) found that a refusal to make concessions contribute to the image of toughness, and that the image of (opponent's) toughness induces large concessions,

Second team's concessions	← — — — — — —	First team's image of opponent as being tough	— — — — — — →	First team's concession

why is it that a refusal to make concessions does *not* cause the opponent to make large concessions? We suspect that we may find that if we average concessions over a longer period than we did in this paper, say over six speeches, we might find a relationship between opponents' concessions. Such a finding would be consistent with our tentative hypothesis that it takes time to create an image in the mind of the opponent.

ACKNOWLEDGMENTS

The experiments on which this paper is based were made possible by a grant from Deutsche Forschungsgemeinschaft (Professor Reinhard Teitz, Principal Investigator) and the Council on Research and Creative Work at the University of Colorado.

NOTES

1. For a good summary of the experimental work dealing with negotiation see McClintoch and Messick (1960) or Swingle (1970).

2. If $0 < aa < 1$, then $(aa)^n$ will grow smaller as n grows larger.

3. If $aa > 1$, then $(aa)^n$ will grow larger as n grows larger.

4. If $aa < 0$, then $(aa)^n$ will be a positive number when n is even, a negative number when n is odd.

5. There are those who would argue that the correct way to take various conditions into account is to test our simple model under various experimental conditions and to identify the conditions under which negotiators are cooperative. We prefer to take another route, that of building into our model additional causes, thus making it a more complex but also more flexible so that it is applicable to a variety of conditions. For a discussion of this methodological issue see, for example, Bartos (1980).

6. See, for example, Forrester (1973).

7. This was shown earlier for our simpler model $C_t = aC_{t-1}$.

8. For example, if parameter a in Equation 1 is positive and the opponent just made a concession, then the negotiator's concession-making is explained, at least in part, by the fact that the opponent just made a concession.

9. For example, if opponent's parameter a is positive, we would counsel the nagotiator to be cooperative (to make concessions); if it is negative, we would counsel him to be tough (to raise his demand).

10. For a good summary of previous research dealing with the impact of personality on negotiation see Terhune (1970). Among the personality measures used are California F-scale Rokeach's dogmatism scale, EPPS, Gough ACL, MMPI, Allport ascendance-submission, Christie's Machiavellianism scale, TAT, Kogan-Wallach risk-taking scale, and Gore-Rotter internal-external control test. (See *ibid*, pp. 200-1.)

11. These characterizations are based on the summary given by Bales (1970). For a more detailed description of each type, one must read the lengthy discussion in the appropriate six chapters.

12. These traits are listed in ibid., Appendix 1.

13. Some of these aspects of negotiation style are suggested by the work of Tietz (1973).

14. For a discussion of this point, see Bartos (1980).

15. While realism was our primary objective, there were some overriding requirements. For example, some payoff matrices were designed so as to make the agreement easy, others to make it difficult.

16. We used principal component analysis with iteration, and rotated the factors orthogonally with VARIMAX rotation. For a description of this procedure, see Nie et al., (1975).

17. They may represent "search behavior," attempting to discover which proposals might be acceptable to the opponent.

18. We used the .05 level of significance.

19. For a good description of this method, see Heise (1975), 168–172.

20. For a discussion of how intervening variables can be "extricated" so that the total influence between two variables can be determined see, for example, Bartos (1980).

21. The computation of total influences involves multiple regression analysis, just as the computation of direct influences does. The only difference is that, when we compute the *total* influence of X on Y, we do *not* control for the intervening variables (i.e., all variables that are potential causes of Y but not of X).

22. For example, Pruitt (1978) found that negotiators who are held accountable negotiate differently than those who are autonomous. One could argue that the "silent" member of the team makes the speaking member feel accountable.

23. At stake is the fact that Figure 2 shows toughness to be in a negative loop: the tougher a negotiator was, the softer was his opponent. This is an unquestionable statistical fact, but before we conclude that it means what it seems to mean, we must answer the following question: could this loop be due to the fact that *all* of the ratings on which our measure of toughness was constructed was done by the experimenter? It seems possible that he had created this difference by striving (without being aware of it) to rate the two teams differently: when he rated one team as "tough", then he might have, for the sake of contrast, rated the other as "soft." We can resolve this question because we have available to us the ratings the *subjects* made of their opponents. And the preliminary analysis is none too encouraging: when we relate the ratings by the subjects, we find that the correlation between the toughness of the opposing teams is not statistically significant.

24. We can have considerable faith in the proposition "The lower is the previous demand, the smaller is the concession." We do not claim that the coefficient of .73 always represents the relationship between last demand and present concession: the size of this coefficient will depend on various conditions, such as the amount of time available for negotiation.

25. This formula is obtained when we convert concessions into demands. Since concession C_t is defined as $D_{t-2} - D_t$, we may write (5) as

$$D_{t-2} - D_t = .73D_{t-2} + \ldots$$

This simplifies to

$$D_t = (1 - .73)D_{t-2} + \ldots$$

Since $1 - .73 = .27$, and since .27 is roughly one-fourth (25 percent), we see that (5) implies that our subjects tended to ask for one-fourth of what they asked for previously.

26. This interpretation is consistent with the view taken by Homans (1950): the person who *initiates* interaction is seen as more powerful than the person who responds to such an initiative.

REFERENCES

Bales, Robert F. (1970) *Personality and Interpersonal Behavior,* New York: Holt, Rinehart and Winston.

Bartos, Otomar J. (1974) *The Process and Outcome of Negotiations,* New York: Columbia University Press.

————(1980) *Sociological Theory,* New York: Columbia University Press, (forthcoming).

Bixenstein, V. E., H. M. Potash, and K. V. Wilson (1963a) "Effects of Level of Cooperative Choice by Other Player on Choices in a Prisoner's Dilemma Game: Part I," *Journal of Abnormal and Social Psychology,* 66, 308-13.

Bixenstein, V. E., and K. U. Wilson (1963b) "Effects of Level of Cooperative Choice by the Other Player on Choices in a Prisoner's Dilemma Game, Part II," *Journal of Abnormal and Social Psychology,* 67, 139-47.

Coddington, A. (1968), *Theories of the Bargaining Process,* Chicago, Ill.: Aldine.

Cross, J. G. (1969), *The Economics of Bargaining,* New York: Basic Books.

Druckman, Daniel (1971) "The Influence of the Situation in Interparty Conflict," *Journal of Conflict Resolution,* 15, 522-554.

Forrester, Jay W. (1973) *World Dynamics,* Cambridge, Mass.: Wright-Allen.

Gillis, John S., and George T. Woods (1971) "The 16PF as an Indicator of Performance in the Prisoner's Dilemma Game," *Journal of Conflict Resolution,* 15, 393-402.

Heise, David D. (1975) *Causal Analysis,* New York: Wiley.

Homins, George C., (1950) The Human Group. New York: Harcourt, Brace & World.

McClintock, C. G., and David M. Messic (1966) "Empirical Approaches to Game Theory and Bargaining," *General Systems,* 11:229-38.

Nie, Norman H., C. H. Hull, J. G. Jenkins and D. H. Bent (1975) *Statistical Package for the Social Sciences (SPSS),* New York: McGraw-Hill.

Pruitt, D. G., J. M. Kimmel, S. Britton, P. J. D. Carnevale, J. M. Magenau, J. Peragallo, and P. Engram (1978) "The Effect of Accountability and Surveillance on Integrative Bargaining," in Sauremann, H. (Ed.) *Contributions to Experimental Economics,* Vol. 7, Tubingen, Germany: Mohr.

Sermat, V. (1968) "Dominance-Submissiveness and Competition in a Mixed-Motion Game," *British Journal of Social and Clinical Psychology,* 79, 43-50.

Siegel, S. and L. E. Fouraker (1960) *Bargaining and Group Decision Making,* New York: McGraw-Hill.

Swingle, Paul (Ed.) (1970) *The Structure of Conflict,* New York: Academic Press.

Terhune, Kenneth W., (1970), "The Effects of Personality in Cooperation and Conflict", in Swingle (1970), pp. 193-233.

Tietz, Reinhard (1973) *Ein Anspruchsannassungs-orientiertes Wachstuns-und-Konjukturmodel (KRESCO),* Tubingen, Germany: J. C. B. Mohr.

INTERLOCKING CONFLICTS
IN THE MIDDLE EAST

Louis Kriesberg

Although international conflicts are generally intractable and persist for long periods, they escalate and de-escalate in intensity—sometimes abruptly. To understand such variations, I argue in this paper, it is necessary to consider how each struggle is embedded within a wide variety of interlocking conflicts. Limiting attention to the over-simplified conception of a struggle as being only between two parties hampers comprehending the changes in the struggle. I will describe the variety of ways in which conflicts are interrelated and the ways in which their interlocking character affects many aspects of international struggles. In the second part of the paper, I will examine how the interlocking character of conflicts in the Middle East has effected the escalation and de-escalation of specific struggles, particularly the ones between the Egyptian and Israeli governments.

Research in Social Movements, Conflicts and Change, Vol. 3, pages 99-119
Copyright © 1980 by JAI Press Inc.
All rights of reproduction in any form reserved.
ISBN: 0-89232-182-2

INTERLOCKING CONFLICTS

In many ways, we carry with us an illusion that a conflict is two-sided. Partisans, of course, often insist on it. They ask, "Which side are you on?" or assert, "If you are not for us, you are against us." Even social scientists, in discussing conflict, for heuristic purposes, assume two sides. It is acknowledged to be an over-simplification, but it is so convenient that the complex reality is ignored. Some theorists—for example, Dahrendorf (1959)—even argue that ultimately every conflict is between two classes or groups. The elaboration of game theory and its application to social conflicts has also furthered the idea that conflicts are between two sides and often zero sum in their payoffs.

When pushed, we acknowledge that many conflicts are not simply a zero sum struggle between two antagonists. But we lack a systematic analysis of the many ways conflicts interlock and the consequences of their interlocking character for the emergence of conflicts, for the use of coercion, for the ways in which struggle escalate and de-escalate, and how they end. In this paper, I begin such an analysis.

Types of Interlocking Conflicts

Every specific social conflict *always* has more than two sides. This is true first because each party of any social conflict is made up of many component groups and those groups have somewhat different interests and views about the specific conflict. Each conflict party, in attacking or otherwise trying to get its adversary to change, could pay attention to the several groups making up the other side, differently attempting to threaten or persuade them. Each party to a conflict has allies or potential allies. Each adversary, therefore, has a somewhat different conflict with each member of the opposing coalition. A conflict generally involves several issues and the set of adversaries varies with the issues in dispute. Finally, conflicts generally occur in a series: each dispute may be seen as part of a long-run struggle.

This discussion does not deny that adversaries and observers generally regard one conflict as primary at a given time. Indeed, as we shall see, the shifts in what is regarded as the primary conflict are critical for changes in conflict intensity. For analytical purposes, here, I will consider one conflict as the primary or focal conflict and examine how it is interrelated with others.

Six ways in which conflicts are interlocked will be distinguished and discussed: (1) serial or nested in time; (2) converging or nested in social space; (3) superimposed or linking of issues; (4) cross-cutting; (5) internal; and (6) concurrent.

First, every conflict may be viewed as one in a series of fights between the same adversaries. Indeed, the adversaries may choose to bracket a given conflict within a variety of time periods. For example, the American-Soviet conflict may be viewed as occurring as a series of struggles, each enduring for several years, or as a series of short, intermittent crises. In any case, each fight may be viewed as following and preceeding others.

Conflicts also converge. Separate groups may coalesce as allies against an adversary or coalition of adversaries. Such coalitions may be based on broadening collective identifications. Thus, the focal conflict may be between two governments, with the leaders of each government trying to mobilize their domestic constituency and other people who may share ethnic, religious, or ideological identifications. Adversary parties may also increase in number or scope as they converge on different sides of the issue in contention. Thus, a fight between one government and another may be defined by other governments, peoples, or political movements as a struggle between developed and developing countries and choose sides accordingly. The focal conflict may be between large entities and encompass a fight between relatively subordinate entities; in that case, we may speak of proxy wars or a struggle between pawns. Every focal conflict, then, may be embedded in a broader set of social conflicts or itself may encompass more limited ones.

Superimposition is the third way in which conflicts are interlocked. Few or many contentious issues may be superimposed on each other (Dahrendorf, 1959). Thus, two adversaries may be in a fight over one issue with other issues added to the struggle; or, conversely, particular issues may be separated out and put aside. In American-Soviet relations, this has sometimes been referred to as "linkage." At different times, issues about arms control, the war in Vietnam, human rights, and others have been linked or have been de-coupled in adversary negotiations.

Cross-cutting conflicts, the fourth type of interlocking conflict, has been particularly studied by sociologists (Simmel, 1955; Ross, 1920; Coser, 1956; Kriesberg, 1973). Cross-cutting conflicts may be based on divisions within and across adversaries or among a set of adversaries allying themselves differently on several issues of contention. In the first case, the protagonists in the focal conflict are each divided on other issues and the adversaries within each protagonist are allied with their counterparts elsewhere. For example, conflicts about petroleum prices and allocations involve governments, managers of multinational oil companies, consumers, and other collectivities which cut across country borders. Cross-cutting conflicts are also based on the multiplicity of issues in contention. Thus, if two governments are adversaries on one issue but on the same side against other governments on a different issue, conflicts related to those various issues are cross-cutting. For example, we can see some signs of East-West issues cross-cutting North-South (developed-developing country) issues.

The fifth kind of interlocking conflicts are the ones which are internal to one of the adversaries. A number of writers have examined the way in which internal conflicts are linked to external ones (Simmel, 1955; Tanter, 1966; Wilkenfeld, 1969; Rosenau, 1973; Kriesberg, 1973). Most of this research has been concerned with countries as units and the relationship between domestic turmoil and conflict with foreign conflict behavior. However, any major actor in international conflict can be considered to have subgroups within it which themselves may be in contention. Thus, a government consists of quarrelling agencies; a government is struggling against the opposition party; or ethnic and class divisions may be the basis for intense and even violent struggles. An internal conflict also may be an international one; it may occur within a coalition which is one side in a larger conflict. For example, consider the Cyprus dispute. The Greek and Turkish governments' fight about Cyprus may be regarded as internal to NATO, which is a protagonist in the focal conflict with the Warsaw Pact countries. If the struggle between Greek and Turkish ethnic organizations on Cyprus is considered the focal conflict, then each group's alliance with the governments of Greece and Turkey is the basis for a converging conflict.

Finally, the sixth kind of conflict I wish to distinguish is the concurrent conflict. A concurrent conflict is an external one occurring along with the focal one, but does not involve the primary adversaries in the focal struggle. Thus, one of the adversaries in the focal conflict has a side fight with another adversary who has no direct relevance to the adversary in the focal conflict. For example, the Egyptian government's involvement in the war in Yemen in the 1960s was concurrent with its conflict with Israel, but insofar as the Israelis were not involved in Yemen, the fight was concurrent to the focal conflict between Egypt and Israel. A concurrent conflict may involve none of the primary adversaries; it may be happening elsewhere in the world and preoccupying major powers elsewhere.

This discussion has pointed out the many ways in which international conflicts are interrelated. Observers and participants may be paying attention to different ones at different times. What we call a particular interlocking fight depends on which conflict we regard as salient or primary. Obviously, the participants in a struggle try to define one or another conflict as primary, depending on what they regard as best advancing their interests in the fight. I will use the term "focal conflict" to indicate that we must focus on one conflict at a time, but that other focuses are also, perhaps equally, valid.

Possible Effects of Interlocking Conflicts

International conflicts, like all social conflicts, have a variety of aspects. We can consider the underlying basis for the conflict, the coercive and non-coercive means used in pursuing the conflict, the processes of escalation and de-escalation, how agreements are reached, and what the terms of settlement are. To illustrate the relevance of taking into account the interrelated character of international conflicts, I will discuss some of the ways in which different kinds of interlocking conflicts can effect these aspects of international struggles.

It can be argued that if a focal conflict is seen as one in a series of fights, the focal conflict will tend to escalate because yielding on the issue in contention will appear to set a precedent for the next struggle and tend to weaken one's reputation (Jervis, 1976: 103). Each adversary would seek to appear tough. On the other hand, it is possible to treat sequential fights as the basis for trade-offs. This tends to limit escalation and hasten agreements which would be balanced. It would make integrative bargaining, rather than distributive bargaining, more feasible (Pruitt and Lewis, 1977: 164).

Whether seeing a focal conflict as one in a series facilitates or impedes de-escalation and integrative bargaining depends on other aspects of the focal conflict. If the issues in contention are viewed as very important, if relatively few common interests are recognized, if communication is sparse and hostility is high, considering the focal conflict as one in a series will make it more difficult to resolve the issues in contention than if the focal conflict were regarded as isolated in time. Under other conditions, viewing the focal conflict as one in a series will facilitate de-escalation and integrative bargaining.

The convergence of conflicts has effects on the means used and on the escalation of the focal conflict. Wallace and Wilson (1978) have studied arms races and found that they move in spurts. What triggers an arms race is the coalition of several powers against another collectivity. The target country or countries rapidly expand their military expenditures and this is met by further adversary expenditures. Convergence of conflicts generally means an expansion and an intensification of the conflict. Hopmann and Wallcott (1977), in their analyses of negotiations, find that when the larger conflict within which the negotiations are being conducted (the focal conflict) becomes more intense, this places a stress on the negotiations and makes them more difficult. This indicates that changes in the larger conflict are reflected in the conduct of the subsidiary ones.

The complexity of relations in any focal conflict arising from the convergence of conflicts also opens opportunities for a wide variety of inducements to be used by partisans in the fights (Kriesberg and Klein, forthcoming). Partisans of each side are aware that their adversaries are trying to gain adherents to their side. The adversaries, for example, are appealing to shared ideological and ethnic identifications. The partisans of each side then may seek to divide the opponents by offering concessions and arguing cogently. Non-coercive inducements, such as promises of rewards and persuasive efforts, are likely to be used to appeal to supporters of the core adversary if not to the core enemy itself.

The next kind of interlocking conflict whose implications I wish to note is superimposed conflict. It is plausibly argued that a dispute which is viewed in isolation is more readily settled than one which is seen as a symptom of a larger set of disputes (Jervis, 1976: 44). Analyses of the nuclear test ban negotiations indicate that when other disputes coincided, reaching agreements in the negotiations was made more difficult (Hopmann and Walcott, 1977). De-escalation and reaching agreements about disputes then, are likely to be enhanced by de-coupling or isolating disputes.

Although, generally, superimposition of disputes hampers settling each dispute, under certain circumstances superimposition or the threat of it can limit escalation or facilitate agreements. Sorenson (1965: 680), for example, notes that during the Cuban Missile Crisis in 1962, U.S. leaders were inhibited from making a military attack on the Cuban missile bases partly because the Berlin crisis had alerted them to the possibility of Soviet pressure being brought on Berlin. Superimposition also seems to promise the possibility of trade-offs among the several matters in dispute. This is the kind of linkage in which a concession by one side on one issue is exchanged for a concession by the other side on another matter. Plausible as this may be, trade-offs among quite separate matters seem too difficult to effectuate, although they occur in the course of negotiating about a single matter, such as an arms limitation agreement.

The implications of cross-cutting conflicts in international relations has been investigated in only a few areas. Most notably, attention is given to the mitigation of the East-West conflict by the increasing salience of the conflicts between industrialized and economically developing nations. The primacy of the Cold War issues in the United Nations, for example, has declined and increasingly voting cleavages are based on other cross-cutting issues. Of course, some of that change is due to the increase in the number of newly independent countries which have become members of the United Nations.

There are several implications of internal conflicts for the way in which a focal conflict is conducted. For example, domestic conflicts may weaken a conflict unit so that it avoids foreign adventures and hostility; but internal disorder and the resulting weakness may lead other conflict units to take advantage of the weakness and act aggressively toward it. Domestic conflict may also lead to external conflict because the country's leaders act aggressively internationally in order to unify the country. If the protagonists of an international conflict come to regard their conflict as internal to a more important shared international conflict, it is likely to be mitigated in intensity and subject to integrative rather than distributive bargaining (Pruitt and Lewis, 1977). Persuasive means will appear more pertinent in this context. On the other hand, an international conflict which is internal to one adversary coalition may be exacerbated when the larger conflict de-escalates. For example, detente between the U.S. and U.S.S.R., loosens cohesion within the blocs led by each. Holsti (1969) analyzed Sino-Soviet relations between 1950 and 1965 and found that during periods of low tension between the U.S. and U.S.S.R., Soviet and Chinese official statements tended to be divergent as regards the U.S. and sharp differences between them emerged. In 1964, Krushchev publically recognized that detente produced divisiveness, not only in the Capitalist camp, but also in the Socialist camp (Zimmerman, 1969: 100).

Finally, I will mention some implications of concurrent conflicts for the way in which a focal conflict is conducted. A concurrent conflict, like an internal one, may weaken a protagonist in the focal struggle and hence limit conflict escalation and hasten a resolution. On the other hand, a concurrent fight may be an inducement to the leaders of one adversary group to escalate the focal conflict as a way cf drawing attention away from the concurrent one; this, however, is less likely since the desire to do this would arise if the concurrent fight were not going well and that would not be viewed as a good time to become more entangled in foreign adventures. Concurrent conflicts may tend to limit conflicts in another way. If major powers are deeply involved in a major conflict, their attention and resources tend to be so engaged that an unconnected focal conflict is more likely to remain localized than if the major powers were less so engaged.

The concurrent conflicts, which each primary adversary has, may develop into a network of cross-cutting conflicts and hence bonds. For example, the United States and the Soviet governments have found in recent years that other powers are growing in significance, and hence in some ways challenging them. Consequently, they have a common interest in not cancelling each other out and retaining their relative power as much as possible (Young, 1967: 163–164). This has been one reason for the U.S. and the Soviet governments to cooperate with each other. But, as we noted earlier, that may lead to members of each camp intensifying their challenge of the dominant leader of their camp.

Interlocking conflicts have a variety of effects on the escalation, de-escalation, emergence, and resolution of international conflicts. Those effects depend partly on which conflict is considered the focal one. Adversaries shift in whatever struggle they regard as primary and those shifts are the basis for changes in the conflict. It is also important to recognize that protagonists may differ in what they regard as the primary conflict. They may also disagree about how many adversaries are involved in the conflict and how many issues are in contention. If protagonists differ in these matters, their bargaining strategies and means of conducting the struggle are likely to be different. For example, insofar as Soviet leaders view the world as made up of two blocs led by the U.S. and the U.S.S.R., they will see each fight between them as converging and superimposed with other conflicts; hence, their bargaining demands are likely to be tougher and they are more likely to rely on coercive inducements. Insofar as they see multiple independent actors and cross-cutting conflicts, they are more likely to see integrative bargaining as possible.

In the second part of this paper, I will examine the escalation and de-escalation of Middle East conflicts and analyze how considering interlocking conflicts helps explain those changes. That analysis should also contribute to specifying the conditions under which particular kinds of interlocking conflicts tend to facilitate conflict escalation, termination, persistence, and de-escalation.

IMPLICATIONS FOR THE MIDDLE EAST CONFLICTS

To assess how the interlocking character of conflicts helps our understanding of Arab-Israeli relations, I first examine the persistence and intractibility of the conflicts and then their escalation and de-escalation. The struggle between Egyptian and Israeli governments will be regarded as the focal conflict.

Persistence of Arab-Israeli Conflict

Conflicts in the Middle East can be traced back to Biblical times. But in discussing the intractable character of the conflicts in the Middle East, I limit the analysis to the period since the establishment of the State of Israel in 1948. The implications of each kind of interlocking conflict on the perpetuation of the struggle between the Israeli and Egyptian governments will be examined.

Conflicts *nested* in each other over time have several effects which tend to perpetuate a struggle. The way in which conflicts have been conducted and the goals for which they were fought tend to become fixed, since they are salient in the minds of all the participants and even observers. The current situation is then viewed through the lenses of the past fights; consequently, the means and, therefore, the appropriate resources tend to be the ones previously used. New circumstances and new kinds of resources are frequently not readily noted and all this contributes to ineffective ways of pursuing a goal. This is true of "victors" as well as "losers" in the preceding fight. For example, the organized violence of 1948 took on more salience than the processes of non-violent mutual adaptation which residents and immigrants to Palestine had been previously conducting. Each war seems to strengthen reliance on armed coercion.

Conflicts nested in each other over time, as in a war series, also tend to generate grievances and so perpetuate conflicts. One way this occurs is that the conduct of a struggle and its outcome may become grievances for at least one party. For example, shame or loss of resources needs to be redressed and losers seek revenge, try to restore honor, or to regain lost territory. As Sadat wrote about planning for the October, 1973 War, "The basic task was to wipe out the disgrace and humiliation from the 1967 defeat" (Sadat, 1978). Thus, too, wars and hostilities have generated Arab refugees whose grievances are the source of uncompromising demands which, in turn, are unacceptable to many Israelis.

Defeats which are viewed as one in a series, rather than as final, are the grounds for new efforts to redress grievances. The defeat of Arab armies in 1948 by Israeli forces contributed to the changes in the governments of Egypt and Syria. The new ruling groups then had a vested interest in renewing a struggle with Israel which they might win (Heikal, 1975). Partisans in the Middle East anticipate recurrent escalations of the conflicts in which they are engaged. Conflicts nested over time also tend to become superimposed as cross-cutting conflicts decrease and more issues become matters of contention among adversaries.

The *convergence* of conflicts in the Middle East has tended to perpetuate Arab-Israeli conflicts in two contradictory ways. On the one hand, the extended coalitions of adversaries associated with the Israeli and Egyptian governments gives them the resources to persist. On the other hand, the diversity of the adherents to each coalition makes it difficult for particular pairs of adversaries to reach an agreement to resolve conflicting issues. Each of these ideas requires some elaboration.

As each adversary seeks wider support from other groups, its adversaries also seek to extend their support. The drive to find allies by one side is an incentive for the other side to seek allies. This tends to perpetuate a struggle, because it broadens the goals and enlarges the resources available for the struggle. The extension of the number of conflict groups engaged in a struggle in itself makes for conflict persistence, because the conflict can pass from one pair of antagonists to another, never allowing the conflict between any one pair to become stabilized. Thus, if Israel is in an adversary relationship with Egypt, Syria, and Jordan, and Syria obtains support from the Soviet Union to counter American support to Israel, stabilization of the conflict between Israel and Jordan could be undermined by Soviet-supported Syrian opposition to Israeli objectives.

Related to this is the effort by each party in the conflict to broaden its collective identity in order to gain support and in so doing generalize its grievance. Thus, one or another party in the Middle East may claim to be representing democracy, socialism, anti-imperialism, national liberation, self-determination, Islam, Arabs, Jews, or Western Civilization. Insofar as groups elsewhere in the world share such identifications, they suffer some of the same grievances that others with the same collective identity do. Reaching an acceptable agreement about an issue in contention, then, is made more difficult.

Interlocking conflicts help perpetuate each other by providing a basis upon which resources are provided to the partisans so they can continue their struggle. This has been true in the Middle East throughout the period we are discussing. In 1948, Jews in Palestine received aid from Jews and non-Jews from elsewhere, while Arabs in Palestine were aided by Arab governments in the area by the dispatch of troops. Without these interventions, the various local groups would have achieved a settlement closer to their immediate interests.

In succeeding years, too, resources were provided to all major parties sufficiently to maintain the expectations of each that it would be able to attain its objectives in the future. The provision of such resources was often linked to other conflicts—for example, American-Soviet rivalry and world-wide divisions about colonialism and national independence (Laqueur, 1969; Campbell, 1961).

On the other hand, the looseness of coalitions and the diversity of interests among all the parties to the conflicts makes it difficult to form a binding conclusion to a major dispute between the Israeli government and representatives of an Arab collectivity. The looseness of the convergence, reflecting in part the ambiguity of which conflict was paramount, has hampered a settlement of the struggles in the Middle East. Thus, in 1948 and 1949, the Arab Palestinians were not clearly bounded and organized with unambiguous representatives. Syria, the Hashemite rulers of Transjordan, and Arabs in general each were in a somewhat different conflict with Jews, Zionists, the newly emerged Israeli government, and the West generally. Consequently, an authoritative agreement was made even more difficult than if the antagonists were not part of such extensive coalitions and were not nested in wider and wider identities.

The accretion of parties to a specific struggle so that it involves extensive coalitions also tends to perpetuate an international conflict since maintaining the solidarity of a broad coalition is difficult. If a coalition is divided by conflicts among its own members, reaching agreement about the terms of settlement with the common enemy is quite difficult. For example, in World War II, the allies insisted on unconditional surrender of Germany and Japan partly to avoid the risks of a separate peace by any of the allies and to avoid disputes among the allies about the peace terms. Similarly, the Arab governments and the Arab Palestinian groups, faced with disputes and mistrust among themselves, have often found it advisable to insist on no compromise with Israel. In the past, this has been a factor in expanding the coalition's objectives against Israel.

Taking the conflict between the Egyptian and Israeli governments as the focal one, many issues have been *superimposed* and made the conflict difficult to resolve. Thus, there have been several ideological or value issues: religious differences, differences in orientation to the West, and ties to various third world collectivities, as well as Arab ones. In addition, issues have existed about military security, rights of passage through territories controlled by the adversary or potentially so controlled, and control of land relevant to security as well as settlement. I will consider in the next section how the extent of superimposition of these and other issues has varied over time, and consequently, the intensity of the conflict.

On the whole, there have been few *cross-cutting* conflicts between Egypt and Israel. As we shall see in the next section, only rarely have significant cross-cutting conflicts emerged, but with important de-escalatory consequences. Thus, the two governments sometimes have shared opposition to Soviet involvement in the Middle East or each thought that economic and political radicals were threats to stability of their own or of the other's governments.

If we consider the conflict between the Israeli and Egyptian governments as the focal conflict, then *internal* conflicts occur within Egypt and Israel. If the focal conflict is between the Arabs and Jews, internal conflicts include those among Arab governments. In the present context, I will discuss such intra-Arab conflicts as concurrent ones. There is systematic evidence about the relationship of domestic conflict behavior with foreign conflict behavior. Wilkenfeld, Lussier, and Tahtinen (1972) conducted a study of conflict interaction in the Middle East between 1949 and 1967, analyzing systematically gathered daily events data. Using regression analysis, they distinguished two major factors of *domestic* conflict: government instability and domestic violence. *Foreign* conflict included the factors of military actions, active hostility, and verbal hostility. Then they regressed on each country's foreign conflict behavior, prior conflict behavior, domestic conflict behavior, and the foreign conflict behavior of other Middle East countries.

For the Arab governments, but not for the Israeli government, domestic conflicts are significantly and positively related to foreign conflict behavior. Thus, Egyptian military activity is significantly and positively related to domestic violence and Jordanian verbal hostility and Jordanian military activities are each related to domestic violence; Syrian verbal hostility, Israeli verbal hostility, and Lebanese verbal hostility are also each related to domestic violence. This suggests that domestic violence leads Arab government leaders to rally support by increasing hostile activity toward Israel or another Middle Eastern country. This is an example of linked conflicts which can foster conflict escalation when there is a ready external target. Domestic conflict, however, is not positively related to Israeli external conflict behavior; in fact, Israeli government instability is slightly negatively related to external conflict. Perhaps, in Israel the existence of competing political parties inhibits government leaders from trying to use foreign conflict behavior as a means to unify the country.

Finally, I comment on the way in which *concurrent* conflicts have perpetuated the Egyptian-Israeli conflicts. As already noted, Arab governments, Arab and Palestinian political organizations, various social strata within Arab societies, and other groupings have diverse interests and goals in their conflicts with Israel. Moreover, they are often in conflict with each other. They struggle with each other to advance their own ideologies and interests and for leadership and deference. As noted in the discussion of converging conflicts, the looseness of the anti-Israeli coalition impedes fashioning a common and realizable set of goals. Conflicts among members of the coalitions have several contradictory effects upon the focal conflict. In some ways they tend to inhibit escalation. This is true insofar as the conflicts drain attention and resources. For example, if Egypt is involved in a war in Yemen or if Jordan and Syria are fighting each other, the possibilities of Egypt alone or in alliance with Jordan and Syria to escalate the conflict with Israel are lessened. On the other hand, conflict among Arab countries has often taken the form of competing for leadership against Israel. One related effect of this is to give a veto power to the most intransigent of the coalition partners. All this tends to prevent de-escalation of the Arab-Israeli conflict and the Egyptian-Israeli conflict.

Variations in Israeli-Egyptian Conflicts

Now I turn to major escalations and de-escalations since 1953 in the struggle between the Egyptian and Israeli governments. I will examine changes in the interlocking character of the conflicts that may have affected the escalations and de-escalations of the focal conflict.

During the summer of 1953 through the spring of 1954, several actions were taken and indirect negotiations conducted which constituted a de-escalation of hostility and movement toward settlement of several issues in contention between the Israeli and Egyptian governments. Negotiations pertained to compensation for Arab Palestinian refugees and a land link between Egypt and Jordan; in the summer of 1953, an agreement was reached regarding shipping (Berger, 1965; Avnery, 1971).

The change in the Egyptian regime, the overthrow of the monarchy by Nasser and his military colleagues in 1952, was critical in this de-escalatory shift. The Israeli government leaders, with their socialist orientation, saw hope of agreement with the new anti-reactionary government. There seemed to be the possibility of a common interest in working toward economic development and allying with each other against the British. One of the most important immediate objectives of the revolutionary Egyptian government was to remove the British troops stationed at the Suez Canal (Sadat, 1978). For the new Egyptian government, the concurrent struggle with the British had the highest priority for their resources and attention.

Negotiations broke down after the July 27, 1954 initialing of the Anglo-Egyptian agreement regarding the departure of British soldiers (Khouri, 1976; 300–301). Propaganda attacks on Israel grew and maurading squads began to make deep penetration raids into Israel (Dayan, 1977: 221–222). The resolution of the concurrent fight with the British freed the Egyptian government to turn its attention to the conflict with Israel. Perhaps, the divided Israeli leadership, with Ben Gurion on the sidelines while Sharett was Prime Minister between January 26, 1954 and June 29, 1955, contributed to a mixed and uncertain effort at de-escalation. In July, 1954, Israeli agents tried to discredit Egyptian efforts to draw closer to the U.S. by committing sabotage against American targets in Cairo and Alexander. This was discovered in Egypt and later became known in Israel as the Lavon Affair (Khouri, 1976; Berger, 1965).

The deterioration in Israeli and Egyptian relations in 1954 and 1955 suddenly escalated with the October, 1956 Israeli attack in the Sinai. That escalation was very strongly linked to the convergence of several wider conflicts. The catalyst for the Sinai war was the offer by the French and British leaders to cooperate with the Israelis in attacking Nasser and Egypt (Dayan, 1977; Brecher, 1975; Berger, 1965). The French and British governments, seeking to overthrow the Egyptian government in order to rescind the nationalization of the Suez canal, sought the aid of the Israeli government, led by Ben Gurion, to initiate hostilities to give a cover for their attack. The Israeli government saw this as an opportunity to get allies in its efforts to open the waterways for the new port, Elath, and to control the attacks being launched particularly from Gaza.

The emergence of concurrent as well as converging conflicts established the conditions which could be triggered into a war. The U.S., led by Dulles, had fostered the Baghdad Pact as a Middle East alliance against Soviet Russia. Egyptian competition with Iraq for Arab leadership contributed to the Egyptian search for military assistance from the adversary of the U.S., Soviet Russia. Pressure from the U.S. (withdrawal of support for the Assawn High Dam) and from France and Great Britain also helped introduce the Cold War dispute to overlap the Egyptian-Israeli conflict. The Egyptian announcement in September, 1955 that it would receive military weapons from Czechoslovakia raised Israeli fears of growing Egyptian military might. The French government had an additional grievance against Nasser, based on his support of the Algerians who were fighting against the French government's control of Algeria.

Upon the insistence of the U.S. government, the fruits of the Israeli defeat of the Egyptian armed forces in the Sinai campaign were denied the Israeli government, with two exceptions. A United Nations Expeditionary Force (UNEF) was stationed at Sharm el-Sheikh to ensure the free passage of Israeli vessels to the port of Elath and forces were also stationed along the Sinai-Israeli border. Between 1956 and 1967, there were no major de-escalatory or escalatory shifts. In the summer of 1963, the new Israeli Prime Minister, Eshkol, did make some statements which suggested de-escalatory possibilities, but they were not pursued and were not built upon by Egyptian officials (Prittie, 1967: 211; Khouri, 1976: 307).

A major and well-documented escalation occurred with the events which led to the war of 1967 when Israeli military forces fought the armies of Egypt, Syria, and Jordan. The escalation began with intensification of hostilities between Syrians and Israelis on local issues pertaining to water rights. The recently renewed coalition of Arab governments was the basis for Arab expectations that Egypt would pressure Israel in order to reduce its pressure on Syria. The convergence of several conflicts, as Israel's neighboring governments coalesced, was the basis for the large-scale escalation. Nasser, as leader of the Arab collectivity, requested the removal of UNEF from the Sinai. UNEF withdrew and then Egypt closed the Strait of Tiran for Israeli passage to Elath. This was understood by Nasser and his aides to inevitably result in war with Israel (Heikal, 1975). The U.S. President did not act to forestall Israeli action and did not warn or move quickly to prevent the UNEF withdrawal or to re-open the strait of Tiran. President Johnson was concerned about the Vietnam war and feared loss of Congressional support (Quandt, 1977). That concurrent conflict was sufficiently distracting to interfere with more active intermediary roles.

Following the Six Day War of 1967, the Israeli armed forces were in control of the entire Sinai, all of Jerusalem, the West Bank, and the Golan Heights. Earlier, there may have been few positive inducements the Israeli government had to offer its Arab neighbors to gain recognition. Now, there was little that the Arabs could offer as valuable as what Israel already controlled. Egypt tried to raise the cost of Israeli occupation of the Sinai by launching a War of Attrition, in March, 1969. Israel reciprocated, the violence escalated, and the costs of the War of Attrition in destroyed Egyptian cities and in the deaths of Israelis and Egyptians mounted.

By the Spring of 1970, a major de-escalatory shift began, culminating in a ceasefire late in the summer. The U.S.-Soviet conflict in some ways cross-cut the Egyptian-Israeli War of Attrition and in some ways converged with it. These interlocking conflicts were critical in the de-escalation. Early in President Nixon's administration, exploratory conversations were held between high U.S.

and Soviet officials about a common policy for the Middle East (Szulc, 1978). The U.S. administration was testing the seriousness of Soviet interest in detente. The efforts to impose an American-Soviet Middle East policy floundered, but the movement toward detente may have helped set some limits on Soviet support for Egypt. Thus, U.S. Secretary of State Rogers, in June, 1970, called for a 90-day cease fire; this was rejected by President Nasser, but following a trip to Moscow, where he failed to win the commitment to the additional military support he requested, he agreed to the cease fire (Kriesberg and Klein, forthcoming).

The convergence of the Soviet-American conflict on the Egyptian-Israeli struggle became more salient with the failure of common U.S.-Soviet policy. For the U.S., this meant increased interest in drawing Egypt away from its dependence on the Soviet Union. The U.S. government could and did influence the Israeli government to accept the cease fire and promised military aid to compensate for the risks and losses entailed by Egyptian respite from the War of Attrition and the possible build-up of Egyptian forces against the Israelis. The Egyptians thought, too, that "a positive approach to the Americans would prevent new shipments of Phantoms to Israel" (Quandt, 1977: 98).

The cease fire led to a further change in the interlocking set of conflicts. The Egyptian acceptance of the cease fire was seen by other Arab groups as conciliatory toward Israel. It probably contributed to the PLO's increased militance which precipitated the violent September showdown between King Hussein and the Arab Palestinian militia units in Jordan. On the Israeli side, Begin and his party, Herut, which had been part of the governing coalition, left the government in protest against acceptance of the cease fire and the possibility of withdrawing from the West Bank (Meir, 1975: 385; Brecher, 1975).

In his autobiography, Sadat (1978) stresses a peace initiative which he launched soon after becoming President in late 1970. On February 4, 1971, Sadat proposed to again extend the expiring cease fire and begin work on clearing the Suez Canal if Israel would make a partial withdrawal in Sinai. Some of his colleagues in the government strongly objected to what they regarded as conciliatory proposals (Heikal, 1975: 116). On the Israeli side, there were also discussions of a partial withdrawal as a step toward a peace settlement. Dayan raised this idea publicly in November, 1970 and it was discussed with Eban who transmitted the idea to the United States President in January (Quandt, 1977: 136; Eban, 1977: 472).

Proposals and counter-proposals were made through U.S. officials, indicating some movement regarding a possible partial withdrawal. In March, 1971, the Israeli cabinet accepted the principle of a partial withdrawal from the Suez Canal (Eban, 1977:474) and after additional arms had been authorized for Israel by the U.S., it offered a formal proposal on April 19. Egypt responded to the Israeli proposal by pointing out the areas of disagreement between the two governments. In hopes of moderating the Egyptian and Israeli positions, Rogers and Undersecretary of State Sisco traveled to the Middle East in May. Rogers and

Sisco continued meeting with Israel and Egyptian officials through August; although the Egyptian government made some conciliatory movement, the Israeli leaders would not budge from their March position. No direct negotiations or even partial agreement was reached, and Rogers and Sisco returned home in defeat. By this time, the Egyptian government had turned its attention to strengthening its relations with other Arab nations and strengthening its internal unity after a government shakeup in May resulting in the removal of anti-Sadat forces.

What accounts for the apparent de-escalatory movements? Sadat in his autobiography explains that it was important as a leader to take action and the war option was not available because his military forces needed to be strengthened. Therefore, he launched his peace initiative. His suspicion of the Soviet Union and his desire to move closer to the United States government were also very significant (Heikal, 1975). If Israel was to be moved, United States support was vital and, therefore, he had to convince the United States government that his objectives were reasonable and did not threaten the existence of the State of Israel. It would be essential to weaken and perhaps break the special bond between the Israeli and the United States government.

Conversely, Dayan reasoned that a partial withdrawal in the Sinai and the reopening of the Suez Canal would reduce pressure for a total withdrawal (Eban, 1977). He thought that the Soviet Union's interest in getting Egypt to try to make Israel abandon the Sinai would be reduced once its vessels could again use the Suez Canal.

Sadat and Dayan each viewed the Egyptian-Israeli conflict as converging with the Soviet-U.S. conflicts. But they each were also shifting to view the Egyptian-Israeli conflict as primary and sought conflicts (and therefore bonds) which cross-cut the U.S.-Soviet conflict.

The next major escalation of the conflict between the Israeli and Egyptian governments was the October, 1973 war, when Egyptian and Syrian forces suddenly attacked Israel. The eruption of that war was premised upon an underlying stalemate and the convergence of a new set of conflicts. Clearly, Egypt, Syria, and Jordan had little to offer to induce Israelis to make concessions and withdraw from Sinai, the West Bank, and the Golan heights. A major military action which would produce a new reality promised a favorable break out of an unsatisfactory deadlock.

Two related shifts in the conflicts in the Middle East preceded war. Sadat had inherited from Nasser a close military and political link with the Soviet Union. This link set the Egyptian-Israeli conflict within the context of the Soviet-American struggle. This meant Soviet support for Egyptian armed forces, but also limits and constraints to avoid a direct Soviet confrontation with the U.S. Sadat, himself, was unwilling to rely on the Soviets. Sadat grew increasingly dissatisfied with the Soviet lack of military support and limits on Egyptian military plans. Sadat broke dramatically with the USSR in 1972, sending the

Soviet military personnel out of the country. Sadat (1978) argues that reducing the bonds to the Soviet Union freed him to escalate the conflict with Israel. He could give it the central importance it had for him, rather than the peripheral role it had in the context of American-Soviet relations.

At the same time, Sadat worked to build a new coalition of Arab countries, including Saudi Arabia and its agreement to use oil as a weapon (McLaurin, Mughisuddin, and Wagner, 1977: 60–61). Egypt then received military and economic aid from several, ideologically diverse Arab states. Coalescence with the Saudis in the struggle against Israel required concessions, including expelling Soviet soldiers. This new Arab united front created obligations for forceful action as well as the support that made it seem more likely to be successful.

The most spectacular de-escalation of the Middle East conflicts was the visit of President Sadat to Jerusalem in November, 1977 and the related negotiations. Underlying as well as precipitating conditions produced those radically new peace efforts. Several basic factors underlie President Sadat's decision to undertake a break with the past. The Egyptian military effort in 1973, although not a clear victory, demonstrated military prowess and the ability to inflict heavy damage and gain political fruits from beginning a war. A concession could more readily appear to be coming from strength and equality and not from weakness and dishonor (Sadat, 1978). The movement of the Egyptian government away from reliance on the Soviet Union, however, limited future military strength. The U.S. could not be expected to replace the Sov⁺ Union as a military supplier without a demonstration of Egyptian ⁀llingness to make peace with Israel. The economic conditions in Egypt were extremely poor and even aid from the oil-rich Arab countries seemed inadequate, especially when tied to military preparedness to wage war against Israel. The U.S. government seemed more and more the essential source for assistance in developing the economy.

The underlying conditions for Israel had also changed since 1971. The costs of the 1973 war and the demonstration of the oil-producing Arab countries' power raised the spector of further costly wars and isolation from allies, even from the U.S. Consequently, Israeli dependence on the U.S. increased as did the importance of seeming reasonable and flexible to the U.S. government and public. The new Israeli government was led by a party and a leader who had always seemed particularly intransigent about making concessions. But the legacy in some ways gave the government more freedom of movement since the opposition was not likely to decry concessions which would make peace attainable (Avishai, 1979). Moreover, the Likud and its coalition partners were particularly concerned with the West Bank for ideological and religious reasons and these were of less significance for the Sinai.

The efforts of President Carter and his new Administration to bring about a comprehensive settlement to the Middle East conflicts posed problems for President Sadat and for the new Israeli government led by Prime Minister Begin. The proposed Geneva conference would bring the Soviet government more actively into the conflict, which both parties would rather not happen. In addition, for

President Sadat, participation, even indirectly, by the PLO, by Syria, and by other hard-line Arab groups would put them in a position to veto any settlement, thus restricting Egypt's freedom of movement. For the Israeli government, the participation of these groups at a Geneva conference would isolate it and might be a step toward recognition of the PLO and toward the creation of a Palestinian state.

Preliminary soundings between Egyptian and Israeli leaders indicated a common interest in a direct bilateral effort to reach an agreement (Zion and Dan, 1979). For Sadat, a dramatic concession such as going to Jerusalem promised to bring the U.S. government and public sufficiently to his side to bring pressure on Israel to make the concessions he sought. For Begin and the Israeli government, welcoming Sadat and making concessions to him, promised to split the Arab camp and ensure Israeli security from a major war. Both leaders viewed the focal conflict as one between Egypt and Israel rather than between Arabs and Zionists or between Communism and the West.

The gains each side might expect from this first step and the likely subsequent ones entailed risks for the other side. Thus, President Sadat risked accusations from other Arab leaders of making a separate peace and facing a reduction or cessation of economic ties and aid. The Israeli government risked giving up real estate and military security for an agreement which might be repudiated by a new Egyptian government.

Once a mutual commitment to conduct negotiations had been made, the representatives of Egypt and Israel could view their conflict as a series of disputes trailing off into the future and amenable to extensive trade offs. Integrative bargaining was more likely if concessions on one dispute could be compensated for by gains in another and even more fundamentally when a problem was seen as shared. The representatives of each side then had an interest in discovering solutions which were at least acceptable to both focal parties and their domestic constituencies. Previously, mistrust and hostility made concessions and any dispute difficult because that seemed to be yielding a hard-won past claim.

The actual consequences of the initial visit and negotiations provided the gains each side would have liked. Sadat won widespread approval from the U.S. public and more active support from the U.S. government; he also convinced many Israelis that he could be trusted and wanted peace. This was essential to gain the kind of concessions he sought from the Israeli government. The Israeli government gained a rupture in the Arab camp which made a war against Israel unlikely and gained a possible Arab ally to influence other Arab groups to make an acceptable settlement.

CONCLUSIONS

Every conflict is always embedded in a set of serial, superimposed, converging, cross-cutting, internal, and concurrent conflicts. At any given moment, we may focus upon a single set of adversaries in dispute over a particular issue. But single-minded attention to the conflict will not prepare us to understand the sometimes sudden and radical changes in a struggle. Even in the Middle East, intractable as its conflicts may be, there are periods of escalation and de-escalation. Some of these shifts occur abruptly. We have seen how attention to the interlocking character of conflicts helps us to understand the rapid changes in the Middle East conflicts in 1949, 1956, 1967, 1973, and 1977. We will be better able to understand, and even anticipate, the terms of settlements in a dispute and the sudden escalatory and de-escalatory shifts if we consider the interlocking nature of conflicts than if we do not.

Paying attention to the interlocking character of social conflicts helps resolve several difficulties. One theoretical problem in the study of social conflicts relates to the distinction between realistic and unrealistic conflict. A realistic conflict refers to one which is based on an objective, underlying condition in which the adversaries have incompatible interests or values. In an unrealistic conflict, one or more parties is acting on the basis of internal factors rather than from those relating to the relationship among collectivities; it appears to result from domestic forces. Whether a particular conflict is realistic or unrealistic seems then to depend on the observer's assessment of the true bases for a social conflict; whether conflicts are realistic or not depends on the theoretical stance the analyst takes. But his conceptualization makes it difficult to assess the theories.

Attention to the interlocking conflict offers a way to extricate us from conceptual and operational difficulties in distinguishing between realistic and unrealistic conflicts. It suggests that when an observer considers a conflict to be unrealistic, he or she is attending to a different conflict than the one the adversaries are considering as most salient. But conflicts always are multiple and interlocking. Adversaries, it should be noted, always characterize the conflict in which they are engaged as realistic: they are mobilizing and organizing themselves in terms of one set of conflicts, even if some obeervers think those are trivial ones. I think it is useful to regard every conflict as having important realistic components, since that is how the partisans see the conflict. Furthermore, there always are some incompatible goals for every pair of adversaries. It is also useful to note the unrealistic components, since they reflect other conflicts to which adversaries are giving attention but are peripheral to the focal one. A shift in the adversaries' views of the set of conflicts that engage them may facilitate the resolution of one or two of them.

Unrealistic conflict sometimes is used in a very different sense; it may refer to excessive means of getting what the adversaries seek. In other words, the observer thinks the partisans are spending more resources in the fight than their ostensible goals warrant. In that sense, many conflicts might well be regarded as unrealistic, but that is a quite different meaning to the term.

In this paper, we have seen how the interlocking character of conflicts in the Middle East contributes to their persistence, escalation, and de-escalation. Shifts in the way conflicts converge and redefine the focal conflict has been particularly important in accounting for changes in the intensity of the Israeli-Egyptian struggle. To what extent interlocking conflicts make for persistence, escalation, or de-escalation of international conflicts depends on a variety of particular circumstances. Specifying those conditions is an important next task.

ACKNOWLEDGMENTS

An earlier, briefer version of this paper was presented at a session of the Section on the Sociology of World Conflicts of the American Sociological Association held in Philadelphia, in conjunction with the meetings of the Eastern Sociological Society, March, 1978.

A Syracuse University Senate Research Grant made possible field trips to Washington, D.C. and New York, N.Y. where I was able to conduct useful interviews with Egyptian, Israeli, and U.S. officials and former officials. I wish to express my thanks for the grant and the cooperation of the persons I interviewed.

I am also indebted to the following persons for their comments about earlier versions of this paper: Ross Klein, Lois A. Kriesberg, Henry Barbera, Allan Mazur, Lewis Coser, and Florence Ridlon.

REFERENCES

Avishai, Bernard (1979) "Begin vs. Begin", *New York Review of Books,* May 31.

Avnery, Uri (1971) *Israel Without Zionism,* New York: Collier Books.

Berger, Earl (1965) *The Covenant and the Sword: Arab-Israeli Relations,* 1948–56. London, England: Routledge & Kegan Paul.

Brecher, Michael (1975) *Decisions in Israel's Foreign Policy.* New Haven, Conn.: Yale University Press.

Campbell, John C. (1961) *Defense of the Middle East.* Rev. Ed. New York: Praeger.

Coser, Lewis A. (1956) *The Functions of Social Conflict.* New York: The Free Press of Glencoe.

Dahrendorf, Ralf (1959) *Class and Class Conflict in Industrial Society.* Stanford, Ca.: Stanford University Press.

Dayan, Moshe (1977) *Story of My Life.* New York: Warner Books.

Eban, Abba (1977) *Abba Eban: An Autobiography.* New York: Random House.

Heikal, Mohamed (1975) *The Road to Ramadan.* New York: Quadrangle.

Holsti, Ole R. (1969) "External Conflict and Internal Cohesion: The Sino-Soviet Case," pp. 337–352. In Jan. F. Triska, (Ed.) *Communist Party-States.* New York: Bobbs-Merrill.

Hopmann, P. Terrence and Walcott, Charles (1977) "The Impact of External Stress and Tensions on Negotiations" pp. 301–323 in Daniel Druckman (Ed.) *Negotiations: Social Psychological Perspectives.* Beverly Hills, Ca.: Sage Publications.

Jervis, Robert (1976) *Perception and Misperception in International Relations.* Princeton, N.J.: Princeton University Press.

Khouri, Fred J. (1976) *The Arab Israeli Dilemma.* Second Edition. Syracuse, N.Y.: Syracuse University Press.

Kriesberg, Louis (1973) *The Sociology of Social Conflicts.* Englewood Cliffs, N.J.: Prentice-Hall.

Kriesberg, Louis and Klein, Ross (Forthcoming) "Positive Inducements in Middle East Peace Efforts," in Joseph Ben-Dak (Ed.) *Peace Thinking and the Middle East Conflict,* Ramat Gan, Israel: Turtledove Press.

Laqueur, Walter (1969) *The Struggle for the Middle East.* New York: The MacMillan Company.

McLaurin, R. D., Mughisuddin, R. D., and Wagner, Abraham R. (1977) *Foreign Policy Making in the Middle East: Domestic Influences on Policy in Egypt, Iraq, Israel, and Syria.* New York: Praeger Publishers.

Meir, Golda (1975) *My Life*. New York: G. P. Putnam's Sons.

Prittle, Terence (1969) *Eshkol: The Man and the Nation*. New York: Pitman Publishing Co.

Pruitt, Dean G. and Lewis, Steven A. (1977) "The Psychology of Integrative Bargaining," pp. 161–192 in Daniel Druckman (Ed.) *Negotiations*. Beverly Hills, Calif.: Sage Publications.

Quandt, William B. (1977) *Decade of Decisions: American Policy Toward the Arab-Israeli Conflict, 1967–1976*. Berkeley, Ca.: University of California Press.

Rosenau, James N.)1973) "Theorizing Across Systems: Linkage Politics Revisited" pp. 25–26 in Jonathan Wilkenfeld (Ed.) *Conflict Behavior and Linkage Politics*. New York: David McKay Co.

Ross, Edward A. (1920) *The Principles of Sociology*. New York: The Century Company.

Sadat, Anwar el (1978) *In Search of Identity: An Autobiography*. New York: Harper & Row.

Simmel, George (1955) *Conflict*. trans. K. H. Wolff and The Web of Group-Affiliations. trans. R. Bendix. Glencoe, Ill.: The Free Press. Originally published in 1908.

Sorenson, Theordore C. (1965) *Kennedy*. New York: Harper & Row.

Szulc, Tad (1978) *The Illusion of Peace: Foreign Policy in the Nixon Years*. New York: The Viking Press.

Tanter, Raymond (1966) "Dimensions of Conflict Behavior Within and Between Nations, 1958–1960," *Journal of Conflict Resolution* 10 (March) pp. 41–64.

Wallace, Michael D. and Wilson, Judy M. (1978) "Non-Linear Arms Race Models: A Test of Some Alternatives" *Journal of Peace Research* 15 (2): 175–193.

Wilkenfeld, Jonathan (1969) "Some Further Findings Regarding the Domestic and Foreign Conflict Behavior of Nations" *Journal of Peace Research*. (2): 147–156.

Wilkenfeld, Jonathan, Lussier, Virginia Lee, Tahtinen, Dale (1972) "Conflict Interactions in the Middle East," 1949–1967, *Journal of Conflict Resolution* 16 (June): 135–154.

Young, Oran R. (1967) *The Intermediaries: Third Parties in International Crises*. Princeton, N.J.: Princeton University Press.

Zimmerman, William (1969) *Soviet Perspectives on International Relations* 1956–1967. Princeton, N.J.: Princeton University Press.

Zion, Sidney and Uri, Dan (1979) "Untold Story of the Mideast Talks," *The New York Times Magazine*. January 21.

THE NEWS AND FOREIGN POLICY:

AN EXAMINATION OF THE IMPACT OF THE NEWS MEDIA ON THE MAKING OF FOREIGN POLICY

Dina Goren

Relations among nations do not necessarily imply conflict. Unless there exists a situation of war between two or more national actors, the very term conflict is avoided as far as possible. With few exceptions, nations today are careful to declare their commitment to the preservance of peace. The containment of conflict and the defusing of dangerous situations where conflicting interests exist among various national actors, are liable to turn a potential conflict into an open conflagration, and are thus among the prime objectives of a nation's foreign policy. However, the formulation of such a policy, the articulation of the diverse and often contrary interests of which such a policy is the end result, is a very complex process, involving a great deal of coordination among numerous factors whose interests eventually combine into such a policy.

The democratic belief system implies, among other things, that a nation's policies be based upon the opinions, desires, and interests of a majority of its

Research in Social Movements, Conflicts and Change, Vol. 3, pages 119-141
Copyright © 1980 by JAI Press Inc.
All rights of reproduction in any form reserved.
ISBN: 0-89232-182-2

citizens. It is more or less taken for granted that these elements should be used as actual inputs in the formulation of policy. How this purpose is to be achieved is less clear. The problem is most acute in the area of a nation's foreign policy, for, as James Rosenau stated in 1961, "Few aspects of public opinion lend themselves more readily to impressionistic and faulty analysis than does the relationship between the foreign policies of a nation and the opinions of its citizenry" [1]. Notwithstanding the volume of the literature dealing with this relationship, "the scholarly community involved in this research—Bernard Cohen was writing 12 years later—is inescapably attributing a fundamental role to public opinion in the formulation of foreign policy in the absence of empirical evidence to that effect . . ." [2]. In his critique of the literature on the subject, Cohen points to the shortcomings of what he calls the "osmosis hypothesis," a term he uses to describe statements and models that obscure the mechanisms by which opinion is absorbed and translated into policy [3]. One of the more neglected aspects of the opinion/policy relationship, which has only rarely been addressed in any systematic fashion, is the role of the news media in relation to both. The news media, to use Cohen's metaphor, are taken for the membrana through which the process of osmosis is taking place.

It is a basic assumption of normative democratic theory that the news media perform a crucial role in the process of opinion formation and of policy formulation. It is further assumed that, in performing such a role, the newsmedia function as independent actors. According to democratic theory, "the public rules, or at least participates extensively in policy making" [4]. The same theory also holds that, with the exception of elections, which are held at long intervals, the news media (we shall henceforth use the term press to cover all of the news media, electronic and printed), are the most important single factor for translating this theory into actual practice. What is more, they do so on a continuing, day-by-day basis which further enhances their prominence.

It would be difficult to find a more eloquent statement of this theory than the following one, provided by Mr. Justice Stewart (1971) in his concurring opinion in the Pentagon Papers case:

> In the absence of governmental checks and balances present in other areas of national life, the only effective restraint upon executive policy and power in the areas of national defence and international affairs may lie in an enlighted citizenry—in an informed and critical public opinion which alone can here protect the values of democratic government. For this reason it is perhaps here that a press that is alert, aware and free most vitally serves the basic purpose of the First Amendment. For without an informed free press, there cannot be an enlightened people [5].

As regards international conflict, the news media are thus assigned a critical role not only in the coordination and mobilization of domestic groups, but also in the determination of policy toward external actors.

The Democratic Model of Press Performance

The democratic model of press performance is based upon the following assumptions: 1) that the press transmits politically significant information from one part of the system to another; 2) that this information is absorbed by the public and helps its members to form opinions on political issues; 3) that, similarly, information offered by the press is used by policy makers as a significant input into their decision making process. As to the nature of this information, it is assumed: 4) that where the public at large is concerned, such information consists mostly of substantive coverage of events and issues, which may or may not be placed within a wider, politically meaningful context; 5) that in the case of decision makers, the press not only is the source of substantive information on the matters at hand, but is also a reflector of the public's opinion on these matters. The press can thus provide decision makers with feedback to be incorporated into their future decisions. Last, but not least, it is also assumed: 6) that in performing the functions listed above, the press does so as an independent actor. Although this point is usually never elucidated sufficiently, the general idea seems to be that even while interacting with the subjects of their coverage and with their sources of information, reporters, and others involved in the process of presenting the news, are working from some kind of Archimedean vantage point which places them entirely outside the system.

In the following pages, I shall attempt what will be an exploratory study concerning the validity of these assumptions. The critical analysis of these assumptions is a very difficult proposition. For one thing, their examination entails a departure from one of the most central tenets of the democratic belief system. The very legitimacy of the press's freedom from governmental restraints depends on maintaining its claim to fulfill a meaningful role in this context. Another difficulty is the scarcity of credible data. Although in recent years the performance of news organizations and of the information networks which make it possible for reporters to operate have been the subject of rigorously conducted research [6], many of the relevant problems have not been touched upon to date. On the other hand, there exists a wealth of material on the subject in the form of personal recollections written by the actors involved, political figures as well as journalists. However, in many cases, these recollections tend to be biased in favor of the very same assumptions, with the validity of which we are concerned. My own experience as a journalist has afforded me with some insights into the processes involved and has, perhaps, somewhat immunized me against accepting statements about the power and the independence of the press at their face value. However, my own experiences do not, unfortunately, amount to a systematic exercise in participant observation. The following analysis of the assumptions underlying the democratic model of press performance will have to rely on what is basically an historical approach.

ENGAGING PUBLIC OPINION—THE AUTOCRATIC AND THE EMOTION AROUSING METHODS

As was well known to Machiavelli and to Hume, concern for public opinion is not necessarily proof of commitment to a democratic belief system. Nor is a respect for the power of the press on the part of government a guarantee of press freedom. In the area of foreign policy, the manipulative use of the press by a ruler, in order to achieve policy aims, was practiced at least as early as the Napoleonic era. Napoleon, himself an avid reader of newspapers, was a strong believer in the power and influence of the press. "I believe that by means of the newspapers, a single pen can cause the world to rise up, while a sole sword can never achieve a similar result" [7]. Accordingly, he was very thorough in asserting his control over the French press, and used various strategems to plant news and commentaries which served his political purposes in newspapers which appeared in countries that were beyond his rule [8]. Newspapers were reporting on international relations from the very first days of their existence, but it is with Napoleon that they began to be exploited systematically in order to achieve definite policy aims. The methods used by Napoleon were clearly those of propaganda: dramatization, distortion, and the suppression of any alternative version. His efforts were directed at moving the public, not at informing it. Coming as soon as he did after the French Revolution, it is not surprising that Napoleon was convinced of the power of mobs, and his purpose was to use the press in order to move them. He seems to have believed in what we would today call a simple "Stimulus-Reaction" theory of press influence. Bismarck, no less than Napoleon, was a staunch believer in the power of the press to influence policy. Like Napoleon, he was a frequent contributor of unsigned articles, and had a special official in his employ whose functions consisted of planting news items and articles, including Bismarck's own writings, in various newspapers in Prussia and elsewhere. This official, Moritz Busch, meticulously chronicled Bismarck's efforts at manipulating the European Press and later published them under the title *Bismarck: Some Secret Pages of his History*. Bismarck's grasp of the possibilities inherent for a politician in manipulating the press is made very clear in the following remark of his, quoted by Busch (1898): "One learns more from newspapers than from official dispatches as, of course, governments use the press in order frequently to say more clearly what they really mean. One must, however, know all about the connections of the different papers" [9]. Busch, incidentally, makes it clear that the often-quoted incident of the Ems Telegram was not the direct cause of the French government's declaration of war on Prussia, as Bismarck had apparently intended it to be. However, it does seem that the Chancellor had engineered the publication of a distorted telegram in order to arouse the emotions of the Parisian mobs, inducing them to mount violent demonstrations in support of declaring war on Prussia.

In the course of the last decades of the 19th century, the mass circulation press was developing rapidly, which, in turn, increased the potential of using it in order to generate emotional mass appeals, which were then directed at governments. As a general rule, the mass circulation press of the late 19th century and early 20th century, devoted only minimal space and effort to the coverage of foreign affairs. Its readers belonged to social strata which not only lacked the capacity to understand the complexities of international affairs, but were usually committed to the belief that such matters did not concern people of their standing. The mass readerships' lack of interest in international affairs, and the concommitant lack of information on the subject, did not, however, preclude an emotional reaction on its part, in the event that such reactions were provoked. The arousal of mass emotions on foreign policy issues was attempted for both political and commercial reasons. An outstanding example of the latter is the role played by the Hearst papers in connection with the Spanish-American War of 1898. In this case, the political decision of declaring war on Spain was taken after a long and concentrated press campaign. The campaign began with dramatic descriptions of Spanish atrocities, some of which, at least, were apparently apocryphal. Later, the campaign was intensified while public feelings were fanned to a pitch by the repeated use of the slogan "Remember the Maine." The tactic of using descriptions of atrocities perpetuated against civilians in order to arouse public emotions may well have suggested itself to Hearst as the result of what had happened in Britain 20 years earlier. On that occasion, the public's emotions had been raised by a feat of genuine investigative reporting: the descriptions of the atrocities by Turkish forces in southern Bulgaria, written by an American correspondent Januarius Aloysius MacGahan, for the *London Daily News* in the summer of 1876. The British public's outrage against the Turks was so intense that Disraeli was forced to qualify his pro-Turkish policy. This, in turn, made it feasible for Russia to declare war on Turkey. It was this war that led to the independence of Bulgaria [10].

It is hardly surprising that in most cases where journalistic treatment of foreign affairs resulted in emotional reactions on the part of the mass public, the subject treated was war. By the end of the 19th century, war correspondence had become a well-paid, high-status profession, whose members' claim to distinction rested more on their literary talents than on their grasp of strategic or political issues [11]. In the course of World War I, both sides made extensive use of sensationalist dramatic eyewitness reports for propagandistic purposes. Arousing hatred toward a cruel enemy, capable of perpetuating terrible atrocities, was among the most important aims of war propaganda [12].

The Press and International Conflict

While the experiences of World War I clearly demonstrated the power of the press to arouse mass emotions and to reinforce discord and hatred, they also served to confirm the beliefs of those who saw the press as capable of guaranteeing peace on earth.

This belief did not emerge as the result of the war. It had its antecedents in the concept of the free marketplace of ideas, which held that public opinion was formed by rational argumentation. If the newspapers could only be prevailed upon to use their enormous power to further this aim, wars would become virtually impossible. "An agency, a world-wide instrumentality as the press is," the editor of the *Wyoming Tribune* told the American Association for International Conciliation in 1913, "which is able to provoke an unnecessary war, certainly is potent enough to prevent one. Acting in unison, with high and patriotic purpose, the newspapers and magazines . . . can place the United States in the vanguard of nations ready, anxious and willing to discard the barbarism of war" [13]. If told the true facts, the public is bound to be opposed to war. Hence, if public opinion does not condemn war, it is the fault of the newspapers, who failed to provide it with enough information, and excited its passions. "No people on earth desire war, particularly an aggressive war. If the people can exercise their will, they will remain at peace," wrote American Secretary of State Robert Lansing, in April, 1918, while fighting was still going on [14].

The Wilsonian commitment to the open conduct of international relations was predicated on the same belief in the capacity of the public to judge correctly if properly informed. It was this belief, no less than a deep aversion toward the manipulative character of 19th-century European diplomacy, that found expression in the first of President Wilson's Fourteen Points, promising "open covenants of peace, openly arrived at after which there shall be no private international understandings of any kind." The second part of this formula was virtually abandoned, even before negotiations at Versailles had properly started [15]. Soon after, the general election which was called in Britain for December, 1918, and the press campaign that preceeded it, were to prove that public opinion can be agitated to respond emotionally on issues of peace negotiation as well as on those of war. Throughout the election campaign, Lord Northcliff's *Daily Mail* inserted the epigraph "The Junkers will cheat you yet" each day at the head of its leading article, and implored its readers not to vote for candidates showing "any tenderness for the Hun" [16]. It was as the result of this campaign, and of the government brought to power by it in England, that the Versailles Treaties became what has been subsequently termed "a vindictive peace."

Notwithstanding such setbacks, belief in the power of public opinion to judge issues on their merit, if properly informed, persisted [17]. In the course of the 1920s and 1930s, considerable efforts were devoted to the cause of bettering the performance of the press.[1] Great importance was placed by the League of Nations on its Information Section, which was the most important part of the League's Secretariat [18].

In 1934, the League's International Institute of Intellectual Cooperation arranged a symposium on the "Educational Role of the Press," in which some of the best known journalists and editors of the day took part. With no exceptions, they all confirmed their belief in the power of the press to engage public opinion in the interest of universal peace. Their rhetoric seems hardly to have been affected by the contemporary triumphs of Fascist and Nazi Propaganda or by the performance of the press under those regimes.

Notwithstanding abundant proof to the contrary, belief in the capacity of the press to exercise a pacifying influence on world politics, persisted even after World War II. In its Report on International Communication, the Commission on the Freedom of the Press stated that "understanding among peoples is one of the four or five primary instruments for promoting world order and peace," a goal which, according to the authors of the report, can be attained by "Taking hold of the improvements that science has affected in all fields of communication" [19].

In 1947, Seymour Berkson, general manager of the *International News Service* wrote as follows: "A peace that is not supported by the free flow of information upon which the peoples of the world can build mutual faith and understanding, is just another armed truce. It makes little difference how cleverly its diplomatic machinery may be designed by governments or statesmen, if this so-called peace can be shattered at will by manipulating the emotions of this or that populace with false information" [20].

PUBLIC OPINION, NATIONAL IMAGES, AND THE NARCISSUS PSYCHOSIS

Article 19 of the Universal Declaration of Human Rights, adopted in 1948 by the UN General Assembly, declared that "Everyone has the right to freedom of opinion and expression, this right includes freedom to hold opinions without interference and to seek, receive and impart information and ideas through any media and regardless of frontiers." However, in the course of consequent attempts to pass a UN Convention on the Free Flow of Information, the concept was carefully qualified so as to accomodate the Soviet Bloc's version of press freedom [21]. Whether or not the concern with a free flow of information across national borders is consistent with the continuous efforts nations make to shape the image which citizens of other countries hold with respect to them, is not made clear. Whatever their purpose, these efforts seem to be based upon the assumption that there exists a causal relationship between image and foreign policy decisions. Kenneth Boulding (1959) defines national images as "images which a nation has of itself and of those other bodies in the system which constitute its international environment," and distinguishes between two representative images—the image of the small group of powerful people who make the actual decisions and the image of the mass of ordinary people. In democratic societies, he says, the aggregate influence of the images of ordinary people is very great, for although the powerful can manipulate to some extent the images which ordinary people hold, they cannot diverge from them too much [22], Louis Kriesberg (1974), in discussing conflict situations between nations uses the terms "feelings of hostility and mistrust between leaders or peoples of a pair of nations"

[23]. The term "image," in this context, should, we believe, be treated with more circumspection than is commonly the case. It should be used differentially in relation to the several audiences concerned. Where the general public, in whatever country, is concerned, images are formed as the result of emotional stimuli as well as, and perhaps more than, on the basis of informational inputs. Both can be used manipulatively. Robert Jervis (1970) [24] uses the term in an entirely different sense, and is concerned mainly with the role of images, as held by or shaped for policy makers themselves. Although in parts of his analysis Jervis does make a distinction between various domestic audiences to whom certain image-oriented efforts are addressed, he is, in general, concerned with images projected from one state to another. The process of making these projections is described in relation to the policy makers actually engaged in it.

It is not unusual for writers on the subject, as well as for practitioners, to use the term "public opinion" on foreign policy issues and images held by the public of foreign states, indiscriminately. As a result, the aim of propagandistic efforts directed by one nation at another, is not always clearly defined.

Attempts by one nation to influence the public in another nation are, as a rule, based on different conceptions of the characteristics of foreign publics, their capacity to hold independent opinions, and the extent to which they are susceptible to holding and forming stereotypes. According to Communist theory, propaganda is a legitimate tool designed to further ideological aims, and is to be used accordingly to influence both domestic and foreign publics. In the case of the United States, its efforts to influence publics abroad, while often aimed at short-term policy ends, seem, basically, to derive from an intense preoccupation with its own image. Proponents of the theory of "media imperialism" believe that there are ulterior political and economic motives behind America's urge to propagate its own image and impose it upon other societies. However, the concern of most Americans for "world public opinion" does appear to transcend immediate concrete policy aims. Dean Acheson described this concern as a "Narcissus Psychosis" when he wrote "An American is apt to stare like Narcissus at his image in the pool of what he believes to be world opinion" [25]. Yehezkel Dror (1971) lists American attitudes toward "world opinion" as one of the major fallacies afflicting the nation's strategic study and analysis: "In its positive form—that world opinion is real and matters a lot—this fallacy is rooted in a positive view of the world cast largely in the image of oneself, and is based, through the convex mirror theory, on an image and ideology which allocated a lot of weight to public opinion . . . this fallacy relies on world public opinion to have real impact on international relations" [26].

On the level of its declared information policy, the United States does indeed appear to be operating on the basis of a convex mirror theory of the impact of public opinion and its role in the formation of foreign policy in other nations of the world. In 1968, at the height of the Vietnam War, a House Foreign Affairs Subcommittee, headed by Congressman Dante B. Fascell, recommended "a comprehensive redefinition of the USIA's mission, and a thorough overhaul of its operations'' as a means to counteract the erosion of American image abroad. Following the subcommittee's report, an Emergency Committee for the Reappraisal of US Overseas Policies and Programs was established. Its members professed a surprisingly naive view on the subject of world public opinion: "The new force of public opinion plays an increasingly important role in affecting action by governments everywhere. The common man plays a part in determining governmental policy in international affairs, even in dictatorial regimes . . . the communications revolution has made him an important individual in the foreign policy decisions of his government . . . Modern technology in communications has furthered the process (of public diplomacy)'' [27]. Following a somewhat bizarre logic, similar assumptions as to the power of public opinion, and the ability of the press to influence policy, in non-democratic regimes, seemed also to have formed the basis of some of the covert attempts at influencing these factors. The extent of the operations undertaken by the CIA which were directed at the mass media in different countries of the world, was only revealed in 1977 [28]. According to Hanna Arendt (1971) American preoccupation with its image abroad, and with the judgment of world opinion, has had far-reaching political consequences. This preoccupation can be so overbearing as to influence the making of policy as such. When this happens, policy makers are no longer concerned only with the manner in which the results of their policies are presented to the world. Psychological considerations, having to do with the images evoked, come to dominate policy making itself. The belief in the importance of images is, according to Arendt, characteristic of "the recent generation of intellectuals, who grew up in the insane atmosphere of rampant advertising and were taught that half of politics is image making and the other half the art of making people believe the imagery'' [29]. Using Neel Sheehan's term, "problem solvers,'' to define the group drawn into government from universities, think-tanks, etc., to "solve'' the problems of foreign policy, these people, according to Arendt, lied, "not so much for their country, certainly not for their country's survival which was never at stake, but for its image.'' The constant shift in the definition of both the strategic aims and the tactical targets involved was the result of the fact that "the ultimate aim was neither power nor profit. Nor was it even influence in the world in order to serve particular tangible interests for the sake of which prestige, an image of the greatest power in the world was needed and purposefully used. The goal was image itself, as manifest in the very language the problem solvers, with their 'scenarios' and their 'audiences' borrowed from the theater [30, 31].[2]

THE DEMOCRATIC MODEL AND THE FORMULATION OF FOREIGN POLICY

Recent developments in electronics and satellite technology have greatly enhanced the ability of the newsmedia to supply their audiences with extensive, almost immediate coverage of world events, As a result, there is little doubt that the citizen of the 1970s is in a better position to know what is happening around the world than were any of his predecessors. Whether or not the media's capacity of spanning geographical distance has also enlarged the public's interest span is less clear. Audience research has supplied us with considerable information about the demographic and social indicators of those who pay attention to the international content of the mass media, and we also know something about the manner in which various segments of the population view the various media as trustworthy sources of news. However, little is known, as yet, about whether the broadcasting of foreign news on television, has had any impact on the general public's interest in foreign affairs.

Alfred Hero (1977–78), a long-time student of public opinion on foreign affairs in the United States, after examining an extensive body of survey and other systematic social research documents, finds that only a small minority of the adult public is much interested in world affairs beyond broad questions of war and peace. "Depending on the rigour of the criteria for knowledge, interest, and political behaviour applied, the issues in question and other standards, this minority is considered to constitute from roughly 10 per cent to fractions of 1 per cent of the adult population. Only a very small minority—perhaps several hundred thousand—manifest a cause and effect, relatively analytical interest across much of the broad spectrum of international issues of continuing importance to the United States" [32]. Most of this minority is interested primarily in a much narrower range of international phenomena, usually related to their own economic, occupational, ethnic, intellectual, or other particular concerns. The global position of the United States and the impact its policies have upon world affairs seem to have little influence on the interest of its citizens in foreign policy issues. In Europe, even where political parties often make foreign policy issues a matter of partisan orientation, interest in foreign affairs is no more widespread than it is in the United States. A recent observer of the French scene, Marie Claude Smouts (1977), has this to say on the subject: "In France, as in a good many countries, public opinion generally takes little interest in foreign policy, except for a few categories of persons directly concerned. . . . Now that daily life depends more and more on decisions taken at an international level, the complexity of subjects treated at that level . . . deflects the public's interest to more immediate preoccupations. The absence of any burning foreign problem reinforces this indifference. In addition, the idea that foreign policy is no concern of the public is very widespread. In a general way, in France, the feeling that politics is a dubious, rather obscure activity, is accompanied paradoxically enough, by a certain respect for the majesty of power." [33]. The lack of interest on the part of the general public in issues of foreign policy, has not discernably affected the tendency of politicians to refer to the preferences of public opinion in their argumentation. Nor has this tendency diminished as the result of the fact that foreign policy issues figure only very rarely on electorial platforms.

For adherents of democracy, the apparent incompatibility of popular control and effective foreign policy poses a serious problem. The problem was clearly stated by de Tocqueville (1835), when he wrote: "I have no hesitation in saying that in the control of a society's foreign affairs, democratic governments do appear decidedly inferior to others.... Foreign policy does not require the use of any of the good qualities peculiar to democracy but demands the cultivation of almost all those qualities which it lacks ... a democracy finds it difficult to coordinate details of a great undertaking and to fix on some plan and carry it through with determination ... it has little capacity for combining measures in secret and waiting patiently for the result" [34]. On the level of daily performance, this has led to the preservation of numerous aristocratic trappings insofar as the exercise of diplomacy is concerned. On the conceptual level, the problem of incompatibility between democratic rule and foreign policy remains a serious one.

INDEPENDENCE OF THE NEWS MEDIA AND THE DEMOCRATIC MODEL

One of the essential components of the democratic model of media performance is the independence of news organizations and of the professionals who work in their employ. In view of the pressures to which news professionals are subjected within their own organizations, it is doubtful whether one can speak in one breath of these two elements—namely, the independence of the organization vis-a-vis the various actors in the political arena and the position of the individual newsman in relation to his sources and subjects of coverage and to the organization for which he works. For the sake of simplicity, however, the distinction between the two kinds of independence shall only be made where it is absolutely necessary to do so.

The tradition of viewing the press as an independent actor in the political arena goes back to the early 19th century, when the phrase "the Fourth Estate"[3] was first coined.

More recently, the concept was elaborated upon by Douglass Cater (1959) in his *Fourth Branch of Government* [35]. Other observers of government-media relationships, like Benjamin Cohen, Dan Nimmo, and, writing much later, Leon Sigal, have described these relationships in terms of an elaborate ongoing exchange system.

While political scientists like Cohen (1963, 1973), Nimmo (1964), and Sigal (1973), are careful to point out that, notwithstanding their dependence on officials as sources of news, journalists are well aware of their constitutionally protected adversary role, other writers, describing the performance of the press from the perspective of the official, take a more cynical view. James C. Thomson, Jr. (1973)—who, as Curator of Nieman Fellowships for Journalists and former Special Assistant to the Secretary of State, is in a position to appreciate the attitude of both reporters and officials—has this to say on their working relationship: "To each, the other is a convenient means, but their ends are usually quite different. The official wants at best to sell an important administration policy, more often to push the case of his faction within the bureaucratic arena, at worst simply to sell himself. . . . The reporter wants at best to ferret out 'the truth', more often to get a few more clues on which to hang a somewhat half-baked story under the gun of a deadline, at worst to feel the warm glow of proximity to power. . . . The crucial social cement is mutual use; also, depending on the nature of the relationship, mutual flattery. Officials use reporters to pass or plant certain messages and thereby win battles. Reporters use officials and thereby get ahead'' [36]. Another former insider, Morton Halperin (1974), views the media as important tools in shaping presidential decisions, which are used accordingly by participants in the policy-making process, to carry to the President such information as will best serve their various objectives [37].

However, there is also an institutional dimension to the problem of government press relationships. Overall editorial policy is not shaped as a rule on the basis of working relationships between officials and reporters. In its broadest sense, the term "editorial policy" means much more than taking positions on concrete policy issues. So-called prestige, or elite newspapers do not periodically redefine their audiences or their thematic preferences, and are what they are more by tradition than as a result of conscious choice. This, too, is ultimately a matter of editorial policy. Developments in recent years, where, in the case of the United States, prestige papers such as the *New York Times* and the *Washington Post* have tended to assume strikingly adversary positions vis-a-vis the administration on foreign policy matters, have obscured the fact that such positions are an exception, rather than the rule.

This fact is further obscured by ideological and constitutional commitments to the concept of an adversary press already mentioned at the beginning of this paper. However, a careful analysis of the positions taken throughout the years by prestige papers on foreign policy issues would reveal a different picture. Prestige papers, in the United States and elsewhere, tended to refrain from "rocking the boat" on foreign policy issues and avoided diverging significantly from the accepted line of policy. Further research is needed in order to identify the roots of this phenomenon.

We were unable to attempt a systematic examination of the output of prestige papers within the present framework, and therefore cannot measure the extent to which they conform to the broader outlines of official foreign policy or accept the basic tenets on which such policy is predicated. The problem is hardly a new one. In what is perhaps the earliest example of applying the method of content analysis to an investigation of press performance, Walter Lippmann and Charles Merz (1920) have come up with strikingly convincing proof of how the *New York Times* consistently and systematically distorted the news from Russia to suit currently accepted interpretations of events [38].

In their analysis, Lippmann and Merz point to what is, perhaps, the classic failing of prestige papers: "Reliance upon official purveyors of information."

They stress that "statements of fact emanating from governments and the circles around governments as well as from the leaders of political movements cannot be taken as judgments of fact by an independent press. They indicate opinion, they are controlled by special purpose and they are not trustworthy news." The far-reaching political significance of such a distortion of the news only becomes evident in retrospect. Lippmann and Merz write from the perspective of 1920, when they say that the *New York Times* "seriously overestimated the willingness of Russia in 1917 to carry on the war. It seriously underestimated the growth of Bolshevik power in the months that followed. It pictured the people of Russia eager for Allied intervention. It developed suddenly the motive of a Red Peril when the end of the war with Germany had banished the need for 'an Eastern front.' It characterized the regimes of Kolchak and Denikin as essentially demo-cratic. It featured the campaigns of these generals when they were progressing, almost ignored them in defeat . . ." [39].

Reading these lines in the 1970s one can think of other situations to which, but with a few substitutions, they might have been applicable.

In 1946, Martin Kriesberg, repeated the study of Lippmann and Merz and brought it up to date. Covering the period from 1918 to 1946, and using a more sophisticated method of content analysis, Kriesberg concludes that "News about Soviet Russia as reported in the *New York Times* is keyed to a concept of American interests. The nature of the themes developed, the amount of attention, and the manner of reporting news of Soviet Russia, are determined by the relationship between American and Soviet interests. . . . News placing the Soviet Union in an unfavorable light receives more attention than news that is sympa-thetic. . . . There is a tendency for unwarranted headlines, loaded words and questionable sources of information when occuring in the *Times* reports, to be consistently unfavorable to the Soviets" [40].

An investigation by Susan Welch (1972) of how four American newspapers had covered the Indochina war in the early fifties has resulted in similar findings. Although, at the time, the Indochina issue was not given much attention by the press " . . . by relying almost solely on administration sources, reporters and editorialists laid the foundation for the way the issue was understood . . . support for the administration was forthcoming not only in editorials, but also, and more importantly, in the phraseology of presumed factual reports" [41]. Three among the four papers examined by Welch - *The New York Times, The Washington Post* and *The San Francisco Chronicle,* are papers commonly recognized as prestige papers and it is these three which were found to echo the administration's posi-tions consistently. The fourth newspaper examined, *The Chicago Tribune,* was found to have challenged these positions persistently. However, this was not the result of the paper's having had superior reporting from the scene but because of its editorial traditions [42].

In his case study of the editorial performance of the *London Times* in the 1930s, Colin Seymour-Ure (1974) shows how the *Times* lent its support to the government's policy of appeasing Nazi Germany and thus smoothed the government's way in implementing this policy [43].

Although conditions in the United States and in Britain differ greatly with regard to the structure of the press and its political role, it is worthwhile to mention the elements of press influence on foreign policy as identified by Seymour-Ure. He analyses four kinds of influence: First, the negative influence arising from the very fact that the paper did not criticize the government's policy. Second, since the *Times* was (at the time) viewed outside Britain as the official mouthpiece of the British Government, the positions it advocated did have direct influence on opinion and action in other countries. The third element identified by Seymour-Ure is termed by him "influence through access." Both Dawson, the editor of the *Times,* and Barrington Ward, his assistant editor and eventual successor, constantly met with and were influenced by the leading politicians of the day. Lastly, Seymour-Ure refers to the influence of the *Times* as a pressure group in its own right. This function, however, was not necessarily exercised through the medium of print. "Dawson's connections imply . . . that . . . for purposes of defining 'influence' over a government, the boundary between what is published and what is left out is more or less arbitrary. Permeating the political atmosphere as he did, Dawson gathered and 'published' news by letter, telephone and word of mouth as much as in his columns" [44].

Several American writers, proceeding on a much less systematic level, have come up with similar findings about the role played by journalists. It is, in fact, far from easy to define the exact position of journalists in the locus of foreign policy making, and to estimate whether their share in the process is the result of their personal status and connections or the result of their having guaranteed access to the media. Thomson (1973) views their role as follows: "The executive branch, in both its domestic and foreign realms, is a congeries of individuals, groupings and agencies. So-called 'policy making' is an ongoing process of argument, negotiation and even guerilla warfare within, and among competing and changing components of the process of 'bureaucratic politics'. Within this process, the press performs an invaluable and probably irreplaceable function: the sending of messages back and forth among individuals, factions and agencies, and the alerting of the public to important battles, unresolved issues, not to mention downright skullduggery" [45]. Another "insider", Leslie Gelb (1973) describes what he calls the "foreign policy community" in Washington in the following terms: "That group of officials, journalists, exiles from power and congressional aides which congregates at conferences and communicates through an intricate ritual that includes telephone calls, lunches, cocktail parties and the columns of purveyors of high-level political gossip like Evans and Novak" [46].

Washington correspondents of prominent newspapers belong, by the very virtue of their appointments, to an elite group with close connections to other elite groups in the capital. Personality, experience, and the nature of the medium they represent may have their bearing on the particular position each of these correspondents occupies within this network of influentials. Several of them have described their experiences in detail, and have analyzed their political significance, others have contended themselves with episodic references [47]. What all these first hand testimonials amount to is a clear picture of Washington correspondents as an elite closely interacting with policy makers. Whether or not they also contribute a significant input of their own into the policy making process is much less clear. Arthur Krock (1968), in his *Memoirs* mentions several occasions on which President Kennedy asked his advice on concrete issues. These, however, had to do in the main with the President's problems in dealing with the press. As has been mentioned, journalists may have à catalyctic effect on some policy making processes as a result of their role in making information circulate. This, however, does not mean that they fulfil an independent role in the process. The furthest they can go is to publicize alternative policy options, which, as a rule, are rarely their own contributions, but represent divergent views from within the system.

The Mutual Re-Inforcement or the Adversary Press Model, Which One Is Applicable?

In recent years, from a post-Watergate and post-Pentagon Papers retrospective, the adversary model of government-media relations, has come to be regarded as the accepted norm. Even on foreign policy issues, it has become common for the media to assume an adversary position. Whether or not such positions are borne out by the actual performance of reporters and editors, in the course of their daily working relations with policy makers, has not been sufficiently investigated [48].[4] However, there seems to be little evidence to warrant a description of media personnel engaged in the coverage of foreign policy matters as independent actors in the process of policy formation. Least of all is this the case where the newsmedia appear to be involved directly in the very process of policy in the making, in what has come to be known as *media diplomacy*. As the result of what seems to be an utter confusion between investigative reporting as practiced by reporters of the printed press, and the on-camera performance of TV personalities who interview political figures, Thomas Griffith (1978) writing in the "Newswatch" section of *Time* magazine, had this to say on the subject: "Perhaps we are witnessing the final reversal of the Watergate era, when the press corps had a hectoring ascendancy over public figures. . . . Currently, in the ongoing contest between leaders who want to put their own viewpoint across and journalists who seek to pin them down or draw them out, the offense prevails." Griffith suggests that this has to do with the fact that "since anchor people are no longer kept at the door or at the curbside but are invited in, deferred to and first-named by heads of state, they may feel themselves part of the diplomatic process, and may be fearful of derailing it. The imperial presidency and jet age diplomacy are producing a matching elite of imperial commentators." [49]

It is our contention that, while "being deferred to and first-named by heads of

state'' may be distinctions reserved for the more celebrated television interviewers, reporters, both for the printed and the electronic media who ''may feel
themselves part of the diplomatic process'' are the norm, rather than an exception.

The social eminence and considerable visibility enjoyed by these reporters do
not, however, protect them from being manipulated on occasion by the policy
makers concerned.

However, the propensity of reporters to be manipulated by decision makers, in
order to serve the latters' policy ends is only part of a much larger problem. It is
the problem of the press's overall dependence on official sources in the area of
foreign policy. Using the term ''dependence'' does not only mean that in this
area of coverage reporters are mostly confined to exchanges with official
sources, although this, no doubt, is the case. What we have in mind is a much
more pervasive dependence, one which results in the creation of a veritable
vicious circle. As one observer has pointed out, ''News stories reinforced the
preoccupations of the Administration largely because most of the stories dealt
with activities and comments of those involved in the decision making'' [50].
Such dependence does not necessarily prevent the press from criticizing the
government. What it does is to reduce the conceptual level of such criticism.
Since the press has little or no access to sources capable of independent assessments of the policies under consideration, all that the press can do is to
criticize the manner in which policy is implemented.

Notwithstanding the fact that, at least in the foreign policy area, the press is
almost structurally dependent on sources who belong within the policy making
system,[5] [51] the subjective assessments of both journalists and decision
makers—at least up to a certain level—tend to view their mutual relationship as
one which is more or less balanced. Bernard Cohen (1973) has shown that decision
makers in the area of foreign policy—i.e., State Department officials—rely on
the newsmedia and on the press in particular, and regard them as an opinion
source. One-third of the respondents interviewed in Cohen's study singled out
''the substantive coverage of issues and events in the press as a prime source . . .
of information on what others think are important questions of the day.'' An
equal number of Cohen's respondents viewed the journalists themselves as a
source of public opinion, or rather as ''representatives of informed American
opinion'' [52]. In his earlier work, Cohen (1963) had shown that officials at both
the State Department and the Department of Defense, at least up to the level of
Assistant Secretary, were updated on events in foreign countries by means of
news agency tickers installed in their offices [53]. In addition, it should also be
kept in mind that a substantial part of what diplomats stationed abroad include in
the reports which eventually reach the desks of decision makers at the Department of State, is based on the local press in the countries where they are
stationed. Foreign correspondents usually use the same sources [54].

It is by no means clear at what level of the decision making hierarchy there no longer is such a dependence on the news media for factual information. The literature abounds in sweeping statements to the effect that the media have a direct impact on presidential decisions. Morton Halperin, in a statement already referred to, believes that the mass media have a direct impact on the shaping of presidential decisions and that it is for this reason that bureaucrats manipulate the press [55]. James Reston (1967) attributes the tendency to be influenced by the media only to some presidents, who as a result are extremely conscious of what both the newswriters and the editorial writers have to say (56). President Johnson, it will be recalled, had had three television sets installed so that he could simultaneously follow the three networks.

CONCLUSION

In the foregoing pages, I have tried to examine some of the assumptions on which the democratic model of media performance is based. We have seen that, on the one hand, the belief in the power of public opinion and in the capacity of the press to influence it, is not necessarily the result of an adherence to the democratic model of government. On the other hand, in the case of democracies, we have seen that some of the more important manifestations of the power of public opinion were divorced from the democratic model, according to which, public opinion intervenes in the policy making process as the result of having been supplied by the press with politically relevant information.

We have also examined what results a doctrinaire adherence to the democratic model might have, and have seen that these range from a naive belief in the power of public opinion to an exaggerated preoccupation with the impacts of what might be called "world public opinion" and with the nature of the "images" nations are said to hold of each other.

An essential component of the model is the independence of the journalistic actors from the system in which they operate. Our examination of their position among the elites who influence the making of policy, particularly in the area of foreign relations, has somewhat undermined the validity of their assuming an adversary posture in relation to the makers of policy.

Although the above analysis is concerned with refuting the democratic model of the function of the newsmedia in democratic regimes, I do not believe that the role of the media is merely of a symbolic nature. To know more about their true function, we shall have to overcome some very difficult obstacles. These concern the patterns of media consumption on the part of policy makers. For one thing, there is little data on the matter. It would probably be possible to cull some information on the subject by carefully screening the personal recollections of major political actors and journalists. Such material, however, would be mostly anecdotal and therefore could hardly contribute to a systematic approach to the problem at hand. There is, furthermore, a problem of credibility involved, since, by virtue of the role assigned to the news media according to the accepted democratic belief system, political leaders may feel bound to show concern for what the media have to say, even when they do not actually do so. In more than one way, a political actor's media behavior is, at present, part of his public image. His interaction with media figures such as interviewers and reporters, to the extent that it gets exposure on the media, is only part of this image. What is known, and often deliberately circulated by the politician's public relations apparatus, about his habits of watching TV and newspaper reading, is also part of that image. In some cases, notably that of Richard Nixon, a political figure's subjective interpretation of the media's attitudes toward him, may constitute an independent input into his process of decision making. On rare occasions, a process of this kind is actually demonstrated.

Also, there is the difficulty of isolating what is the political figure's genuine media behavior from the layers added to it by his own media specialists— namely, his spokesman, and perhaps no less important, whoever is in charge of collecting the press clippings, which are routinely presented to political leaders as a mirror not only of media opinion, but also as a reflection of public opinion as such.

Even though we do not know much about the true pattern of media consumption on the part of top echelon policy makers, we do know that, unlike lower placed officials, they do, or can have, access to all the information available within the system which they head. According to Joseph Frankel (1963), access to important sources not generally available is, in fact, among the criteria which define top-level status [57]. Although this access does not in and of itself guarantee that decision makers of the top level will always have at their disposal all the information pertinent to their decisions, it seems doubtful that what information they lack should be found in the newsmedia. In other words, it is hard to maintain that policy makers of the top echelon depend on the newsmedia for any substantive informational inputs.

However, as has been shown by researchers involved in the exploration of political decision making, decisions—particularly in the area of foreign policy—are not necessarily based on rational information-seeking processes only. As has been pointed out by Roberta Wohlstetter (1965), in writing about the Cuban missle crisis, "... Once a predisposition about the opponent's behavior becomes settled, it is very hard to shake. In this case ... it was reinforced not only by expert authority but also by knowledge, both conscious and unconscious, that the White House had set down a policy for relaxation of tension ... this policy background was much more subtle in its influence than documents or diplomatic experience ..." [58]. Robert Jervis (1977) has shown that the search for information, on the part of decision makers, is in itself limited by the cognitive processes of inference which they employ in order to construct balanced belief systems. In the interest of maintaining this balance, decision makers, once having accepted an organizing assumption, then limit their search for additional information [59]. Some of the processes described by Jervis in his discussion of how decision makers perceive reality and organize their information search, bear what we believe to be very interesting similarities to how journalists perform their own tasks. Although the two perform under very different conditions, these similarities deserve further elucidation, in the course of which some of the subtler modes in which the news media influence decision making, might become apparent. Thus, for example, it might prove interesting to compare the way journalists distort their presentation of reality to comply with accepted news values [60] with the way decision makers act when, after having accepted certain assumptions, they limit their information seeking to what is consistent with these assumptions. Both journalists and decision makers are often subject to the same inclination to simplify, to engage in unwarranted deductions, and to submit to premature closure. The extent to which the decision makers' continuing exposure as media consumers, to processes of deduction as practiced by journalists, may have an effect on their own deductive powers could however only be verified empirically. Another interesting similarity concerns the tendency of both journalists and decision makers to engage in what Jervis defines as the "personification function". In the case of reporters, particularly those who work for the electronic media, personification is a routine convention justified by both stylistic needs and organizational convenience. For decision makers, it serves, according to Jervis, as an aid to decision making in complex situations where, by means of "vicarious identification" it helps them to speculate on how their adversaries might react.

Another fascinating aspect of interaction between news media and decision makers involves the time element. Although, as we have pointed out, decision makers rarely depend on information conveyed by the media, for their assessments of a given foreign policy issue, they may, particularly in the case of crisis situations, get their first intimidation of certain developments through the news media. Little is known about how the primacy thus gained by the news media in defining the issue, may influence decision makers in their subsequent processes of information search. The news media, or rather the timetable imposed by them, may influence decision making on yet another level. The fact that, at least in part, decision making in the area of foreign policy is exposed to news coverage on a continuing basis, may well constitute a constraint on the decision making process itself. Although the meeting of deadlines and the need to report new developments at fixed intervals are the concern of the reporter and not of the decision maker, the former's insistence may sometimes affect the latter's timetable as well. This is true especially in situations where policy makers, for a variety of reasons, find it convenient to engage in "media diplomacy," or to put it more generally, in "on the air" decision making.

No less interesting is the further exploration of the role of ambiguity in the context under discussion. Ambiguity may be said to be an almost inbuilt feature of the presentation of news. Although not usually conceived of in this manner, a so-called balanced presentation of issues, events or personalities, involves a large measure of ambiguity. In pursuing the normative goal of objectivity, a reporter may often end up in presenting his readers or viewers with a series of conflicting statements which, in turn, will greatly hinder them in the process of making up their minds as to the merits of the case. Except for special cases, such as elections, the consumers of news are not expected to make decisions on the basis of information conveyed by the media. Continuing exposure to the ambiguous manner in which the news media present reality, however, may well enhance a tendency to abstain from clear-cut decisions.

The above are but a few examples of what we have in mind in referring to the subtler modes of interaction between news media and decision makers. Further empirical research is indicated, along the lines here suggested, which may call for a combined effort on the part of political scientists, sociologists, social psychologists, and experts in mass communication. The problems we have stated at the beginning of this paper can only be answered if and when such research is completed, for, in the last analysis, it would seem that the influence of the news media on policy making is to be judged mainly in terms of their impact on those who make the ultimate decisions.

ACKNOWLEDGMENTS

This paper was written while the author was a Visiting Scholar at the Yale Law School.

NOTES

1. Some particularly damaging evidence concerning the French press had been published in the mid 1920s by the then Socialist organ *L'Humanité*. On information supplied by the Soviets, it was shown how Count Islovsky, the Russian ambassador to Paris, had consistently paid French newspapers before World War One, to insert articles favorable to Russian policy. [18].

2. Although it is probably true that considerations of image were given an exaggerated importance in the course of the Vietnam War, efforts at manipulating image were addressed to the domestic audience of the United States, no less than to world opinion. On the domestic scene, insofar as the American newsmedia were concerned, these attempts were eventually proven to be counterproductive. Arendt's argument that a preoccupation with image is characteristic only of wars waged in a media-saturated age can also be challenged. Raymond Aron (1966) makes the distinction between what he calls *struggle for glory* and *struggle for power* and shows how military victory can become a goal to itself, causing political objectives to be forgotten. "The desire for absolute victory is often more the expression of a desire for glory than of a desire for force, and it derives from the amour-propre that animates men, once they measure themselves against other men" [31].

3. The editors of the O.E.D. say that they "have failed to discover confirmation of Carlyle's statement (1841) attributing to Burke the use of this phrase in the application now current. A correspondent of *Notes & Queries* . . . states that he heard Brougham use it in the House of Commons in 1823 and 1824 and that it was at that time considered original . . . ''

4. With regard to at least one occasion, which occurred after Watergate, there exists ample documentation of how the newsmedia agreed, for a long period, to follow the CIA's directives and forego the publication of a news story which, among other things, also had foreign policy implications. We refer to their agreeing to keep out of print any reference to the attempts by the *Glomar*

Explorer to raise a Soviet submarine in the Pacific. These documents were eventually released under the Freedom of Information Act, in October, 1977 [48].

5. This should not be taken to mean that officials are the only sources reporters use in covering foreign affairs. Research institutes, think tanks, and academic institutions are among those who generate considerable information which journalists use when writing on foreign policy. Recently the term "foreign policy counterestablishment" has been coined to cover the activities of these bodies [51]. However, very little in the way of hard facts originates from these sources.

REFERENCES

1. Rosenau, James. *Public Opinion and Foreign Policy*. New York: Random House, 1961, p. 3.
2. Cohen, Bernard. *The Public's Impact on Foreign Policy*. Boston, Mass.: Little Brown & Co., 1973, p. 22.
3. *Op. cit.* p. 11.
4. *Op. cit.* p. 20.
5. *New York Times Co. v. U.S.,* 403 U.S. 713 (1971) at 728.
6. Cohen's *The Press and Foreign Policy* Princeton, N.J.: Princeton University Press, 1963; Dan Nimmo's *Newsgathering in Washington* New York: Atherton Press 1964; Leon Sigal's *Reporters and Officials,* Lexington, Mass.: D.C. Heath & Co. 1973; and William Chittick's *State Department, Press and Pressure Groups,* New York: Wiley 1970, should be mentioned in this context.
7. Periviér, A. *Napoléon Journaliste*. Paris: Libraire Plon, 1918, p. 412.
8. Everth, Erich. *Die Oeffentlichkeit in der Aussenpolitik*. Jena: Gustav Fischer, 1931, pp. 416–420.
9. Busch, Moritz. *Bismarck: Some Secret Pages of his History*. London: Macmillan, 1898, pp. xv–xvi.
10. Knightley, Phillip, *The First Casualty*. New York: Harcourt, Brace, Jovanovich, 1975, pp. 50–52.
11. Mathews, Joseph. *Reporting the Wars*. Minneapolis, Minn.: University of Minnesota Press, 1957, pp. 141–45.
12. Lasswell, Harold D. *Propaganda Techniques in the World War,* Macmillan, 1927.
13. Deming, William C. "The Opportunity and Duty of the Press in Relation to World Peace" *International Conciliation,* May 1913, No. 66.
14. Letter from Robert Lansing to Edward M. House, April 8, 1918, quoted by Lawrence Gelfand in "American Foreign Policy and Public Opinion," *Reviews in American History,* Sept. 1977.
15. Nicholson, Harold. *Peacemaking,* 1919. London: Constable, 1934, p. 13.
16. *Op. cit.* pp. 57–63.
17. Spender, J. A. "The Press and International Affairs" *Yale Review* Vol. 17 1927–28, p. 490.
18. Desmond, Robert W. *The Press in World Affairs*. London: Appleton Century, 1937, p. 162.
19. Commission on Freedom of the Press *Peoples Talking to Peoples,* Llewelyn White and Robert D. Leigh, (Eds.). Chicago, Ill.: 1947.
20. Berkson, Seymour. "Freedom of the Press and American Foreign Policy" in Quincy Wright, (Ed.) *A Foreign Policy for the United States*. Chicago, Ill.: University of Chicago Press, 1947, p. 339.
21. Eek, Hilding. *Freedom of Information as a Project of International Legislation*. Uppsala, 1953 pp. 77–117.
22. Boulding, Kenneth E. "National Images and International Systems", in *International Politics and Foreign Policy,* James Rosenau (Ed.) New York; The Free Press, 1969, pp. 423–424.
23. Kriesberg, Louis "International Decisionmaking", in *International Systems*. Michael Haas, (Ed.) New York: Chandler Publishing Co. 1974, p. 241.

24. Jervis, Robert. *The Logic of Images in International Relations.* Princeton, N.J.: Princeton University Press, 1970.
25. Quoted by Lloyd A. Free, in Statement Before House of Representatives Committee on Foreign Affairs, Subcommittee of International Organizations and Movements, Meeting on "US Image Abroad", July 22, 1968.
26. Dror, Yehezkel. *Crazy States* Lexington, Mass.: Heath Lexington Books, 1971.
27. Bernays Edward L. and Burnett Hershey, (Eds.) *The Case for Reappraisal of U.S. Overseas Information Policies and Programs.* New York: Praeger, 1970, p. 5.
28. *New York Times,* Dec. 25, p. 1; Dec. 26, p. 1; Dec. 27, p. 1; 1977.
29. Arendt, Hanna. "Lying in Politics: Reflections on the Pentagon Papers" *The New York Review of Books,* Nov. 18, 1971 p. 31.
30. *Op. cit.*32.
31. Aron, Raymon. *Peace and War.* New York: Doubleday, 1966, p. 73.
32. Hero, Alfred O. "Non Profit Organizations, Public Opinion and United States Foreign Policy" *International Journal,* vol. 33, no. 1, Winter 1977-78 pp. 159-60.
33. Smouts, Marie Claude. "French Foreign Policy: The Domestic Debate" *Interntional Affairs,* January 1977, p. 38.
34. de Tocqueville, Alexis. *Democracy in America,* New Translation by George Lawrence J. P. Mayer and Max Lerner (Eds.) New York: Harper & Row, 1966 p. 211.
35. Cater, Douglass. *The Fourth Branch of Government.* Boston, Mass.: Houghton Mifflin & Co. 1959.
36. Thomson, James C. Jr. "The Relationship of Government and Media". *The Requirements of Democratic Foreign Policy: Pacem in Terris III.* Washington, D.C. Center For the Study of Democratic Institutions, 1973, p. 67.
37. Halperin, Morton. *Bureaucratic Politics and Foreign Policy.* Washington D.C.: The Brookings Institution, 1974. Ch. 10 "The Uses of the Press".
38. Lippmann, Walter and Charles Merz. "A Test of the News" *The New Republic* August 4, 1920 pp. 1-42.
39. *The New Republic,* September 15, 1920, p. 61.
40. Kriesberg, Martin. "Soviet News in the 'New York Times' ". *Public Opinion Quarterly,* Vol. 10, 1946, Winter 1946-47, p. 540.
41. Welch, Susan. "Vietnam" How the Press Went Along" *The Nation,* October 11, 1971, p. 329.
42. Welch, Susan. "The American Press and Indochina", *Communication in International Politics.* Richard L. Merritt, (Ed.) Urbana, Ill.: University of Illinois Press, 1972. pp. 339-230.
43. Seymour-Ure, Colin. *The Political Impact of the Mass Media.* London: Constable. 1974. Ch. 3 "The *Times* and the appeasement of Hitler. *passim.*
44. *Ibid.* p. 52.
45. Thomson, *op. cit.* pp. 68-69.
46. Gelb, Leslie, and S. Lake "Washington Dateline: Watergate and Foreign Policy" *Foreign Policy,* No. 12 Fall 1973.
47. For example, to mention but a few among the volumes devoted to the subject: Krock, Arthur. *Memoirs: Sixty Years on the Firing Line.* New York: Funk and Wagnall's, 1968, Reston, James, *The Artillery of the Press.* New York: Harper & Row, 1967, and Alsop, Joseph and Stewart, *The Reporter's Trade,* New York: Reynal, 1958.
48. *Harriet A. Phillipi v. C.I.A. et al.* U.S. District Court, D.C.C.A. No. 75-1265.
49. *Time,* January 30, 1978, p. 61.
50. Welch, *The American Press in Indochina,* p. 223.
51. *New York Times,* March 27, 1978, p. A-4.
52. Cohen, *The Public's Impact on Foreign Policy,* 1973, pp. 108-09.
53. Cohen, *The Press and Foreign Policy,* 1963, pp. 133-168.

54. Goren, Dina. Akiva A. Cohen and Dan Caspi. "Reporting the Yom Kippur War" *Journalism Quarterly,* Summer 1975, 199–206.
55. Halperin, *Op. cit.* p. 173.
56. Reston James, *op. cit.* pp. 67–68.
57. Frankel, Joseph *The Making of Foreign Policy: An Analysis of Decision Making.* Oxford University Press, 1963, p. 96.
58. Wohlstetter, Roberta. "Cuba and Pearl Harbor: Hindsight and Foresight" *Foreign Affairs,* vol. 43, no. 4. July 1965, p. 699.
59. Jervis, Robert. *Perception and Misperception in International Politics.* Princeton: Princeton Univ. Press, 1977. ch. 4.
60. The problem of news-values, is too complex to go into at this point. Cohen (1963) suggests that journalists are incapable of supplying a definition of news which is not tautological. A comprehensive list is suggested by Johan Galtung and Mari Holmboe Ruge, in "The Structure of Foreign News" *Journal of Peace Research,* 1965, 1 pp. 64–91 as well as by Einar Ostgaard, "Factors Influencing the Flow of News", pp. 39–63 of the same issue. A much older but still valid definition is given by Charles Merz, "The Big News of 1926", *The New Republic,* vol. 49 January 12, 1927 pp. 213–215 "But in the last analysis, we come down to the fact, I think, that the surest element of all is conflict, Big news is really news of flying fists". p. 214.

THE ARISTOCRACY OF LABOR:

AN EMPIRICAL TEST

Peter Dreier and Al Szymanski

One of the most persistent themes in social science has been the question of the failure of the working class in Western societies to foster a socialist revolution, or in some cases such as the U.S.A., even to develop a socialist class consciousness. The failure of Marx's predictions that such would be the case in all the advanced countries has been attributed to a wide variety of causes. (See Lipset and Laslett, 1974, for a good summary of the major arguments of why a socialist consciousness did not develop in the U.S.) This paper will be concerned with only one such explanation—the labor aristocracy thesis. This hypothesis holds that a relatively *small segment* of the working class (1) receives special privileges, especially significantly higher pay, because of its involvement with those industries that make "super profits" from imperialism, (2) because of its privileges are relatively conservative (i.e., supportive of the status quo), and (3) because its domination of the union movement and the political organizations of the working class has a conservatizing effect on the working class as a whole. The popular version of this argument is that the politically influential upper strata of the working class is "bought off" or "co-opted."

Research in Social Movements, Conflicts and Change, Vol. 3, pages 143-168
Copyright © 1980 by JAI Press Inc.
All rights of reproduction in any form reserved.
ISBN: 0-89232-182-2

143

The theory of the "labor aristocracy" was first used to explain the political and economic development of the British working class in the last half of the 19th century. Until Lenin's work, *Imperialism: The Highest Stage of Capitalism* (first published in 1916 with a new preface in 1920), however, the theory focused on the hierarchial division of labor within capitalism, rather than imperialism, as the cause of the conservative role of this strata. Engels lamented the relative conservative role of the British working class which became apparent after 1850. "The British working class is actually becoming more and more bourgeois," he wrote in a letter to Marx in 1858 (Marx and Engels, 1956:133). He explained this phenomenon in what he saw as the development of a conservative elite within the working class.

In an 1885 article called "England in 1845 and 1885," written for the socialist newspaper *Commonweal* and later incorporated as the preface to the 1892 edition of *The Condition of the Working Class in England,* Engels used the already current term "labor aristocracy" to refer to improved conditions of two sectors of the working class. First, the factory hands' position was improved by Parliament's fixing of the workday. Second, the "great trade unions"—particularly among the engineers, bricklayers, and carpenters and joiners—were successful "in enforcing for themselves a relatively comfortable position and they accept it as final." It was in those crafts, not threatened by female or child labor or by mechanization, that trade unions were most successful, Engels argued, and they "form an aristocracy among the working class." (Engels, 1968:368).

Although Engels placed this development in the context of England's central position in the world economy, particularly due to the success of free trade in the second half of the century, the focal point of this theory was the *initiative* of the working class through Parliament (fixing the workday) and trade union bargaining (higher wages and job security) to better its conditions. The "great mass" (Engels, 1968:367) of the working class was still in miserable shape, separated from the working class elite, because conditions did not yet permit the development of class consciousness, solidarity, and organization.

It is in Lenin, however, that we see the 20th century popularity of this thesis as well as its specification. Lenin linked the theory of the aristocracy of labor as the source of working class conservatism to imperialism and generalized it as a characteristic of the most advanced capitalist countries during the most mature phase of capitalism.

Because of the British empire, Lenin argued, a segment of the British working class "enjoy crumbs from colonial advantages" (cited in Pelling, 1968:39). It was to British imperialism that Lenin attributed the "economism" and "reformism" of working class politics—the trade unions and the Labour Party in particular.

In an oft-cited quote from *Imperialism,* written in 1916, Lenin noted:

"Obviously, out of such enormous super-profits (since they are obtained over and above the profits which capitalists squeeze out of the workers of their 'home' country) it is quite possible to bribe the labor leaders and the upper stratum of the labor aristocracy. And the capitalists of the 'advanced' countries are bribing them; they bribe them in a thousand different ways, direct and indirect, overt and covert.''

"This stratum of bourgeoisified workers of the 'labor aristocracy,' who are quite philistine in their mode of life, in the size of their earnings and in their outlook, serves as the principal prop of the Second International, and in our days, the principal social (not military) prop of the bourgeoisie. They are the real agents of the bourgeoisie in the labor movement, the labor lieutenants of the capitalist class, the real channels of reformism and chauvinism. In the civil war between the proletariat and the bourgeoisie they inevitably, and in no small numbers, stand side by side within the bourgeoisie, with the 'Versaillese' against the 'Communards.' ''

"Not the slightest progress can be made toward the solution of the practical problems of the Communist movement and of the impending social revolution unless the economic roots of this phenomenon are understood and unless its political and sociological significance is appreciated.'' [Lenin, 1939 (1916):13-14.]

"The causes are: 1) exploitation of the whole world by this country (Britain); 2) its monopolist position in the world market; 3) its colonial monopoly. The effects are 1) a section of the British proletariat becomes bourgeois; 2) a section of the proletariat allows itself to be led by men bought by, or at least paid by, the bourgeoisie. [Lenin, 1939 (1916):107.]''

It is clear that Lenin's theory posits a link between imperial activity and the development of a strata within the working class which exhibits at least two characteristics: (1) their "outlook" (attitude) is more conservative, and (2) they have a significantly higher income than other segments of the working class. In this paper, we will examine whether or not these two factors are characteristic of segments of the U.S. working class today. If we find that they are, this will be considered substantial support for (but not definitive proof of) the aristocracy of labor thesis as advanced by Lenin. If one or both are not true of the U.S. working class, on the other hand, this would seem to be proof that the labor aristocracy thesis, at least as advanced by Lenin, is *not* the explanation of the lack of a socialist consciousness in the U.S. working class.

This paper will *not* attempt to test other hypotheses that have been used to explain the relative conservatism of the U.S. working class. One thesis argues that U.S. working class conservatism is a product of the higher living standards of either most, or the elite, of the American working class compared to other working classes in the world. (Sombart, 1906; Goldethorpe, et al., 1969.) (This higher living standard is attributed to the U.S.'s leading role in the world capitalist system and/or to the greater productivity and natural resources of the U.S.) This paper, however, is examining variations *within* the American working class, not comparisons of working classes between nations. A second thesis argues that the relative conservatism of the U.S. working class is due to the cultural hegemony of capital in the U.S. due to the absence of strong working class culture, especially when compared with European working class culture (Hoggart, 1957; Mann, 1973; Parkin, 1971). The absence of a strong working class culture, in turn, is often attributed to the higher level of ethnic and racial diversity in the American working class and to higher levels of individual socio-economic or geographic mobility (or the belief in mobility) in the United States. (Aronowitz, 1973; Thernstrom, 1964.) Again, our concern is with variations within the U.S. working class itself.

More relevant to our analysis, however, is the popularity of a modified version of the labor aristocracy thesis. This version claims that rather than a *small* especially privileged segment, *most* of the U.S. working class benefits from imperialism, either directly or indirectly through cheaper imports or a leveling of wages at a higher level than would be the case in the absence of imperialism. During the mid-1960s, in good part because the stimulus of the war in Vietnam provoked renewed interest in issues of imperialism, this version of Lenin's theory became current once again in the U.S. The support of union leaders for the war became apparent. Attention was focused on the alleged "hardhat" support for the war and military spending, although it was often disproved (Wright, 1972; Hamilton, 1975; Patcher, 1970). Many linked prosperity to the necessity of a "war economy" (Baran and Sweezy, 1966), while others insisted that the permanent war economy wasted resources and actually resulted in a lowered standard of living (Melman, 1965 and 1974; Dreier, 1976). It became quite common to argue that the other side of the coin from rebellion and national liberation movements in the Third World was the conservatism of working classes in the advanced countries. According to the arguments of such influential authors as Andre Gunder Frank (1967), Paul Baran (1962), Samir Amin (1974), and Arrighi Emmanuel (1972), material wealth was transferred from the poor peripheral countries of Asia, Africa, and Latin America to the advanced countries of North America, Western Europe, and Japan to the detriment of the productive classes in the former countries, but to the benefit of those in the latter. This notion, which became central in the "dependency theory" popularized in the U.S. by the journal *Monthly Review* and most recently by the "world system" school around sociologist Immanual Wallerstein (1974), has been widely used to account for the relative conservatism of the working classes in the advanced countries.

In this context, much of the student movement of the late 1960s came to accept the arguments of those who argued that the U.S. working class was hopelessly "bourgeois," "bought off," and part of the "establishment." Students in the 1960s turned away from the working class and tended to look instead to minorities, youth, and women as the source for social change in general and opposition to the war in particular. (Gintis, 1970; Flacks, 1971; Rowntree and Rowntree, 1968; Allen, 1970; Boggs, 1970; Mitchell, 1971.) The idea that at least the white male industrial working class, especially those in strong unions and in basic industries, were benefiting from imperialism, and thus tended to be conservative supporters of the status quo, became virtually hegemonic within the movements of the late 1960s and early 1970s.

The hypothesis that most of the U.S. working class benefits from imperialism has been examined by one of the authors in an earlier article and found to be invalid (Szymanski, 1972).

This paper will thus focus solely on the version of the aristocracy of labor thesis developed by Lenin in 1916 that maintains that a *small segment* (the most privileged stratum) of the working class of the leading imperalist countries receive material privileged *because of* their countries' imperial involvements and that they *therefore* become supporters of the established institutions. They, in turn, use their central position in the unions and political organizations of the working class to transmit conservative ideas to the working class as a whole. (Evansohn, 1977.)

RESEARCH DESIGN

If the material benefits of imperialism trickle down differentially to segments of the industrial working class in industries which secure the biggest share of their profits from imperialism (as Lenin predicted was the case for Great Britain), then we would expect that the productive workers in such industries (or perhaps just the craftworkers in these industries, as Lenin suggests), would materially benefit relative to workers in industries who profit relatively little from activities related to dominating the Third World. Further, we would expect that workers in those industries which are most involved in imperial activities would be more conservative than other workers. Even if workers in those sectors of the economy most directly tied into imperial activities do not actually benefit materially from imperialism relative to other sections of the working class, they still might be more conservative, either because they *think* they benefit or because they are concerned about a high level of employment in their industries and feel that without imperialism they might lose their jobs.

To test whether or not there are segments of the U.S. manual working class which benefit differentially from the effect of U.S. imperialism, we located three measures of an industry's involvement in imperial activities: (1) repatriated income on U.S. direct investments in Third World countries per production worker; (2) the exports to Third World countries per production worker; and (3) the percentages of total product shipments to the U.S. military. These measures are indicators of the potential trickle down effect from overseas investments, export markets in Third World countries and military contracts. A fourth possible avenue of benefit from imperialism, imports from Third World countries per production worker, cannot, of course, be differentially distributed by different segments of the manual working force, since all workers are able to buy such goods with an equal probability (at least, those at the same income level). The effect of cheap imports from the Third World can only be captured by designs such as those in Szymanski's article (1972) which look at the aggregate effects of imperialism (including any leveling of wages through the labor market at levels higher than they would be in the absence of imperialism) and include as well estimates of the gain from cheap imports.[1]

Our measures of repatriated profits and exports are those from and to the Third World only (not from and to the advanced capitalist countries.) This is because both Lenin's original theory and the contemporary modification of it argue that the superprofits of imperialism come mostly from Asia, Africa, and Latin America. These theories also suggest that the relatively high living standards of the working classes in the advanced countries is a product of the relatively low living standards of the working classes in the less developed countries of the Third World. Neither Lenin, nor contemporary theorists of the aristocracy of labor school, argue that U.S. workers are conservative (either as a whole or an elite segment of them) because of profits being drained out of Canada or Western Europe (areas in which for the most part the working classes now have a living standard equivalent to that of the U.S. working class).

There are serious problems with the reliability of statistics on international capital flows such as repatriated earnings, because profits can be easily transferred within a transnational corporation in order to minimize taxes. The actual transfer of money in the form of repatriated profits is only one way that the surplus generated in the Third World could reach the U.S. and hence trickle down to workers. Two other important ways are through royalties, rents, insurance payments, pattern fees, etc., *and* through goods sold by a corporation's overseas subsidies to its domestic parent at prices less than the going rate; i.e., a loss created for tax purposes in Chile can appear as a profit in the corporation's domestic operations. However, statistics on either process are not available and we must thus rely exclusively on formally repatriated profits. Thus, while we should be somewhat cautious about the interpretation of this indicator, the wide range of values among industries combined with the large magnitude of repatriated profits suggests both that repatriated profits itself can well be a significant source of a differential trickle-down effect *and* that it is further a good indicator of the degree to which value can be transferred by either of the other mechanisms (since it roughly reflects the overall involvement of an industry in Third World investments).

We examined the basic industrial subsectors of the U.S. economy for which data on foreign investments are available: aircraft, chemicals, electrical machinery, fabricated metals, foods and kindred, lumber, mining, motor vehicles and parts, non-electrical machinery, ordinance, paper, petroleum, primary metals, printing, rubber, stone, clay and glass, and textiles and apparel.

It perhaps would have been better to use firms or corporations rather than whole industries as our units of analysis, comparing those corporations that are heavily involved overseas or with the military with those that are not, on the grounds that this would produce a greater variation in the independent and, hence, dependent variables; i.e., more of the unit is involved in imperial activities and, hence, workers there might benefit more. However, neither the government nor the corporations generally release the type of data required on the firm or corporate level. Further, because of the gigantic size of the corporations that do most of the business with the Department of Defense or are involved overseas, the proportion of total sales exported or sold to the government or total profits made on Third World investments is little different for the major corporations than for industries as a whole. A number of studies have shown that Department of Defense contracts are concentrated in a relatively few firms. One hundred corporations receive over two-thirds of all prime contract awards each year and 50 corporations receive 60 percent. The list of the top 100 defense contractors has changed little during the past two decades. These top Department of Defense contractors are also among the largest corporations. Among the top 100 firms, 65 are significantly involved in military contracting. All but five of the largest 25 industrial corporations in 1968, for example, were among the 100 largest contractors for the Department of Defense. This pattern has not changed. (Lieberson, 1971; Galloway, 1973; Reich, 1973.) In either the case of firms or whole industries, then, we make the reasonable assumption that the higher the proportion of imperial-related activities, if the aristocracy of labor thesis holds, the higher the average level of working class benefit (since the benefits for the proportion of workers that benefits brings up the overall industrial average). These same arguments hold equally for the case of political attitudes as well as for that of material benefits.

Within the 17 basic industrial sectors, we located indicators that measure potential gain for craftworkers and for operatives. As measures of material gain from imperial activities, the median annual earnings of employed craftsmen and foremen, and the median annual earnings of employed operatives, were used. As measures of a differential gain of craftsmen and foremen relative to operatives, the ratio of the median income of craftsmen and foremen to operatives was examined.

The degree of unionization is also examined since part of Lenin's theory argues that the aristocracy of labor is both more unionized than other workers and dominates the labor movement. It might be argued that the rate of profit of our industries should be examined as well, since the theory maintains that the "superprofits of imperialism" trickle down to workers in good part, perhaps, because they have strong unions to take their share. We might expect then that those industries which are most involved in imperialism should have higher profit rates than others. However, this should not necessarily be expected to be the case. The "superprofits" referred to by the theory is all "surplus value" (rents, loan payments, executive salaries, royalties, taxes, distributed and undistributed profits, reinvested earnings, etc.) and not just book profits reported in government statistics (a rather small proportion of the total surplus). Further to the extent that "superprofits" trickle down to workers, they, of course, are *not* part of the surplus (or of book profits) at all but, rather, part of wages. It would even be logically possible that a firm could earn twice as much in its Third World operations as it does in identical operations in the U.S., but that higher domestic wages and salaries made possible by these *potentially* higher profits take up all the extra earnings and thus that the firm's overall rate of surplus or profit is no different than that of firms not involved in imperial activities; i.e., to the extent that workers benefit from imperialism, the realized surplus or profits of their firms will be less than otherwise. These factors, combined with the tendency of the rate of profit to equalize across industries, suggests that any expectation about imperialist-oriented industries having a consistently higher profit rate may be misdirected. If there is a tendency for the overseas operations of certain firms to result in especially high rates of surplus value which trickles down to domestic workers, this will be fully captured in the dependent variables we employ; i.e., there is no need to attempt to explicitly measure the intermediate variable of potential surplus value.

As control variables, we use the factors which are most often cited in the literature as alternative explanations of the *higher level of wages* in different industries, either because of their direct or indirect effect. Three key structural factors were controlled for (1) the percentage of the value of total shipments accounted for by the four largest shippers in each industry as a measure of degree of monopolization (and hence an industry's ability to grant wage increases due to the ability to pass wages on the consumers); (2) the capital investment per production worker (which is reflected in the skills and responsibilities of workers and the relative unimportance of wages in total costs); and (3) the production workers per enterprise (i.e., workplace) as a measure of both the socialization of the labor process (or extensiveness of the division of labor) *and* the ability of workers to establish a working class subculture independent of management domination (which is manifested in more militant unions and leftist political attitudes) (Kerr and Seigel, 1964; Lipset, 1960).[2]

For any of the independent variables for which a significant positive relationship was found in the direction of that predicted by the aristocracy of labor thesis, the relationships were further examined, controlling for the effects of strikes and unions. While it might be the case that time lost in strikes and proportion of the labor force in unions are intermediate variables, accounting for at least part of why the independent variables effect the dependent variables, they might also be autonomous variables which themselves might produce a possible spurious relationship between imperial involvements and material gain.

It is necessary to control for these five factors, since all of them can be expected to produce higher wages for both craftworkers and operatives independently of the operation of an aristocracy of labor effect, and because they, or at least most of them, can well be considered to be themselves related to an industry's degree of imperialist involvement and thus be responsible for spurious results. We would be justified in regarding a correlation between higher wages and imperial involvements as spurious if the relation is caused, for example, by higher imperial involvement which facilitates domestic monopolization (by giving certain firms a market edge through cheaper raw materials or special access to markets) and hence gives a firm the ability to pass on domestic wage increases through price rises. The same would be the case if higher imperial involvements and consequent higher profits and available domestic investment funds lead to technologically more advanced plants and hence to a lower ratio of wages to total costs, thus decreasing reluctance to grant wage increases. Likewise, if greater imperial involvement results in higher profits reinvested in larger plants and hence a more militant working class which becomes more insist on, and better able to secure, higher wages. However, a relationship between higher wages and imperialism should *not* be regarded as spurious (unlike as with the above three variables) if it disappears when controlling for either percentage in unions or time lost in strikes (especially if it persists while the above three factors, all of which affect both degree of unionization and militance, are controlled for). If such were to be the case, it should be taken to mean that greater imperial involvements lead to stronger unions and more militant workers who effectively demand their share of imperial profits; i.e., that these latter two processes represent intermediate variables through which the effect of imperial involvements operates.

Controlling for the first three structural factors also controls for the effect of industrial differences in occupational differentials in worker's characteristics and pay having nothing to do with imperial involvements; i.e., are caused by differences in technological development, size of operations, or degree of protection from competitive market forces. Controlling for degree of unionization and worker militance likewise removes the effect of class action on occupational differentials having nothing to do with imperial activities. Consequently, differentials in the figures for the income of both craftworkers and operatives, when all these factors are controlled for, can be considered to accurately reflect imperial involvements.

For each of the above indicators, we attempted to secure data for years as close as possible to 1970, because this was the year of the last census (which reports necessary information for our analysis). Data on the numbers of operatives and craftworkers are for 1970; for mean annual earnings, 1969; for repatriated earnings on U.S. investments, 1966 (the last year in which the U.S. government has issued a detailed report which breaks data down by detailed industries on foreign direct investments); for exports and imports, 1970; for time lost in strikes as a percentage of total work time, the annual average from 1964 to 1972; for the ratio of union members in an industry to total production workers, 1970; for percentage of the value of total shipments accounted for by sales to the Department of Defense, 1976; for capital investment per production worker, 1970; for the percentage of the value of total shipments accounted for by the four largest shippers in each industry, 1970; and for production workers per enterprise, 1972.

Because our indicators are measured over as much as a ten-year time span because of the differential availability of data, as well as because the years for which data are available may not be typical of the period as a whole, it is important to get some idea of the stability of the figures used. There is a Spearman's rank order correlation of .93 between the exports of our 17 industries in 1966 and 1976, indicating an extremely high level of stability for exports to the Third World in our period. There is a rank order correlation of .75 in repatriated income for the half of our 17 industries for which data is available for both 1966 and 1976, suggesting a high level of stability for all 17 industries. There is a rank order correlation of .67 in the value of shipments to the government from the leading eight defense-oriented industries from 1966 and 1976, again suggesting reasonable stability in the levels of military shipments. Lastly, there was a Spearman's rho of .80 between the ranking of average hourly earnings for our 17 industries in 1966 and 1976, reflecting considerable stability in relative earnings over our period. In conclusion, we can be reasonably confident that the correlations among the dependent and independent variables are based on typical figures for the period of the late 1960s and early 1970s and thus reflect real underlying tendencies operating during this time.

If the trickle-down effect of imperialism is manifested in benefits both to the skilled craftsmen and less skilled production workers, then we would expect a significant positive relationship between any or all of the three measures of imperial involvement of industries and the mean annual earnings of both operatives and craftsmen. If the trickle-down effect, as Lenin seems to suggest, effects mainly the more skilled in those industries with the highest involvement in imperial activities, then we would expect the ratio of craftsmen to operative earnings to be greater in those industries that are most imperially involved.

Pearson's zero order correlation co-efficients were examined for the relationship between the independent variables (the measures of imperial involvement) and the dependent variables (the measures of gain for craftsmen and operatives). Pearsonian r co-efficients are justified by the absence of any cases extreme enough to make such co-efficients unreliable and distributions, as shown by scattergrams, that manifest no curvilinear relationships. Partial correlation co-efficients were employed to control for the number of employees per enterprise, the degree of monopolization of an industry, capital invested per worker, percentage in unions, and time lost in strikes. These variables were included as controls individually and as a group. Pearsonian correlation co-efficients are fully adequate to determine whether or not there is material benefit from imperial involvements. We are concerned solely with the question of the existence and direction (positive or negative) of a relationship, not with exactly how much of the total variance is shared by different variables or what the exact equation is which relates different variables. If we were interested in the latter, which we are not, regression analysis would be required. Actually, the Pearsonian co-efficients provide us with more information than a test of the theory requires, since these co-efficients, when squared, indicate the proportion of total variation explained when all we need to know is whether or not there is a significant relation of *any* magnitude between our variables.

In addition to examining the effect of the three independent variables on the measures of economic gain and the degree of unionization, their effect on a wide range of political attitudes obtained from the 1975 and 1976 N.O.R.C. General Social Surveys were also examined. Opinion data were analyzed through secondary analysis for the following questions: presidential preference in 1972, self-definition of political views as a conservative or liberal, amount of trust in business, attitude about national expenditures on the military, attitude about national expenditures on welfare, feeling about the People's Republic of China, feelings about whether or not Communism might not be good for at least some countries, and attitude about the right of a Communist to speak.[3]

Of course, Lenin was concerned with attitudes along a reformist-revolutionary continuum, and our measures of political attitudes reflect more a conservative-liberal continuum. However, both continuums can well be considered part of a broader progressivist dimension, and social forces that benefit from (or belief that one benefits from) imperialism can legitimately be considered to push one to the right along this single dimension. The homogeneity of the dimension tapped by our questions with the continuum tapped by revolutionary versus reformist attitudes is suggested by the fact that three of the eight questions we use explicitly deal with Communism (and thus clearly tap revolutionary attitudes). Further, one deals with business, one with military spending, and one with welfare spending. Again, revolutionaries would clearly give progressive answers to these questions as well as to the question about support for McGovern in 1972 (when the primary issue of the campaign was withdrawal from Vietnam).

It should be noted that, since the theory of the aristocracy of labor argues that those workers who benefit from imperialism politically influence the mass of the working class, the difference in attitudes between them and the rest of the working class would not be expected to be as great as if they had no influence. However, we would not expect the political difference between the two groups to disappear altogether, even with considerable influence from the aristocracy of labor, since the work and life experiences of the masses of workers, including their lack of material interest in imperialism, pushes their attitudes in a direction opposite from that of the aristocracy. In other words, if the aristocracy thesis holds, we should observe a significant political difference between the two groups, even while the masses of workers are more conservative than they would be in the absence of a labor aristocracy.

In order to increase the number of cases for analysis, we combined the cases for all attitudinal questions which were asked in both 1975 and 1976. The N.O.R.C. did not begin collecting data on detailed industrial classifications until 1975. Thus, 1975 and 1976 are the years closest to the 1970 census year for which sufficient attitudinal data are available. Using attitudinal data collected in the mid-1970s to correlate with structural data mostly collected in 1966 and 1970 *is* appropriate, since we would expect somewhat of a lag between changes in the social structure and the formation of political attitudes.

In analyzing the effect of income from Third World investments, exports to the Third World and military contracts on these eight attitudinal variables, we used the simple method of dividing the 17 industrial categories into that half which ranked the highest and that half which ranked the lowest on each of the three independent variables.

Dichotomization of the independent variable makes sense, since this provides us with averages for the high and low halfs on the dependent variable, which thus reflect the effect of strong and weak presence of the independent variable under conditions where the mean variation in both variables are minimized (and thus the probability of arbitrary results minimized). In addition, we compared the average of those *three* industries that ranked the highest on the independent variables and examined whether there was a significant difference between them and the half of the cases with the lowest scores on the independent variables. Here, we are taking the cases where the effect of an aristocracy of labor phenomenon is expected to be greatest—i.e., the most homogeneous cases—and comparing them with those industries where the effect is expected to be least. A judgment taking into account both types of comparisons should be more valid than looking either at dichotomized variables or just the three most extreme cases.

In addition to examining the relation between each of the independent variables and the eight attitudinal measures, an attempt was made to rank the 17 industries by degree of involvement in imperial activities considering all three aspects. Because some industries that are heavily involved in imperial activities (such as aircraft and ordinance) had no overseas investments in the Third World to speak of, it was decided that the most accurate reflection of imperial involvement was first to give each of the 17 industries an individual ranking on each of the three independent variables and then to sum the *two* highest rankings for each industry to give an aggregate score (used as the rank on this combined index), which could then reasonably be considered a valid measure of overall involvement in imperial activities.

Results

None of the zero order correlations between repatriated income from the Third World per production worker and worker gain are greater than $+.09$, and none are statistically significant at the .05 level (see Table 1). When production employees per enterprise, degree of monopolization of an enterprise, and capital per production worker are held constant, the only statistically significant relations to emerge (with capital per worker held constant), was with operative and with craftworker income (both relations are significant at the .05 but not at the .01 level). When all three structural control variables are controlled for simultaneously, *no* relationships were significant at the .05 level. The relationships which emerged when capital per worker is held constant were in the opposite direction from that predicted by the aristocracy of labor thesis. There seems to be no tendency for repatriated profits from foreign direct investments of American industries to be reflected in higher wages for either operatives or craftworkers in those industries most involved. In fact, if anything, there is a slight reverse relationship. Income for both operatives and craftworkers are somewhat lower in those industries which are repatriating the most profits from their overseas investments. Likewise, there is no tendency for there to be relatively more craftworkers or for craftworkers to earn relatively more, compared to operatives in those industries repatriating the most from overseas investments. Nor is there any tendency for the percentage in unions to be correlated one way or the other with repatriated income per production worker.

Even though tests of statistical significance are not strictly applicable here, since we are dealing with almost the universe of industries in the U.S. rather than a sample, the lack of statistically significant positive correlations between income repatriated per worker and the dependent variables demonstrates the absence of any effect predicted by the aristocracy of labor thesis. No support whatsoever can be found for the aristocracy of labor thesis from these data, whether or not the effect on all the workers in an industrial sector or just craftworkers is examined.

Similar results are found when the relationship between the percentage of an industry's shipments to the military and the dependent variables is examined (see Table 1). When the zero order Pearsonian correlation co-efficients are examined, the only statistically significant relationship is with the percentage of the work force in unions—+.64 (which is statistically significant at the .01 level). The relationship between percentage in unions disappears when production workers per enterprise are controlled for (suggesting that the zero order correlation was a spurious relation produced by a relationship between military contracting and large enterprises). When either degree of monopolization or capital per enterprise is held constant, the relationship between the wages of operatives becomes statistically significant at the .05 level, but disappears altogether when production employees per enterprise is held constant, again suggesting that any apparent relationship between higher wages and military-oriented industries is, in fact, spurious and caused by the association of military contractors with large scale operations.

When all three factors are held constant, there is a −.41 relationship with the ratio of craftworker to operatives income (significant at the .08 level). This means that there is a slight relationship *opposite* to that suggested by the aristocracy of labor thesis; i.e., the more involved a firm is in military contracts, the *lower* the differential between craftworkers and operatives. When all *three* factors are controlled for simultaneously, we see that there is no relationship at all between either craftworker or operative income and degree of military contracting. Workers in "defense industries" thus do *not* make more than workers in other industries because of military contracting. The slight tendency to higher wages in these industries is entirely a product of the fact that military production tends to occur in larger factories than non-military production; i.e., it is due solely to the effect of size of plant. Likewise, when all three factors are simultaneously controlled for, it is seen that there is no relationship whatsoever with the degree of unionization. In summary, no evidence whatsoever can be found for the thesis of the aristocracy of labor when the impact of involvement in military sales is examined.

A different picture emerges when we look at the relation between exports to the Third World per worker and the dependent variables (see Table 1). There is,

Table 1. The Effect of Imperial Involvements of Industries on Production
Workers Circa 1970 ((Partial Correlation Co-efficients)

	Ratio of Craft to Operative Annual Income[7]	Annual Income of Operatives[8]	Annual Income of Craftworkers[8]	Percentage of Production Workers in Unions[9]
Repatriated Profits from Third World Direct Investments per Production Worker. [1]				
Controlling for:				
Zero Order:	−.34	+.09	−.07	−.00
Workers per enterprise: [2]	−.37	+.23	+.05	+.19
Degree of Monopolization:[3]	−.35	+.17	+.01	−.01
Capital per worker: [4]	+.13	−.48*	−.54*	−.02
All three simultaneously:	+.12	−.33	−.35	+.05
Shipments to the Military as a Percentage of Total Shipments. [5]				
Controlling for:				
Zero Order:	−.27	+.37	+.32	+.64**
Workers per enterprise:	−.28	−.10	−.30	+.17
Degree of Monopolization:[3]	−.28	+.43*	+.39	+.64**
Capital per worker:	−.37	+.43*	+.34	+.65
All three simultaneously:	−.41	+.07	−.14	+.03
Exports to the Third World per Production Worker: [6]				
Controlling for:				
Zero Order:	−.48*	+.63**	+.54**	−.07
Workers per enterprise:	−.46*	+.64**	+.54**	−.29
Degree of Monopolization:	−.52**	+.56**	+.41	−.07
Capital per Worker:	−.45*	+.62**	+.54*	−.07
All three simultaneously:	−.49*	+.59**	+.43	−.20

*Statistically significant at the .05 level.
**Statistically significant at the .01 level.

Sources: 1. U.S. Department of Commerce, *U.S. Direct Investment Abroad,* 1966, Table C-5; and U.S. Census, 1970 *Special Reports Occupation by Industry,* Table One.
2. U.S. Department of Commerce, Census of Manufacturing, 1972. Volume One, *Subject and Special Statistics General Summary,* Table 5.
3. U.S. Department of Commerce, *Annual Survey of Manufacturers,* 1970, Table 4.
4. U.S. Department of Commerce, *Statistical Abstract of the U.S.,* 1975, p. 762.
5. *Current Industrial Reports,* Bureau of the Census, *Shipments of Defense Oriented Industries,* 1975, Table 3.
6. U.S. Department of Commerce, *Highlights of the U.S. Export and Import Trade,* December 1970, Table E-6.
7. U.S. Department of Commerce, *U.S. Census, 1970, Special Reports: Occupation by Industry,* Table One.
8. U.S. Department of Commerce, *U.S. Census, 1970, Special Reports: Occupation by Industry,* Table Four.
9. U.S. Department of Labor, *Handbook of Labor Statistics,* 1973, Tables 1 and 150.

in fact, a strong positive relationship (in the direction predicted by the aristocracy of labor thesis) with the income of operatives and the income of craftworkers and a statistically significant relationship in the *opposite* direction from that predicted with the ratio of the income of craftworkers to the income of operatives. There is no significant relationship with the percentage of the work force in unions. In fact, there is a very slight negative relationship; i.e., opposite from that predicted by the labor aristocracy thesis. All of these relationships hold up when the three structured control variables are included individually or as a group, although some are weakened. When degree of monopolization is controlled for, the relationship between the income of craftworkers is no longer statistically significant, suggesting that much of the relationship between craftworkers' income and exports to the Third World is spurious and due to a relationship between monopolization and export industries—the more monopolized industries being the biggest exporters. This weakening of many of the relationships is also seen when all three control variables are included simultaneously. Here, as well as when monopoly alone is controlled for, the level of statistical significance of the relationships with the level of craft income is reduced to the .06 level, while that for the income of operatives is also reduced slightly. Nevertheless, a real relationship emerges even with all the controls. The more an industry exports to the Third World, the higher the level of wages for both operatives and craftworkers, although the degree of equality between operatives and craftworkers is greater in the export oriented industries. The first relationship is consistent with the labor aristocracy thesis, but the second would seem to be the opposite.

The relationship between exports to the Third World per worker and the two measures of income levels, and the ratio of craftworker to operative income was examined controlling for the percentage of the work force in unions and the time lost to strikes (see Table 2). When percentage of the labor force in unions is controlled for, all the relationships are *strengthened,* indicating that the positive relationship between export industries and material benefit are neither a spurious result of greater unionization in export industries nor the effect of exports operate *through* unions. When time lost to strikes is controlled for, the relations are diminished somewhat, suggesting that part of the relationship between export industries and income levels is either a spurious result of the greater militance of the workers in export-oriented industries, or perhaps greater militance in these industries gains workers a greater share of the profits of exporting. However, when time lost in strikes and percentage of the labor force in unions are *simultaneously* controlled for, the relationships between income levels and export industries are stronger than the zero order relationships, and when these two factors—together with the structural control variables (production workers per enterprise, degree of monopolization and capital per worker)—are all simultaneously controlled for, the correlations are almost as strong as they were without any controls. In summary, then, the relationship between exports to the Third World and income levels persists through all the controls. Industries oriented to

Table 2. The Effect of Exports to the Third World per Production Worker Controlling for Membership in Unions and Time Lost in Strikes Circa 1970 (Partial Correlation Co-efficients)

	Ratio of Craft to Operative Annual Income	Annual Income of Operatives	Annual Income of Craftworkers
Zero Order	−.48*	+.63**	+.54**
Controlling for:			
Percentage in Unions	−.51*	+.82**	+.74**
Time Lost to Strikes	−.31	+.44**	+.32
Both Percentage in Unions and Time Lost to Strikes	−.35	+.71**	+.62**
Percentage in Unions, Time Lost to Strikes, Degree of Monopolization, Capital per Worker, Workers per Enterprise Simultaneously	−.40	+.63*	+.50*

*Statistically significant at the .05 level.
**Statistically significant at the .01 level.
Sources: Same as Table 1.

exporting to the Third World have higher average incomes (both skilled workers and operatives) because of their export orientation, even though there is greater economic equality between skilled workers and operatives in such industries. This does not necessarily mean that *all*—or even a majority of craftworkers and operatives in industries, which on the average are more export-oriented than other industries—get higher wages because of exporting. The observed relations could, of course, merely reflect exceptionally high wages among the workers for the corporations or firms within the industries which are the most heavily involved in exporting (and those exceptionally high wages bring up the overall industrial average). Thus, one should be conservative in attempting to estimate the size of anything like an American "aristocracy of labor" from estimates based on studies such as this, which out of necessity use industrial rather than firm statistics.

We found no positive relationship between degree of imperial involvement and percentage in unions, and in the case of exports per worker even a slight negative relationship. This shows: (1) that the gain of workers in export-oriented industries does *not* appear to be secured through higher levels of unionization, contrary to what Lenin suggested; and (2) that workers in imperial-oriented industries do not appear to be disproportionately represented in the labor movement and thus are not in an especially advantageous position to dominate it for conservative ends (again, contrary to what Lenin suggested). There is thus no support for the aristocracy of labor thesis here, even in the case of export-oriented industries where production workers appear to gain economically.

In order to provide a baseline for the analysis of the aristocracy of labor theory,

Table 3.   The Effect of Imperial Involvements of Industries on Production
Workers' Income (1970) (Partial Correlation Co-efficients)

	Hourly wages of all production, non-supervisory workers
Repatriated Profits from Third World Direct Investments per Production Worker.	
Controlling for:	
Zero Order	+.43*
Workers per enterprise	+.52*
Degree of Monopolization	+.48*
Capital per Worker	−.35
All three simultaneously	−.30
Shipments to the Military as a Percentage of Total Shipments.	
Controlling for:	
Zero Order	+.17
Workers per enterprise	−.09
Degree of Monopolization	+.18
Capital per worker	+.31
All Three Simultaneously	+.01
Exports to the Third World per Production Worker:	
Controlling for:	
Zero Order:	+.49*
Workers per enterprise:	+.47*
Degree of Monopolization:	+.48*
Capital per Worker:	+.48*
All three simultaneously:	+.47*

*Statistically significant at the .05 level.
Sources: Same as Table 1 and (for hourly wages) *1979 Handbook of Labor Statistics* U.S. Department of
       Labor, Table 94.

we examined the relationship between three independent variables and the hourly
wages of *all* production, nonsupervisory workers. (See Table 3). The results are
strikingly similar to the relationships with the annual income of craft workers and
operatives when all controls are made. There is *no* statistically significant relationship between repatriated profits from the Third World when capital per
worker and all three control variables are held constant simultaneously, although
there *are* significant relationships for the zero order correlations and when workers per enterprise and degree of monopolization are controlled. There is *no*
significant relationship between shipments to the military and hourly wages
under any circumstances. There is, however, a significant relationship, in the
direction predicted by the aristocracy of labor thesis, between exports to the
Third World and hourly wages under *all* circumstances. These figures for *all*
production, non-supervisory workers suggest that not only do the "aristocracy"
among production workers fail to benefit from imperial involvements, but all
production workers fail to benefit, except in the heavily export-oriented industries.

POLITICAL ATTITUDES

There is very little relationship of any kind between our eight measures of political attitudes and income on direct investments from the Third World.

The indicators of vote for McGovern or self-defined political identity (liberal or conservative) show no significant difference from the mean for all production workers (as measured by the t-test for differences between proportions). Neither do workers' attitude of trust in business, their feelings that the government is not spending enough money on welfare, or too much on the military. Friendliness to China, belief that the Communist form of government is okay (or at least for some), and their feelings that a Communist has a right to speak are also not significantly correlated with income from foreign investments. While there is not significantly correlated with income from foreign investments. While there is

Table 4. The Relationship Between Income of Direct Investments in Third World Countries Per Production Worker and Political Attitudes (1975–1976)

	The Eight Industries with the Least Repatriated Profits Per Production Worker	The Eight Industries with the Greatest Repatriated Profits Per Production Worker	## The Three Industries with the Greatest Repatriated Profits Per Production Worke
Percent of Those with Opinions Who:			
Define themselves as liberals	50% (202)#	42% (170)	40% (65)
Supported McGovern in 1972	42% (381)	43% (267)	43% (95)
Do not trust business	22% (419)	24% (304)	24% (107)
Support greater welfare spending	18% (409)	20% (345)	22% (107)
Support reduction in military budget	28% (402)	25% (297)	21% (105)
Think that Communism might be all right at least for some countries	20% (222)	16% (164)	13% (61)
Are favorably inclined towards the People's Republic of China	40% (221)	34% (147)	31% (51)
Support the right of Communists to speak	45% (219)	51% (386)	56% (63)

*Statistically significant at the .05 level.
**Statistically significant at the .01 level.
#The numbers in parentheses are the number of cases on which the percentage is based.
##Petroleum, Mining, Food.
Source: National Opinion Research Center, *General Social Survey,* 1975 and 1976.

a slight (not statistically significant) tendency for workers in the three industries most involved in overseas investments to be less progressive in terms of self-definition as liberals, feelings that Communism might be all right at least for some, friendship towards China, and belief that the government ought to spend more on the military, they have somewhat more progressive (but not statistically significant) attitudes on support for the right of a Communist to speak publicly and to support greater welfare spending.

We see that an industry's involvement in overseas investments seems to have no effect on the political attitudes of its workers. Thus, not only do such workers fail to receive any special material benefits from such involvements, but the fact that their employers are involved overseas does not result in any higher than average identification with imperial activities (as seen by the measures of support for military spending, attitude about Communism and feelings toward China), nor does it seem to lead to any general conservatism.

When we examine the correlates of the percentage of an industry's production that goes to the U.S. military, we see no statistically significant results supportive of the aristocracy of labor thesis (see Table 5). While one political attitude is significantly related to the degree of military contracting, it is in the direction of the production workers being *more* progressive in the industries more involved in the armament industry. Thirty-one percent of the production workers in the three industries which are most involved in military production (aircraft, ordinance, electrical machinery) think that the government is not spending enough on welfare compared to 21 percent of those workers in the eight industries which are the least involved in military contracting.

Slightly fewer of the workers in the three industries most involved in military contracting define themselves as liberals, or support the right of a communist to speak or think too much money is being spent on the military. But slightly more than the average preferred McGovern over Nixon and were positive towards China. Thus, there was no pattern that would suggest that workers in war industries are more supportive of imperialism than others. While they are slightly more likely to support more military spending, they are no more hostile to Communism as a form of government, or to China than the mean of all production workers. And there certainly is no tendency whatsoever for workers in this sector to be more conservative than average because of any identification with their companies' stake in military contracts.

When the relationship between exports to the Third World per production worker and the eight political attitudes is examined, we see that in no case do the attitudes manifest a statistically significant difference (see Table 6), although slightly fewer of the workers in the three industries most involved in Third World exports support expanded federal welfare spending, and support the right of Communists to speak. An industry's involvement in exports to the Third World, while it does result in higher income for both operatives and craftsworkers, does *not* produce a greater identification with imperial policies. Workers in the indus-

Table 5. The Relationship Between Shipments to the Military as a Percentage of Total Shipments and Political Attitudes (1975–1976)

	The Eight Industries with Least Proportion of Shipments to the Military	The Eight Industries with the Greatest Proportion of Shipments to the Military	The Three Industries with the Greatest Proportion of Shipments to the Military ##
Percent of Those with Opinions Who:			
Define themselves as liberals	47% (240)#	43% (182)	40% (48)
Supported McGovern in 1972	45% (402)	41% (262)	48% (64)
Do not trust business	24% (445)	20% (298)	24% (76)
Support greater welfare spending	21% (438)	16% 340)	31% (80)**
Support reductions in military spending	26% (426)	28% (295)	21% (77)
Think that Communism might be all right at least for some countries	18% (236)	20% (159)	17% (35)
Are favorably inclined towards the People's Republic of China	38% (224)	44% (160)	50% (56)
Support the Right of Communists to Speak	52% (236)	40% (159)	35% (37)

*Statistically significant at the .05 level.
**Statistically significant at the .01 level.
#The numbers in parentheses are the number of cases on which the percentages are based.
##Ordinance, Aircraft, Electrical Machinery.
Source: Same as Table 3.

tries most involved in exporting were no more supportive of military spending than the average, nor were they any less likely to express a favorable attitude to China or towards Communist regimes than the average. Overall, there is no evidence that workers in export-oriented industries have any special identification with imperial policies or are more conservative than any other workers. Thus, even though this segment of the working class does benefit materially from exporting to the Third World countries, it is not a special source of either pro-imperialist or conservative sentiments within the working class.

When the industries that are most involved in imperialist-related activities overall are examined, we see only one of the eight political attitudes are correlated significantly with imperial involvement: 12 percent of the workers in the three most involved industries compared to 20 percent of the workers in the eight least involved industries supported expanded welfare payments. Slightly less than the average number of workers in the three most imperially involved indus-

Table 6. The Relationship Between Exports to Third World Countries
per Production Worker and Political Attitudes (1975–1976)

	The Eight Industries with the Least Exports to the Third World	The Eight Industries with the Most Exports to the Third World	The Three Industries with the Most Exports to the Third World
Percent of Those with Opinions who:			
Define themselves as liberals	49% (160)#	45% (233)	47% (111)
Supported McGovern in 1972	44% (288)	45% (329)	44% (165)
Do not trust business	23% (314)	23% (389)	22% (193)
Support greater welfare spending	20% (307)	20% (388)	15% (190)
Support reductions in military spending	28% (301)	25% (381)	28% (187)
Think that Communism might be all right at least for some countries	23% (162)	16% (202)	17% (106)
Are favorably inclined towards the People's Republic of China	37% (166)	43% (206)	38% (100)
Support the right of Communists to Speak	49% (160)	45% (204)	41% (104)

*Statistically significant at the .05 level.
*Statistically significant at the .01 level.
#The numbers in parentheses are the number of cases on which the percentages are based.
##Non-Electrical Machinery, Aircraft, Motor Vehicles.
Source: Same as Table 3.

trial sectors supported McGovern and thought that Communist regimes might be all right in some cases.

There is no difference between the workers in the most imperially involved industries and others in respect to their attitude about military spending, or China (see Table 7). There is then no tendency for workers in the most imperially involved industries to be more supportive of imperialism than others. Nor is there any substantial tendency for these workers to be any more conservative overall than others. Such workers are thus *not* a special source of either pro imperialist or conservative ideology within the working class.

We have not tried to examine the sources of variation in opinion regarding political and military questions. If one's immediate economic position vis-a-vis imperial activity does not significantly effect such attitudes, what does? Alternative explanations for such opinions focus on how social learning—years of schooling, political party identification, trade union membership, and similar factors—

Table 7.   The Relationship Between Aggregate Involvement in Imperial Activities
in the Third World and Political Attitudes (1975–1976)

	The Eight Industries with the Least Imperial Involvement in the Third World	*The Eight Industries with the Greatest Imperial Involvements*	*The Three Industries with the Greatest Imperial Involvements##*
Percentage of Those with Opinions who:			
Define themselves as liberals	48% (202)#	43% (205)	48% (79)
Supported McGovern in 1972	42% (349)	43% (291)	37% (119)
Do not trust business	21% (382)	22% (336)	21% (136)
Support greater welfare spending	20% (372)	20% (378)	12% (134)**
Support reductions in military spending	28% (365)	26% (332)	28% (133)
Think that Communism might be all right for at least some countries	20% (196)	18% (178)	16% (79)
Are favorably inclined towards the People's Republic of China	39% (200)	43% (180)	37% (68)
Support the right of Communists to Speak	47% (194)	42% (178)	44% (78)

*Statistically significant at the .05 level.
**Statistically significant at the .01 level.
#The numbers in parentheses are the number of cases on which the percentages are based.
##Aircraft, Ordinance, Non-Electrical Machinery.
Source: Same as Table 3.

help shape the political outlooks of working class Americans (Kriesberg and
Klein, 1980; Hamilton, 1975).

SUMMARY AND CONCLUSIONS

We found that there is no tendency for the workers (whether operatives or
craftsworkers) in those industries which are the primary military contractors or in
those industries which are the most involved in overseas investments to gain
materially because of their industry's overseas involvement. We did find that the
workers, especially the operatives in those industries which export the most to
the Third World, *did* gain materially because of such exports. When we examined the relation between war industries, investments in the Third World, exports
to the Third World, and overall involvement in imperial activities, we found no
tendency for either the workers in these industries to be more supportive of
imperialism than the average for production workers, or for them to be consis-

tently more conservative than the average for workers. There are just as many cases of such workers being more progressive. In general, we found very little relation one way or the other between the imperial involvements of an industrial sector and political attitudes.

In conclusion, we can find little evidence in support of Lenin's theory of the aristocracy of labor in the contemporary U.S. working class. The only finding in support of this thesis is that workers in export-oriented industries benefit from exporting to the Third World, although the craftworkers (as Lenin suggests they should) do *not* benefit disproportionately and unions (again as Lenin suggests) are *not* expecially strong. No other measures of imperial involvement produces a material gain for either all the production workers or just craftworkers. Thus, the first part of the aristocracy of labor thesis, the existence of a material gain, is only partially supported. The weight of the evidence, however, is against this hypothesis. The second part of the aristocracy of labor thesis, the idea that because some workers gain materially because of a trickle-down effect from imperial activities, they are both more supportive of imperialist policies and generally a fount of conservative ideas within the working class, is consistently *not* supported. There is no evidence whatsoever that the workers, whether they gain materially or do not gain materially because of their corporation's involvements in overseas imperial activities, are any more pro-imperialist or conservative than the average or that they are in an advantageous position to dominate the labor movement. Thus, the theory of the aristocracy of labor must be rejected.

The policy implications of this research bear further research as well as testing in the political arena. While workers in industries with high imperial involvement do not seem to develop more jingoistic, militaristic, or conservative attitudes, there is nevertheless an *overall* high level of support for U.S. military spending and overseas investment among the American working class. This must be explained by larger political and cultural factors beyond industry-specific patterns. In particular, the role of political leaders, business pressure groups, the mass media, and labor officials in fostering an ideological climate favorable to defense spending and imperial economic activity, must be examined. Despite our finding that there is little *material* basis for this support, the political and cultural hegemony of the business class has been able to offset any countervailing learning process among the working class.

On the other hand, the past several years has witnessed some significant cracks in this ideological consensus. A number of major labor union leaders and their political allies have recognized the long-term negative impact of "runaway shops" to Third World nations in terms of overall job loss and have called for legislative efforts to restrict plant closings and tax breaks for overseas investment. They have also taken strong stands to "transfer" funds from the military budget toward more labor-intensive social programs in health care, mass transit, and other areas. While neither of these initiatives have so far met with much success, they perhaps represent the initial stirrings of a wider recognition that the long-term interests of American working people do not coincide with the imperial objectives of the capitalist class.

ACKNOWLEDGMENTS

The authors wish to thank the following people for their helpful comments on an earlier draft of this paper. Chris Chase-Dunn, Richard Hamilton, Paul Joseph, Louis Kriesberg, Rosemary Taylor, Maurice Zeitlin, Sam Friedman and Jim Robbins.

NOTES

1. A brief updating of the data in Szymanski's 1972 article follows. In 1975–76, net income on U.S. Investment in the Third World was $2.2 billion, net gain from trade with the Third World because of unequal trade relations was roughly $19.1 billion, and the costs of the military above the legitimate costs of defense was $96.8 billion. The net loss per employee in the U.S. can thus be estimated at about $600 a year, or approximately five percent of employee compensation. See Szymanski (1972) for an explanation of the calculations.

2. These authors argue that the larger the size of a factory, the more class homogenous a community, and the more isolated workers are both on the job and in their living situation from cross-class pressures, the more likely they are to develop a distinctively working class subculture and hence the more likely they are to form militant unions and develop a radical working class political consciousness.

3. The wording of the NORC questions are as follows:

1975, #31; 1976, #30: We hear a lot of talk these days about liberals and conservatives. I'm going to show you a seven-point scale on which the political views that people might hold are arranged from extremely liberal to extremely conservative. Where would you place yourself on this scale? (We recoded the percent liberal as a percent specifying extremely liberal, liberal, or slightly liberal).

1975, #80; 1976, #59: We are faced with many problems in this country, none of which can be solved easily or inexpensively. I'm going to name some of these problems, and for each one I'd like you to tell me whether you think we're spending too much money on it, too little money, or about the right amount.

   I. The military, armaments and defense (percent specfying too much)

   K. Welfare (percept specifying too little)

1976, #63: Thinking about all the different kinds of governments in the world today, which of these statements comes closest to how you feel about Communism as a form of government? (We recoded percept that think Communism might be all right for at least some countries as the percent specifying "Its all right for some countries" and "Its a good form of government.")

1976, #66: Now, I should like to ask you some questions about a man who admits he is a Communist. Suppose this admitted Communist wanted to make a speech in your community. Should he be allowed to speak, or not? (Percent saying "Yes, allowed to speak.")

1975, #77B; 1976, #74B: I am going to name some institutions in this country. As far as the people running these institutions are concerned, would you say you have a great deal of confidence, only some confidence, or hardly any confidence at all in them? Major companies: (percent saying "heardly any.")

1975, #81: You will notice that the boxes on this card go from the highest position of "plus 5" to a country which you *like* very much to the lowest position of "minus 5" for a country you *dislike* very much. How far up the scale or how far down the would you rate the following countries?

   F. China (percent answering with a positive response between 1 and 5 inclusive).

REFERENCES

Allen, Robert (1970) *Black Awakening in Capitalist America*. Garden City, N.Y.: Anchor Double-day.

Amin, Samir (1974) *Accumulation on a World Scale,* Volumes I and II. New York: Monthly Review Press.

Aronowitz, Stanley (1973) *False Promises*. New York: McGraw-Hill.

Baran, Paul (1957) *The Political Economy of Growth*. New York: Monthly Review Press.

Baran, Paul and Paul Sweezy (1966) *Monopoly Capital*. New York: Monthly Review Press.

Bell, Daniel (1973) *The Coming of Post-Industrial Society*. New York: Basic Books.

Boggs, James (1970) *Racism and Class Struggle*. New York: Monthly Review Press.

Dreier, Peter (1976) ''The Politics of Peace Conversion.'' Paper presented at the meetings of the Society for the Study of Social Problems.

Emmanuel, Arghiri (1972) *The Political Economy of Growth*. New York: Monthly Review Press.

Engels, Friedrich (1968) *The Condition of the Working Class in England*. Stanford, Calif.: Stanford University Press.

Evansohn, John (1977) ''Workers and Imperialism: Where is the Aristocracy of Labor?'' *Insurgent Sociologist* 7:54-63.

Flacks, Richard (1971) *Youth and Social Change*. Chicago, Ill.: Markham.

Foster, John (1974) *Class Struggle and the Industrial Revolution*. London: Weidenfeld and Nicholson.

Galloway, Jonathan F. (1973) ''Multinational Corporations and Military-Industrial Linkages.'' Pages 267-290 in Steven Rosen (ed) *Testing the Theory of the Military-Industrial Complex*. Lexington: D.C. Heath and Company.

Gintis, Herbert (1970) ''The New Working Class and Revolutionary Youth.'' *Socialist Revolution* 1:13-44.

Goldthorpe, John H., David Lockwood, Frank Bechhofer and Jennifer Platt (1969) *The Affluent Worker in the Class Structure*. Cambridge, Mass.: Cambridge University Press.

Gorz, Andre (1967) *A Strategy for Labor*. Boston, Mass.: Beacon Press.

Habermas, Jurgen (1970) *Toward a Rational Society*. Boston, Mass.: Beacon Press.

Hamilton, Richard F. (1975) *Restraining Myths*. Beverly Hills, Calif.: Sage Publications.

Handlin, Oscar (1951) *The Uprooted*. Boston, Mass.: Beacon Press.

Hobsbawm, Eric J. (1974) ''The Labor Aristocracy of Nineteenth-Century Britain.'' Pages 138-176 in P. Stearns and D. Walkowitz (eds.), *Workers in the Industrial Revolution*. New Brunswick: Transaction Inc.

Hoggart, Richard (1957) *The Uses of Literacy*. New York: Oxford University Press.

Jones, Gareth Stedman (1970) ''Class Struggle and the Industrial Revolution.'' *New Left Review* 90:35-69.

Kerr, Clark and Abraham Siegel (1954) ''Inter-Industry Propensity to Strike.'' In Robert Dubin, Arthur Kornhauser and Arthur Ross (eds.) *Industrial Conflict*. New York: McGraw-Hill.

Kriesberg, Louis and Ross Klein (1980) ''Changes in Public Support for U.S. Military Spending.'' *Journal of Conflict Resolution* 24:79-110.

Leslett, John H. M. and Seymour M. Lipset (eds.) (1974) *Failure of a Dream?* Garden City, N.Y.: Anchor Doubleday.

Lenin, V. I. (1939) *Imperialism: The Highest Stage of Capitalism*. New York: International Publishers.

Lieberson, Stanley (1971) ''An Empirical Study of Military Industrial Linkages.'' *American Journal of Sociology* 76:562-584.

Lipset, Seymour M. (1964) *The First New Nation*. Garden City, N.Y.: Anchor Doubleday.

Lipset, Seymour M. (1960) *Political Man*. Garden City, N.Y.: Doubleday.

Mann, Michael (1973) *Consciousness and Action Among the Western Working Class*. London: MacMillan.

Marcuse, Herbert (1964) *One Dimensional Man*. Boston, Mass.: Beacon Press.
Marx, Karl and Friedrich Engels (1956) *Selected Correspondence*. Moscow: Foreign Languages
    Publishing House.
Melman, Seymour (1965) *Our Depleted Society*. New York: Dell.
Melman, Seymour (1974) *The Permanent War Economy*. New York: Simon and Schuster.
Mitchell, Juliet (1971) *Women's Estate*. London: Penguin.
Nicholaus, Martin (1970) "The Theory of the Labor Aristocracy." *Monthly Review* 21:90-21.
Parkin, Frank (1971) *Class Inequality and Political Order*. New York: Praeger.
Patcher, Martin (1970) "Social Class and Dimensions of Foreign Policy Attitudes." *Social Science
    Quarterly* 51:649-674.
Pelling, Henry (1968) *Popular Politics and Society in Late Victorian Britain*. New York: St. Martin's
    Press.
Reich, Michael (1973) "Military Spending and the U.S. Economy." Pages 85-102 in Steven Rosen
    (ed.), *Testing the Theory of the Military-Industrial Complex*. Lexington: D.C. Heath and
    Company.
Rineheart, James W. (1971) "Affluence and the Embourgeoisement of the Working Class: A Critical
    Look." *Social Problems* 19:150-162.
Rowntree, Michey and John Rowntree (1968) "Youth as a Class." *Our Generation* 6:155-190.
Sombart, Werner (1906) *Why is There No Socialism in the United States?* Tubingen, Germany:
    J.C.V. Mohr.
Syzmanski, Albert (1973) "American Imperialism and the U.S. People." *Social Praxis* 1:81-91.
Thernstrom, Stephan (1964) *Poverty and Progress*. Cambridge, Mass.: Harvard University Press.
Wallerstein, Immanuel (1974) "The Rise and Future Demise of the World Capitalist System."
    Comparative Studies in Society and History 16:387-417.
Wright, James D. (1972) "The Working Class, Authoritarianism and the War in Vietnam." *Social
    Problems* 20:133-149.

MULTINATIONAL CORPORATE EXPANSION AND NATION-STATE DEVELOPMENT:

A GLOBAL PERSPECTIVE

Richard G. Braungart and Margaret M. Braungart

ABSTRACT

This study examines the relationship between multinational corporate expansion and nation-state development. Measures of US-based and non-US-based multinational corporate growth and national development are chosen from two independent reference sources and merged into a global data set of 133 countries. Findings indicate that both US-based and non-US-based subsidiaries are likely to be located in the more developed or core nation-states around the world, and less likely to invest in the developing or peripheral regions. The results of stepwise regression analysis reveal that seven indicators of nation-state development explain 51 percent of the variance for US-based foreign investment, and 16 percent of the variance in non-US-based corporate expansion. Significant variables related to US-based penetration are gross national product and communications. Important predictors of non-US-based corporate growth include year of independence, gross national product, literacy, and defense rank. In general, national development indicators are more closely related to multinational corporate expansion into core areas than in peripheral regions of the world.

Research in Social Movements, Conflicts and Change, Vol. 3, pages 169-186
Copyright © 1980 by JAI Press Inc.
All rights of reproduction in any form reserved.
ISBN: 0-89232-182-2

Two parallel developments are influencing the global order: the growth of multi-national corporations and the proliferation of nation-states. Working under different sets of values and goals, the struggles and tensions created by these two historical movements are transforming the world of the future. Innovations in technology and management allow organizations such as corporations to operate on an international scale. At the same time, ideological and political developments make it difficult to expand or exercise political authority beyond national borders.

Much of the previous research offers descriptive and discursive explanations of how multinational corporations interact with nation-states (Gilpin, 1975, 1976; Hopkins-Paul, 1975; Kimmel, 1975–1976; U.S. Senate Committee on Finance, 1973; U.S. Senate Committee on Foreign Relations, 1974; Wilkins, 1970, 1974). Although these works made an important contribution, there is a growing body of literature that provides the basis for more systematic understanding of the topic (see Rubinson, 1976; and the 16 studies summarized in Bornschier, et al., 1978). Our task is to continue in this direction by examining the patterns and structures of these two global forces and how they affect each other. The present study has two objectives: first, to determine which indicators of national development are most closely related to the establishment of foreign subsidiaries by multinational corporations; and second, to assess whether national indicators are differentially associated with multinational corporate investment into core versus peripheral areas. Multinational corporations and nation-states are defined and described, followed by a discussion and empirical test of their influence on one another.

MULTINATIONAL CORPORATE EXPANSION AND NATION-STATE DEVELOPMENT

A firm is considered multinational if its principal operating facilities are located in two or more countries (Modelski, 1972). Multinational corporations are also defined as companies that attempt to carry out their activities on an international scale, on the basis of a common strategy directed from a corporate center (Vernon, 1971). The unprecedented growth of multinational enterprises occurred after World War II when the United States established the political, military, and economic framework for capitalist world order. Under these post-war conditions, multinational corporations spread quickly throughout the industrialized nation-states. Today, most multinational corporate businesses originate in four countries: the United States (US), United Kingdom (UK), West Germany, and Japan. Of the 300 giant multinational corporations that dominate the world economy, two thirds are American-based. The increasing concentration of power into fewer private hands is documented by the United States Trade Commission (Segal, 1973). Between 1960–1968, the top 200 US corporations organized with other corporations to establish over 700 jointly-owned subsidiaries. In 1967, US-based firms accounted for 55 percent of all foreign direct investment, surpassing that of the second highest investor UK at 16.2 percent, followed by home countries whose direct foreign investment was rising rapidly—West Germany at 2.8 percent and Japan at 1.3 percent (Bergsten, et al., 1978:15). By 1969, US multinational corporations placed two-thirds to three-fourths of the book value of foreign direct investment in developed nation-states and the balance in developing countries (Solomon, 1978). Von Krosigk (1972) argues, if present trends continue, by the year 1990 over 60 percent of the non-communist world's gross national product will be owned, controlled, and financed by US-based companies. Multinational corporations do not merely establish retail outlets in foreign countries; they are increasingly involved in operating their own factories, setting up subsidiaries, and buying out local competition.

The resources of multinational corporations are extensive. Their total sales exceed the gross national product of every country in the world, with the exception of the US and Soviet Union (Barnet and Mueller, 1974; Barnet et al., 1974). With economic power comes political power, and many large multinational corporations possess more influence than do most sovereign states. These giant businesses have the ability to affect people's values, aspirations, life styles, their work and consumer habits, leisure, tastes, and what knowledge schools will encourage (Kumar, 1979). It has even been suggested that multinational corporations may someday replace nation-states as the primary socio-political unit around the world (Ball, 1975; Modelski, 1972).

The growth of nation-states, or nationalism, is another major historical movement directly influencing the world order. Dating back to the 17th century, the nation-state has emerged as the dominant form of political organization and power. Since the turn of the 20th century, nationalism and the rise of new nations has become one of the prime movers of international politics. Nationalism represents a sense of common destiny, goals, and responsibilities for citizens of a nation. The rapid growth of nation-states occurred after World War II, when membership in the United Nations grew from 50 states in 1945 to 149 member states today. With the decline of European power and fading colonialism, nationalist movements have increased, especially throughout Asia and Africa.

The development of nation-states is determined by a number of factors, one of which is growing popular political and economic awareness. More than ever before, people around the world see their personal futures linked to a new sense of national identity, particularly among the recently established Third World nations. Urbanization is another factor that affects nation-state development, as large numbers of people concentrate in cities in search of higher standards of living. In the more advanced countries, urban centers exhibit an advanced division of labor with greater economic and political specialization. A third trend is toward increased levels of literacy, with even the poorest countries making noticeable strides in this area, and as populations become more literate, they place greater demands on their political leaders. One of the most significant forces in the development of nation-states is the political drive for economic independence, income stability, and mass consumption. Accompanying this desire for economic power is the concern with national communications development and increased military expenditures, both of which demonstrate the ability of nation-states to control and defend national territory (Dowse and Hughes, 1972; Lipset and Schneider, 1973; Orum, 1978).

The accelerating development of multinational corporations and nation-states since world War II has resulted in what Vernon (1977) terms a "shrinkage of international space." Operating under different sets of values and principles, tensions are created by these two global actors as they pursue their own goals. Critics of multinational corporations depict these giant enterprises as conspiratorial organizations, whose major concern is with profit and their own well-being. Remaining aloof and unresponsive to the interests of the nation-states in which they establish subsidiaries, multinational corporations threaten the autonomy of host countries, and force them into a state of "dependency" (Amin, 1974; Frank, 1969; Hopkins-Paul and Martin, 1975). The defenders of multinational corprations view the new global enterprises as loose affiliations of interacting units, rather than as unified and conspiratorial. Supporters see multinational corporations as part of an international trend toward increasing efficiency, technology, and interdependence (Ball, 1975; Maisonrouge, 1974). According to Vernon (1977), these polemic caricatures, while appealing in their simplicity, fail to shed light on the precise nature of the relationship between multinational corporations and nation-states. Given the paucity of empirical information, it is difficult to generalize about this global problem. The evidence that is available indicates there is a complex association between these two forces.

A GLOBAL PERSPECTIVE

The world stratification system that results in part from the relationship between multinational corporations and nation-states takes two forms. The first represents a global division of labor with clearly identifiable core and peripheral regions (Chirot, 1977; Wallerstein, 1974). Empirical evidence suggests that multinational corporate penetration varies along lines of national development. Within metropol or core areas, national development correlates strongly with multinational corporate growth—to a much greater degree than in peripheral areas. That is to say, parent corporations are more likely to invest in and locate subsidiaries in older established, more socially advanced, and wealthier nation-states than in the younger, less developed, and poorer countries around the world.

The second characteristic of global stratification concerns the pattern of economic exchanges within and between core and peripheral areas (Morse, 1972;

Gilpin, 1975). A high incidence of interdependent or symmetric exchanges exists among the core states, with parent corporate enterprises more likely to locate subsidiaries within other advanced nation-states rather than in less developed regions. A good example of the symmetric linkages of multinational corporations within select nation-states and geographic regions was demonstrated when comparing the total number of manufacturing subsidiaries entered into by parent systems. Data collected during 1965–1967 identified two distinct world cores: the first consisted of the US-UK-European core; the second a US-Japanese core. A greater number of reciprocal or two-way manufacturing investments occurred within these two core regions than was evident outside these areas (Braungart and Braungart, 1979). On the other hand, core relations with peripheral areas were characterized as one-way or asymmetric; that is, while corporations from core nations established subsidiaries in peripheral nations, the latter did not have the capacity (technology, capital, organization) to invest in core regions. Regarding multinational corporate manufacturing subsidiaries, the US-UK-European core penetrated all areas of the Western world, while Japanese subsidiaries were located mainly in Asia and Oceania (Braungart and Braungart, 1979).

Although previous research was able to identify and differentiate global core and peripheral areas, much is still unknown about the exact form or structure of this relationship. Select social, political, and economic indicators of national development correlate strongly with multinational corporate growth in core states. The US, UK, West Germany, and Japan comprise the major core countries throughout the Western world. Within each of these countries, modalities of multinational corporate strength vary positively with indicators of national political development. These core countries represent older political regimes, highly urbanized, literate populations, wealthy economies, and control most of the world's corporate business (Braungart and Braungart, 1979).

Multinational corporate penetration is motivated by a number of factors, including the quest for greater profits and corporate efficiency, fear of foreign competition, lower labor and production costs, and the need to diversify product lines in order to avoid fluctuations in earnings (U.S. Senate Committee on Finance, 1973). Of course, underlying these corporate motives is the search for stable and secure environments in which to operate. Friendly nation-states with large literate and urban populations and having steady growth in their gross national product provide ideal investment opportunities. While previous research had identified correlates of political and economic development, the problem that remains unresolved at the present time is which nation-state indicators best predict or exert the strongest independent effect on where multinational corporations locate their foreign subsidiaries? Since two-thirds of the multinational subsidiaries around the world are US-based, this question needs to be examined to see whether the patterns of multinational corporate expansion for US firms differ from non-US firms. Previous studies demonstrated that parent multinational enterprises were more likely to establish foreign subsidiaries in advanced or core areas, even though the profits are higher in peripheral regions (see Chirot, 1977:153). For example, the interpenetration of multinational manufacturing corporations within core states is indicated by the fact that from one-half to three-fourths of the United States, United Kingdom, and European-based subsidiaries were located in the areas of North America and Europe—forming an unprecedented network of reciprocal corporate linkages (Braungart and Braungart, 1979). It has yet to be determined whether penetration patterns for US-based enterprises differ significantly from the non-US firms. Another unanswered question is whether the national development characteristics associated with multinational corporate penetration into core areas differ from those related to corporate investment into peripheral regions?

This study addresses these questions in order to gain a greater understanding of the relative impact of a set of national indicators on the establishment of multinational corporate subsidiaries throught the world. Specifically, the results are intended to give a more precise assessment of: (1) how closely national development is associated with the multinational corporate expansion of US-based and non-US-based firms; and (2) whether the relationship between national development and the establishment of multinational corporate subsidiaries is different for core versus peripheral areas.

METHODS OF RESEARCH

Information concerning multinational corporations was obtained from Vaupel and Curhan's *The World's Multinational Enterprises* (1973), while the data for national development were taken from Taylor and Hudson's (1972) *World Handbook of Political and Social Indicators*. Data on the subsidiaries of multinational corporations were gathered from public records by the Harvard Business School, which began the project in 1965, and represents information on more than 28,000 foreign subsidiaries of the world's largest enterprises.[1] For purposes of comparison, data were collected on US and non-US firms through 1967, or the "world subset of data," which includes the subsidiaries of 133 US-based and 128 non-US-based enterprises (Vaupel & Curhan, 1969, 1973).[2] The *World Handbook* provided a compendium of political, social, economic, and cultural indicators from 136 nations for use in cross-national analyses. Included were nations with a population of one million or more in 1965 and nations that were members of the United Nations in June, 1968 (Taylor & Hudson, 1972). Variables measuring multinational corporate growth and national development were selected from the two reference sources and merged into a single data set, using the nation-state as the unit of analysis. The result is a global "working" sample of 133 countries.

The variables that represent multinational corporate penetration include the percentage of US-based and non-US-based manufacturing and sales subsidiaries established in foreign nations. US-based subsidiaries are measured by the percentage of the total number of foreign subsisidaries of American enterprises located in a host country. Non-US-based subsidiaries are operationalized as the percentage of the total number of non-American foreign subsidiaries located in a host country.

Direct foreign investment occurs mainly in industries characterized by certain market structures in both the home and host countries. Corporations make horizontal investments to produce abroad the same kinds of goods they produce for the home market. Many multinational corporations are in high technology industries heavily involved in manufacturing, research, and development. As a result, they tend to establish foreign subsidiaries in areas of least social and political resistance, characterized by favorable markets and congenial values. Since home countries are among the most highly developed capitalist countries in the world—with urbanized, literate, technologically sophisticated, politically stable, and wealthier economies—it makes sense that multinational corporations will invest in host countries with similar structural features as their own. The issue raised here is which of these structural characteristics are the most significant predictors of multinational corporate growth? While multinational corporations gravitate toward developed nation-states in establishing foreign subsidiaries, they also invest in less developed regions of the world. It is assumed that the same political, social, and economic conditions associated with investment in core areas will also influence multinational corporate investment in peripheral nation-states.

Nation-state development is based on the capacity of a political regime to respond to a wide range of legal, historic, social, and economic problems. Measures of national development used in this study involve political structure and performance, social patterns, and national resources. For example, age of institutions and budget allocation for defense are important indicators of national political structure and performance. The longevity of a political system and its legal foundations have long been considered to have important bearing on a nation's stability and order. The longevity of a political system is measured by the year a nation gained independence from an occupying or colonial power, while its legal foundation is determined by the year in which a nation's current constitution was put into effect. Nations defend their boundaries against internal and external threats by allocating a certain proportion of their gross national product to defense expenditures. National defense is measured by the rank order (from low to high) of the percentage of national resources devoted to defense.

Social patterns of nation-states influence the operation of a political system. One of the most significant dimensions of national development is urbanization, which involves the movement of people from isolated rural areas into cities. Since urban dwellers are easily exposed to new ideas, urbanization breaks down old ties to make way for new ones, thus facilitating the politicization process. Urbanization is operationalized as the percentage of a nation's population living in cities of 100,000 or more in 1960. Literacy is also related to development and concerns the extent to which a population has been formally educated. In an important way, literacy reflects the potential of a nation-state to utilize new skills as a force for social and political change. Literacy is represented by a score (ranging from 1–100) which indicates the percentage of a national population 15 years of age and older able to read and write.

Another social characteristic of national development is reflected in the level of media technology. Communications, like the other social factors, serve as agents for social change. The ability to spread information quickly encourages higher aspirations, a desire for better life, and increases pressure on governments to be more responsive to their citizenry. Cutright (1963) was among the first to demonstrate that communications development was closely associated with political development, while more recently Vernon (1977) cited advancements in communications as facilitating the growth of multinational corporations. A key aspect of communications development is the technical means available for transmitting personal or business messages by telephone. For our research, communication is measured by the number of public and private telephone installations connected to a central exchange per 1,000 population.[3]

Economic resources are important components of a nation's development, since they play a crucial role in determining national goals and their means of achievement. The measure most often used to indicate overall wealth and productivity of a nation is Gross National Product (GNP). This indicator of development is operationalized as GNP per capita converted into US dollars. For a detailed discussion of the coding, reporting, and accuracy of the measures used in the analysis, see Taylor & Hudson (1972), and Vaupel & Curhan (1969, 1973).

This investigation into the global relationship between national development and multinational corporate growth is a continuation of an earlier study undertaken by the present authors (see Braungart, 1978; Braungart & Braungart, 1979). In previous research, zero-order correlational analysis indicated a simple association between national political development and the establishment of multinational corporate subsidiaries. The national indicators of year of independence, literacy, and GNP were each related to US and non-US multinational corporate growth. The task now is to determine which of the national development indicators are most closely associated with multinational corporate expansion in a predictive and cumulative sense. This objective necessities a multivariate framework controlling several factors simultaneously in order to identify the most significant national indicators of multinational corporate growth.

Stepwise regression analysis is used to determine which of the national political indicators represent the strongest predictors of multinational corporate growth. In employing this statistical method, national indicators are entered one at a time into the regression equation to determine the particular variable or set of predictor variables that best explains variation in US and non-US multinational corporate penetration (Blalock, 1972; Nie, et al., 1975). Since the national indicators are measured in different units (dollars, scores, per capita, rank), beta coefficients rather than regression coefficients are compared for their explanatory power. Stepwise regression also provides an estimate of total explained variance for the set of national indicators (R^2), along with the incremental change in R^2 with the addition of each variable into the analysis.

In order to test the relationship between national development and multinational corporate growth by US and non-US-based firms, and for core and peripheral areas, the following procedures are employed. First, the zero-order correlation matrix for all the variables in the study is presented for the purpose of determining: (1) the simple association between each indicator of national development and multinational corporate expansion; (2) the extent of intercorrelation among the national development indicators; and (3) a basis for comparison with stepwise results. Second, stepwise regression is performed to determine the strongest national predictors of US and non-US multinational corporate growth, as well as assessing how well the national development indicators in the study can account for variance in the expansion of corporate subsidiaries throughout the world. Third, data are subdivided into those advanced nations having multinational corporate parent enterprises and those nation-states without parent firms.[4] Differences in national development between these two groups are demonstrated by comparing t-test scores and stepwise regression coefficients.

FINDINGS

Table 1 identifies the zero-order correlations between national development and multinational corporate expansion for the world at large. The pattern of relationships suggests three generalizations. First, both US and non-US corporate subsidiaries are likely to be located in nation-states that are older, with more advanced social, economic, and communications development; while rank on defense expenditure does not appear to be related to either US or non-US multinational corporate expansion. Second, these associations (coefficients) are generally stronger for US-based enterprises than non-US-based firms. Third, the strong intercorrelations among the national development indicators make it difficult to establish any clear pattern for their association with US and non-US multinational corporate growth.

In order to address the shortcomings of zero-order correlation analysis, a multivariate analysis is performed using stepwise regression to specify the predictive relationships between national development and multinational corporate expansion. The results of the analysis for US-based and non-US-based enterprises around the world can be seen in Table 2. The set of seven national indicators selected for this study accounts for 51 percent of the total variance in

Table 1. Zero-Order Correlation Matrix for Nation–State Development and Multinational Corporate Growth

		YI	YC	DF	UR	LIT	COM	GNP	USS
YI:	Year Independence								
YC:	Year Constitution	.420**							
DF:	Defense Rank	−.065	−.093						
UR:	Urbanization	−.110	−.230*	.107					
LIT:	Literacy	−.415**	−.413**	.134	.549**				
COM:	Communications	−.303**	−.516**	.103	.436**	.502**			
GNP:	Gross Nat. Product	−.316**	−.368**	.222*	.190	.254**	.370**		
USS:	US subsidiaries	−.408**	−.505**	.194	.199*	.384**	.589**	.510**	
NUS:	Non-US Subsidiaries	−.283**	−.142	−.042	.166	.249*	.280**	.220*	.196*

*significant at .05.
**significant at .01.

Table 2. Stepwise Regression Summary Table for the Relationship Between Nation–State Development and US and Non-US Multinational Corporate Growth

Variable Ranking	R	R^2	R^2 Change	Beta
Nation–State Development and US Multinational Corporate Growth				
GNP	.589	.347	.347	.384
Communications	.668	.456	.099	.227
Year Constitution	.695	.482	.037	−.176
Year Independence	.705	.497	.015	−.111
Defense Rank	.708	.501	.003	.058
Literacy	.709	.502	.002	.091
Urbanization	.712	.507	.004	−.082
Nation–State Development and Non-US Multinational Corporate Growth				
Year Independence	.283	.080	.080	−.191
GNP	.347	.120	.041	.222
Literacy	.366	.134	.014	.111
Defense Rank	.385	.148	.014	−.121
Year Constitution	.390	.152	.004	.100
Communications	.394	.156	.004	.067
Urbanization	.397	.157	.002	.049

US multinational corporate penetration ($R^2 = .507$). When all other indicators are held constant, GNP emerges as the strongest predictor (beta = .384) of US multinational corporate investment, followed by level of communications development (beta = .227). In fact, these two indicators together account for the majority of explained variance in US multinational corporate expansion (46 percent). US multinational corporate growth is most pronounced in nations that are economically powerful and contain advanced levels of technical communications.

With regard to the establishment of non-US-based subsidiaries, substantially less variance (16 percent) can be attributed to the set of indicators measuring national development in this study ($R^2 = .157$). The development factors ranked highest, in a relative sense, predicting non-US penetration are: year of independence (beta = $-.191$), GNP (beta = .222), literacy (beta = .111), and defense rank (beta = $-.121$). While both US and non-US-based enterprises are likely to establish subsidiaries in older, more stable nations with high GNPs, the social factor of urbanization is not related to either US or non-US corporate expansion.

Table 3. Means, Standard Deviations, and T-Tests for Differences in Nation–State Development Between Core and Peripheral Areas

	Mean	*Standard Deviation*	*N*	*T-Test*
Year Independence				
Core	1815.8	62.1	14	−4.87***
Peripheral	1907.5	67.0	117	
Year Constitution				
Core	1881.4	61.5	14	−7.70***
Peripheral	1949.9	29.7	117	
Defense Rank				
Core	74.5	25.9	14	1.73
Peripheral	60.6	35.9	107	
Urbanization				
Core	38.3	17.5	13	2.63**
Peripheral	20.3	23.8	96	
Literacy				
Core	92.4	22.9	14	4.61***
Peripheral	50.0	33.3	116	
Communications				
Core	230.1	139.5	14	7.44***
Peripheral	36.4	84.0	108	
GNP				
Core	91814.1	177909.6	14	4.81***
Peripheral	7212.8	29662.7	121	

**significant at .01.
***significant at .001.

One important change can be observed from the zero-order correlations, in that defense rank gains in its ability to explain variance in US and non-US multinational corporate growth when other national indicators are held constant.

It has been suggested that the penetration of multinational corporate subsidiaries differs in developed versus less developed countries (Vernon, 1977). In order to test this assumption, data are first divided into core nations (those nations containing multinational corporate centers) and newly developed or peripheral countries (those nations without multinational corporate enterprises originating within their boundaries). As seen in Table 3, the t-tests for the difference between means for these two groupings indicate that core nation-states differ substantially from peripheral nations. Not only are the core nations older and more highly developed than peripheral states, they are also more homogeneous, as indicated by their smaller standard deviations for year of independence, defense expenditure, urbanization, and literacy. While there is clear evidence differentiating a global core and periphery in our research, we do not know whether the pattern for US versus non-US multinational corporate growth is similar or different within each area.

To determine whether different national indicators are associated with US and non-US penetration into core and peripheral nations, stepwise regression is employed. The results can be seen in Tables 4 and 5. According to Table 4,

Table 4. Stepwise Regression Summary Table for the Relationship Between Nation-State Development and US Multinational Corporate Growth in Core and Peripheral Areas.

Variable Ranking	R	R^2	R^2 Change	Beta
Nation–State Development and US Multinational Corporate Growth in Core Areas				
Communications	.651	.424	.424	.940
Defense Rank	.753	.567	.142	.467
GNP	.781	.611	.044	−.359
Year Constitution	.804	.646	.035	.285
Urbanization	.809	.654	.008	.267
Literacy	.821	.674	.020	−.312
Year Independence	.823	.678	.004	−.101
Nation–State Development and US Multinational Corporate Growth in Peripheral Areas				
GNP	.433	.188	.188	.361
Year Independence	.516	.267	.079	−.208
Year Constitution	.551	.304	.037	−.192
Defense Rank	.556	.310	.006	−.085
Literacy	.558	.311	.002	.083
Communications	.560	.313	.002	−.038
Urbanization	.561	.314	.001	−.040

subsidiaries of US-based firms are most likely to be established in other core nations that exhibit advanced communications development (beta = .940), and devote large proportions of their national resources to defense expenditires (beta = .467). GNP is a powerful predictor (beta = .361) of US corporate expansion into peripheral nations, along with the political factors of year of independence (beta = −.208) and year of constitution (beta = −.192). Multinational corporations originating from the United States are much more likely to locate their subsidiaries in the peripheral nations that are older, more stable, and wealthier rather than in the newer, poorer nations around the world. However, while 68 percent of the variance in US multinational corporate penetration into core states can be attributed to the seven indicators of national development included in this study ($R^2 = .678$), only 31 percent of the variance in peripheral growth is explained by the same set of indicators ($R^2 = .314$).

As seen in Table 5, non-US expansion into core and peripheral regions is somewhat similar to that of the United States; that is, the set of national development indicators is better able to predict non-US penetration into core states ($R^2 = .770$) than in peripheral regions ($R^2 = .376$). Defense rank (beta = −.908) is an important factor associated with the establishment of non-US subsidiaries in core states, but in the reverse direction that that for US multinational corporate growth, with non-US subsidiaries more likely to be located in nations that rank

Table 5. Stepwise Regression Summary Table for the Relationship Between Nation-State Development and Non-US Multinational Corporate Growth in Core and Peripheral Areas.

Variable Ranking	R	R^2	R^2 Change	Beta
Nation–State Development and Non-US Multinational Corporate Growth in Core Areas				
Defense Rank	.538	.290	.290	−.908
Urbanization	.709	.503	.214	.565
Year Independence	.797	.635	.132	−.543
Literacy	.846	.716	.082	−.322
GNP	.863	.745	.029	.240
Year Constitution	.877	.770	.025	.210
Communications	.878	.770	.001	.042
Nation–State Development and Non-US Multinational Corporate Growth in Peripheral Areas				
GNP	.537	.288	.288	.542
Year Constitution	.575	.331	.043	−.186
Communications	.600	.360	.029	.214
Literacy	.606	.367	.008	−.085
Defense Rank	.610	.372	.004	−.063
Year Independence	.612	.375	.003	−.051
Urbanization	.613	.376	.002	−.048

low on defense expenditures. Similar to the findings for US multinational corporate growth, GNP (beta = .542) and year of constitution (beta = −.186) both strongly predict non-US expansion into peripheral nations. Unlike the pattern of US multinational corporate expansion, social factors such as literacy and urbanization play a stronger role in influencing non-US multinational growth for core areas.

DISCUSSION

The intent of this paper is to go beyond previous research and offer a more precise picture of the relationship between multinational corporations and nation-states. By employing multivariate regression techniques, we are able to evaluate which of a series of national development measures best predicts US and non-US multinational corporate expansion, and whether the ranking of national indicators is different for core versus peripheral nation-states. Our findings suggest certain patterns in the establishment of foreign subsidiaries by US and non-US firms, with important differences noted for penetration into core versus peripheral regions around the world.

One strong pattern that emerges is both US and non-US multinational enterprises invest their operations and resources where the benefits can be expected to outweigh the costs. Business expenses increase relative to the social, geographic, and political distances separating parent firms from host countries (Bergsten et al., 1978; Buckley & Casson, 1976). For example, communications costs rise substantially where there are technical, social, and political differences between source and recipient nations. As a result, corporate investors favor nation-states exhibiting similar socio-economic characteristics as their own. In our research, we identify a bloc or core of nations containing multinational corporate parent enterprises, and these nation-states are more highly developed and homogeneous than the less developed countries without parent firms. These findings support the "structuralist theory" of foreign corporate investment, which maintains that multinational corporations pursue the principle of least resistance by locating foreign subsidiaries in countries that closely resemble their own (Caves, 1971; Madden, 1977).

Contrary to the notion that multinational corporations attempt to penetrate and exploit peripheral nation-states, we find that US and non-US corporations are more likely to establish subsidiaries in the highly developed core regions than in peripheral areas; that is, core nations dominate world trade and trade primarily within themselves (Chirot, 1977). Direct corporate investment does not flow from the "capital abundant" nations to "capital scarce" countries. To the contrary, resources are channeled into nations that are already highly developed— thus widening rather than reducing differences between rich and poor nations.

The historical roots of this global differentiation can be traced to the European commercial ties established in the 15th and 16th centuries, and to the British colonial system which emerged during the 17th and 18th centuries. The geographic proximity of the northern European nation-states facilitated trade and economic exchanges, providing the basis for the capitalist world economy. These nation-states (Belgium, France, Italy, Luxemburg, Netherlands, Sweden, Switzerland, and Germany) shared not only trade but numerous social and political features as well, including an energetic bourgeois class, vibrant urban centers, and rapidly developing economies. A number of the other core states, such as Australia, Canada, United Kingdom, South Africa, and the United States, shared a common language, culture, and political systems. The ties among these English-speaking countries were firmly grounded in the British colonial empire. Today, the regular and substantial network of reciprocal multinational corporate exchanges within the core nation-states reflects the continuation of commercial and colonial linkages dating back hundreds of years.

Multinational corporate enterprises are concentrated in high research and development industries, where, with their vast resources, they can maintain a competitive edge in the world market. These "research-intensive" industries require environments that are technically advanced, have strong economic growth potential, along with an educated labor force capable of performing complex skills. Our data clearly demonstrate that level of national development is a significant factor influencing the establishment of subsidiaries throughout the world, particularly in core nations; and that defense expenditure is a crucial variable related to corporate expansion. The intertwining of government policy, defense expenditures, and corporate operations in developed nations is well documented (Vernon, 1977). It is therefore not surprising that the core states are not only linked by economic interdependence, but by strong military alliances as well. Clear differences exist in our data identifying US and non-US multinational corporate expansion into core nations. Communications development proves to be a powerful predictor of US corporate penetration, while urbanization is more closely associated with non-US multinational corporate expansion into core nation-states.

The movement of US and non-US multinational corporations into peripheral nation-states is not strongly evidenced in our research. However, when penetration does take place, the national development factor of political stability emerges as an important condition for the establishment of US and non-US subsidiaries. With the spector of nationalization hovering over corporate management, multinational corporations gravitate toward older, established, and stable political regimes, particularly in rapidly developing and changing areas of the world. In fact, Vernon (1977) reports that multinational corporations are known to curtail their operations soon after a left-wing government has taken power. We also find that within the newly developed areas of the world, US and non-US corporations are much more likely to establish subsidiaries in the relatively wealthier rather than poorer nation-states.

The present-day pattern of non-reciprocal or asymmetric linkages of multinational manufacturing corporations into peripheral nation-states is selective and also reflects historical influences. For example, most of the foreign manufacturing subsidiaries in Central and Latin America are established by parent enterprises from the US or Japan. Multinational manufacturing firms from the United Kingdom are much more likely to locate foreign subsidiaries in Africa and Asia, while Japanese foreign investment dominates peripheral nations in Asia and Oceania (Braungart & Braungart, 1979).

SUMMARY

The results of this study demonstrate that multinational corporate expansion is related to nation-state development in a number of specific ways. First, both US and non-US firms establish subsidiaries in economically advantaged nation-states with long histories of political independence. Communications development is an important condition for US-based corporate expansion, while literacy level and defense expenditure rank are strong predictors of non-US corporate growth.

Second, empirical results suggest that the relationship between national development and multinational corporate expansion differs in core and peripheral areas around the world. US-based subsidiaries locate in core nation-states characterized by advanced communications technology, high defense expenditure rank, and high GNP; US-based corporations invest in peripheral nation-states with high GNP, a longer history of independence, and older constitutions. Non-US-based multinational corporate enterprises establish subsidiaries in core areas that rank low on defense expenditure, are urbanized, and are more likely to have gained independence; non-US-based corporations expand into peripheral nation-states with high GNP, older constitutions, and communications development.

Finally, nation-state development, as defined in this study, is better able to explain variance in US-based corporate expansion, and both US and non-US corporate growth into core versus the peripheral areas of the world.

ACKNOWLEDGMENTS

This is a revised version of a paper presented at the 73rd Annual Meetings of the American Sociological Association, San Francisco, California, September, 1978. We wish to express our thanks to Louis Kriesberg for his helpful comments and suggestions.

NOTES

1. Specifically, 187 US-based businesses comprising 11,742 subsidiaries in other nations were tracked from 1900 until 1968, while 226 non-US-based firms were traced from 1900 until 1971 representing 16,576 subsidiaries of one or more major enterprises located outside the US. A foreign firm was considered to be a subsidiary of an enterprise if it had at least 5 percent of its equity held by the enterprise or by companies in which the enterprise held at least 25 percent of the equity (Vaupel and Curhan, 1969, 1973).

2. The "world subset of data" for US-based and non-US-based enterprises were selected to provide a greater comparability between US and non-US data by eliminating certain differences in selection criteria. Criteria for inclusion into the world subset included firms having: (1) sales of $400 million or more in 1967; and (2) an equity interest of at least 25 percent in manufacturing subsidiaries in at least six foreign countries by January 1, 1968 (Vaupel and Curhan, 1969, 1973).

3. Telephone installation correlated highly with other measures of communication development, such as newspaper circulation (r = .801) and television receivers (r = .804). These high inter-correlations suggest that we are not only looking at telephone communications but communications development in a general sense as well.

4. The advanced or core nations in this sample include Australia, Belgium. Canada, France, Italy, Japan, Luxemburg, Netherlands, South Africa, Sweden, Switzerland, United Kingdom, United States, and West Germany.

REFERENCES

Amin, Samir (1974) *Accumulation on a World Scale: A Critique of the Theory of Underdevelopment,* 2 vols. New York: Monthly Review Press.

Ball, George W. (1975) *Global Companies.* Englewood Cliffs, N.J.: Prentice-Hall.

Barnet, Richard J. and Ronald E. Mueller (1974) *Global Reach.* New York: Simon and Schuster.

Barnet, Richard J., Ronald E. Mueller, and Joseph Collins (1974) "Global Corporations: Their Quest for Legitimacy." Pages 55-74 in Philip Brenner, Robert Borosage, and Bethany Weidner (Eds.), *Exploring Contradictions.* New York: McKay.

Bergsten, C. Fred, Thomas Horst, and Theodore H. Moran (1978) *American Multinationals and American Interest.* Washington, D.C.: Brookings Institution.

Blalock, Hubert M. (1972) *Social Statistics,* 2nd ed. New York: McGraw-Hill.

Bornschier, Volker, Christopher Chase-Dunn, and Richard Rubinson (1978) "Cross-national Evidence of the Effects of Foreign Investment and Aid on Economic Growth and Inequality: A Survey of Findings and Reanalysis." *American Journal of Sociology* 84:651-683.

Braungart, Richard G. (1978) "Multinational Corporations: New Dimensions in Community Power." *Sociological Symposium* 24:117-135.

Braungart, Richard G. and Margaret M. Braungart (1979) "Axes of World Structure and Conflict: Multinational Corporations and Nation-States." *Humboldt Journal of Social Relations* 6:4-45.

Buckley, Peter J. and Mark Casson (1976) *The Future of the Multinational Enterprise.* New York: Holmes and Meier.

Caves, Richard E. (1971) "International Corporations: The Industrial Economics of Foreign Investment." *Economics* February:1-27.

Chirot, Daniel (1977) *Social Change in the Twentieth Century.* New York: Harcourt Brace Jovanovich.

Cutright, Phillips (1963) "National Political Development: Measurement and Analysis." *American Sociological Review* 28:253-264.

Dowse, Robert E. and John A. Hughes (1972) *Political Sociology.* London: Wiley.

Frank, Andre Gunder (1969) *Latin America: Underdevelopment or Revolution.* New York: Monthly Review Press.

Gilpin, Robert (1975) *U.S. Power and the Multinational Corporation.* New York: Basic Books.

———(1976) "The Political Economy of the Multinational Corporations: Three Contrasting Perspectives." *American Political Science Review* 70:184-191.

Hopkins-Paul, Karen (1975) "Multinational Corporations: Impact and Control." Paper presented at the Southern Sociological Society meetings.

Hopkins-Paul, Karen and William C. Martin (1975) "Transnational Organization: Multinational Corporations and the Nation-State." Paper presented at the American Political Science Association meetings.

Kimmel, Michael S. (1975-1976) "The Negation of National Sovereignty: The Multinational Corporation and the World Economy." *Berkeley Journal of Sociology* 20:91-111.

Kumar, Krishna (1979) *The Social and Cultural Impacts of Transnational Enterprises.* Sydney, Australia: University of Sydney, Faculty of Economics, Information and Research Project on Transnational Corporations, Working Paper No. 6.

Lipset, Seymour M. and William Schneider (1973) "Political Sociology." Pages 399-491 in Neil J. Smelser (Ed.), *Sociology: An Introduction,* 2nd ed. New York: Wiley.

Madden, Carl H. (Ed.) (1977) *The Case for the Multinational Corporation.* New York: Praeger.

Maisonrouge, Jacques G. (1974) "The Mythology of Multinationalism." *Columbia Journal of World Business* 9:7-12.

Modelski, George (Ed.) (1972) *Multinational Corporations and World Order.* Beverly Hills: Sage.

Morse, Edward L. (1972) "Transnational Economic Processes." Pages 23-47 in Robert O. Keshane and Joseph S. Nye Jr. (Eds.). *Transnational Relations and World Politics.* Cambridge, Mass.: Harvard University Press.

Nie, Norman H., C. Hadlai Hull, Jean G. Jenkins, Karin Steinbrenner, and Dale H. Bent (1975) *Statistical Package for the Social Sciences,* 2nd ed. New York: McGraw-Hill.

Orum, Anthony M. (1978) *Introduction to Political Sociology.* Englewood Cliffs, N.J.: Prentice-Hall.

Rubinson, Richard (1976) "The World-Economy and the Distribution of Income Within States: A Cross-National Study." *American Sociological Review* 41:638-659.

Segal, Ronald (1973) "Multinational Corporations I: Everywhere at Home, Home Nowhere." *The Center Magazine* May/June:8-14.

Solomon, Lewis D. (1978) *Multinational Corporations and the Emerging World Order.* Port Washington, N.Y.: Kennikat Press.

Taylor, Charles L. and Michael C. Hudson (1972) *World Handbook of Political and Social Indicators,* 2nd ed. New Haven, Ct.: Yale University Press.

U.S. Senate Committee on Finance (93rd Congress) (1973) *Multinational Corporations.* Washington, D.C.: U.S. Government Printing Office.

U.S. Senate Committee on Foreign Relations (93rd Congress) (1974) *Multinational Corporations and United States Foreign Policy.* Washington, D.C.: U.S. Government Printing Office.

Vaupel, James W. and Joan P. Curhan (1969) *The Making of Multinational Enterprise.* Boston, Mass.: Harvard University Graduate School of Business Administration.

———(1973) *The World's Multinational Enterprise.* Boston, Mass.: Harvard University Graduate School of Business Administration.

Vernon, Raymond (1971) *Sovereignty at Bay.* New York: Basic Books.

———(1977) *Storm over the Multinationals: The Real Issues.* Cambridge, Mass.: Harvard University Press.

Von Krosigk, Friedrich (1972) "Marx, Universalism, and Contemporary World Business." Pages 128-146 in George Modelski (Ed.), *Multinational Corporations and World Order.* Beverly Hills: Sage.

Wallerstein, Immanuel (1974) *The Modern World-System.* New York: Academic Press.

Wilkins, Mira (1970) *The Emergence of Multinational Enterprise.* Cambridge, Mass.: Harvard University Press.

———(1974) *The Maturing of Multinational Enterprise.* Cambridge, Mass.: Harvard University Press.

INTERVENING IN SCHOOL DESEGREGATION CONFLICTS:
THE ROLE OF THE MONITOR

James H. Laue and Daniel J. Monti

INTRODUCTION

Dramatic societal changes and the creation of new social roles often result from intensive conflict in communities and institutions. The emergence of a range of conflict intervention roles—including the school desegregation monitor—is one important societal response to the conflict and social movements of the 1960s and 1970s.

In this paper, the authors examine the role of the school desegregation monitor and various types of monitoring bodies as a special case of the broader phenomenon of community conflict intervention, a field which has developed formally during the last two decades. Monitoring structures and behavior are analyzed in the light of one of the major ongoing social conflict issues facing United States society—school desegregation.[1]

Monitoring is viewed as a process whose manifest goals are to gather data,

Research in Social Movements, Conflicts and Change, Vol. 3, pages 187-218
Copyright © 1980 by JAI Press Inc.
All rights of reproduction in any form reserved.
ISBN: 0-89232-182-2

analyze, evaluate, and communicate findings regarding the extent of a school system's compliance with a desegregation order, and whose latent functions may include advocacy, mediation, and enforcement. Monitoring bodies and monitors also may play critical roles in determining whether court-ordered (or in rare cases, "voluntary") school desegregation is implemented and receives broad community acceptance, or whether it remains a paper policy which never finally impacts educational institutions and their racial practices.

The aims of this paper, then, are: (1) to present an emergent model for understanding school desegregation monitoring as a type of conflict intervention; (2) to assess relevant dimensions of four different types of monitoring and develop criteria for "effective" or "successful" monitoring; (3) to empirically examine monitoring activities in two school districts; and (4) to discuss the implications for school desegregation policy in the United States and for strategies of conflict intervention.

Following the introduction, section II contains definitions of the major terms of the analysis: school desegregation, conflict intervention, and monitoring. Section III examines in more detail the sociological dimensions of monitoring and develops a typology of monitoring as an intervention strategy. In section IV, desegregation and monitoring activities in the St. Louis Public Schools and the Ferguson-Florissant Reorganized School District in St. Louis County are analyzed, followed by a concluding section on implications for social policy and intervention strategies.

DEFINITIONS AND PERSPECTIVES: SCHOOL DESEGREGATION, CONFLICT INTERVENTION, MONITORING

A Sociological Approach to School Desegregation

Social scientists have approached the study of school desegregation from a variety of perspectives, among them human relations, ethnographic, social-psychological, organizational development, social movements, law-and-society, political sociology, social change, diffusion of innovations, conflict management, and complex organizations (see Coleman et al., 1966; Crain et al., 1968; Foster, 1973; Kirby, 1973; St. John, 1975; Weinberg, 1975; Pettigrew and Green, 1976; Kirp, 1977; Monti and Laue, 1977; Orfield, 1978; Ross and Berg, 1978; Crain and Mahard, 1979; Wilkinson, 1979; Monti, 1979a).

Our perspective is primarily that of the political sociologist. We focus on school desegregation as a complex process involving the struggle of various interest groups (boards of education, school administrators and staff, white and minority students and parents, government agencies, and community leaders, for example) for control of the resources and the resource-allocation process in school systems which are facing the issues of discrimination and segregation.

Desegregation usually becomes an issue in school systems where a significant number of schools are racially or ethnically identifiable. In a purely technical sense, school desegregation may be defined as actions taken by a school system, either voluntarily or under order of a court or direction of an agency, to reduce or eliminate racial or ethnic separation in the system's schools. The impact of these actions on the everyday lives of students and parents (and their friends and relatives) and ı a wide range of community interest groups gives school desegregation ι . h salience for all segments of the community.

The school desegregation process has three analytically distinct stages, which we have labeled the Decision to Desegregate, Formulation of a Desegregation Plan, and Implementation of the Plan. The issues, the actors, and the ensuing conflicts vary at each stage—as do the intervention techniques applied.

Stage 1: *The Decision to Desegregate.* This stage encompasses all activity up to and including the actual decision that the school district(s) involved will undergo some form of desegregation, whether the decision is the result of litigation or some less formal process. Stage 1 is among the most highly politicized phases, for, until the final decision is made, the major activity of the parties is to use their power to achieve a formal decision that is perceived to be of greatest benefit to their interests.

Often, parent groups file suit in an attempt to obtain redress for alleged violation of constitutional rights[2] and to "settle" some of the political questions raised at this stage, and the presence or absence of litigation often becomes the most important variable in determining the outcome of Stage 1. While litigation often is viewed as an alternative to the political process for arriving at crucial policy decisions, the introduction of litigation into school desegregation cases can have the effect of more dramatically politicizing the process as the trial's proceedings provide daily media exposure on the issue.

The pre-Decision phase, then, is one of maneuvering for political advantage on the part of all the parties to desegregation: school system, teachers, parents, advocate groups, city, state, and federal agencies. Litigation makes the maneuvering more regularized, expensive, and adversarial, and virtually assures that the school system will not take immediate and forthright action on alleged segregative practices until the final legal appeal is exhausted. Litigation also is an extremely lengthy process, with six to eight years often elapsing from filing to final adjudication.[3]

Most monitoring activity at this stage is internal to the school system; the formal role of the monitor does not fully emerge untion a later stage.

Stage 2: *Formulation of a Desegration Plan.* Stage 2 of the school desegregation process formally begins when a school district and all the constituent parties have recognized the existence of a decision to desegregate and thus become involved both in formulating a *plan* to implement the decision and in making specific *preparations* to implement the plan. The plan-formulation process may be accomplished by one person (a judge, a master, an outside expert, or a school district official, for example) or by many and diverse parties. It may be an open process to the community or it may be secretive, and it may have a short or long lead-time to implementation.

Recognition or acceptance that desegregation *will* occur is the critical cueing mechanism for Stage 2 in this framework, and the clarity and level of that recognition is a key to effective planning and, therefore, effective implementation. Unless there is broad community acceptance of the decision, conflict and perhaps violence will follow, and serious planning for implementation is not possible. The "massive resistance" movement in the South following the 1954 Supreme Court ruling is a primary example of the inability of the process to move from Stage 1 to Stage 2 if broad community acceptance is not present. Boston is a more recent and more relevant example: for more than a year following the formal decision by the courts to desegregate, official and vocal resistance existed in the school system and the city council, and the mayor's office was not willing to take an unequivocal stance in support of court-ordered desegregation. Therefore, planning for effective implementation was impossible, for efforts were still being directed to the macro-political activities of Stage 1.

Frequently, one of the by-products of the desegregation process is the opening-up of the school system to closer scrutiny by a number of persons and interest groups external to the system. This weakening of traditional system boundaries is a prerequisite to the emergence of the fully-legitimated role of the external monitor. During Stage 2, the many interest groups aroused in Stage 1 political activities often turn their attention to the planning process, and extend and regularize some of the activities begun in Stage 1, notably attending hearings and committee meetings, taking notes, and reporting back to the constituency. Formal monitoring of the process of formulating the desegregation plan is a logical but little-used extension of these activities.

Stage 3: *Implementation of the Plan.* For analytical purposes, Stage 3 includes all those activities conducted in the school system and its communities in response to the decision to desegregate and the plan which is developed. This phase usually appears *publicly* with the start of classroom desegregation; in reality, it often begins earlier with less visible administrative actions such as teacher and staff workshops or changes in budgets and tables of organization.

The implementation of any school desegregation plan has two major thrusts. One is primarily logistical and involves the operational changes a school system must make to implement the plan—construction or remodeling of physical facilities, drawing transportation plans, changes in instructional materials, staff placement, and related activities.

The other primary component of the implementation phase is the political process through which the schools relate to parents, other concerned citizens, and students in developing and amending desegregation policies. *It is at this stage that such mechanisms as a monitoring commission and/or a broadly-based citizens coalition typically come into play, although planning for their work may begin in Stages 1 and 2.*

If monitors and other intervenors are to fulfill their role expectations effectively, they must understand the interplay (1) between the technical decisions and political decisions alluded to above, and (2) between school system expertise (and the understandable urge to recapture the process for the inside administrators and experts) and community members' desire to control the conditions in which their children are to receive education.

All three stages—Decision, Planning, and Implementation—are highly politicized, with an ongoing struggle for control over the resources to be allocated in the public education of the community's children. During each of the three stages, different variables come into ascendancy, and they must be fully understood and dealt with by intervenors. In Stage 1, litigation often is the key variable predictive of the process toward decision. In Stage 2, the struggle for control of the planning process is a major dynamic. In Stage 3, the central question is the nature of the relationship between school system owners and managers and the system's clients and constituents—again, a struggle for control of the process and the outcomes.

The Emergence of Community Conflict Intervention

Monitoring is analyzed in this paper as an example of a community conflict intervention technique. The field of community conflict intervention has emerged formally in the last 20 years, largely in response to the racial, community, and service-delivery disputes that came into prominence during that period (see Burton, 1969; Laue, 1970; Chalmers and Cormick, 1971; Kelman, 1972; Nicolau and Cormick, 1972; Deutsch, 1973; Spiegel, 1973; Chalmers, 1974; Gant, 1974; Goldaber and Porter, 1974; Bartunek, Benton, and Keys, 1975; Likert and Likert, 1976; Ford Foundation, 1978a, b; Laue, 1978a; Laue and Cormick, 1978; and Wehr, 1979).

Community conflict intervention is the deliberate and systematic entering into a situation by an outside or semi-outside party or parties (persons or organizations) with the aim of influencing the direction or the outcome of the conflict in a way deemed desirable by the intervenor. All intervention alters the power configuration of the situation; therefore, all intervention is a form of advocacy—whether for a particular party, outcome, or process of conflict resolution (Laue, 1978b).

All intervention activity starts with a goal—or, at least, a conception on the part of the intervenor of the nature, causes, and desirable directions of the conflict. Merely by entering a conflict situation, an intervenor expresses a position. The strategies one pursues in conflict intervention are largely a result of the position the intervenor takes vis-à-vis the parties, the issues, and the values involved in the conflict. Neutrality is impossible, whether or not the intervenor *feels* neutral.

Laue and Cormick (1978) have analyzed community disputes and intervention, identifying the five basic roles which are played individually or in combination by intervenors in all conflict situations: Activist, Advocate, Mediator, Researcher, and Enforcer. The roles are differentiated in terms of the intervenor's organizational and fiscal base, relationship to the parties, and skills.

Activist. Based in one of the parties actively in conflict and so strongly identified with that party that he or she is not able to emphathize, negotiate, or compromise with the other party or parties. Skills generally include organizing, public speaking, strategizing, etc. A welfare mother leading a welfare rights protest is a good example. This type of intervenor may become so closely identified with the out-party that he or she must deal with the challenge "going native" presents to effective intervention. A counterpart, the Reactivist, is aligned with the more established party in community disputes.

Advocate. Works in behalf of an interest group in a conflict, and is supported either by that group or an independent, generally sympathetic source. Promotes the party's cause to wider constituencies, and may serve as a negotiator. Skills include those of the Activist in addition to the ability to envision and achieve conflict-termination on what the Advocate's party defines as good terms. A typical in-party Advocate is the management consultant, and a typical out-party Advocate is the community organizer.

Mediator. Based in an advocacy for "good process" (participatory, jointly-determined, leading to win/win outcomes), rather than for any of the parties per se. Since mediation is a voluntary process, the mediator's fiscal and organizational base must be acceptable to all the parties. Skills include facilitation of negotiations, organizing, communicating, seeking additional resources, and packaging settlements.

Researcher. With an independent or semi-independent base, the Researcher may be a social scientist, policy analyst, media representative, lay observer, or monitor, whose role is to provide an independent description (and, if prescribed, evaluation) of a given conflict situation. Observation, data-gathering, objectivity, writing, and oral communication are some of the requisite skills. The interests of the Researcher include the activities of each of the other parties described above, as well as the ongoing dynamic of the conflict. Occupants of the Researcher intervention role often perceive themselves as neutral, but they alter the power configuration of the situation by their presence and may be used by parties on all sides to further their objectives.

Enforcer. With an independent power base, the Enforcer has the power to enforce conditions on conflicting parties irrespective of their wishes, often in the institutional form of a formal agency of social control of the larger system in which the conflict is set—the courts, the police, a funding agency, or an arbitrator. The Enforcer brings formal coercive power to the situation; no other intervenor does. The Enforcer carries the right to specify behavior or impose sanctions which may support the goals of none, any, or all the parties.

Community conflicts are about *resources* (goods, services, jobs, facilities, land, etc.) and *power* (the control of decisions about the allocation of resources). Community conflict intervenors become part of this dynamic, and the base, background, and ideology of the intervenor is critical to the impact and direction of intervention.

There are a number of persons and organizations currently practicing community conflict intervention, among them human relations commissions, religious groups, government agencies at all levels, individual professionals (including psychologists, sociologists, labor arbitrators, and lawyers), civil rights groups, and university research and training centers.[4]

Monitoring School Desegregation

One of the more recent conflict intervention roles to emerge is that of the *school desegregation monitor*. Formally and structurally, the monitor is a variant of the Researcher role described by Laue and Cormick. *Monitoring school desegregation may be defined as a process in which designated individuals collect data on a school system (through observation, documents, and interviews), analyze and evaluate the data, and report to an authorizing body on the content and quality of the system's efforts to comply with that body's standards for desegregation.*[5]

The characteristics and components of monitoring school desegregation may be further elaborated as follows:

1. Monitoring typically emerges as a well-defined and extensive activity during Stage 3 of the desegregation process—Implementation. The task is to assess how well the system is complying with the desegregation plan, whether established by the court or voluntarily.

2. School systems continuously conduct a range of monitoring activities of their own performance in a number of areas, and organizations outside the system also may begin to monitor performance during the Decision or Planning stages. Formal monitoring often is an extension of activities in Stages 1 and 2.

3. The organizational or authorizing base of the monitoring activity may be the courts, a citizens' coalition (with or without a court sanction), the school system, federal or state agencies, or independent organizations (universities or private research centers, for example).

4. Monitoring bodies vary in their size, specific objectives, complement of professional staff, technical and research skills, longevity, and effectiveness.

The individual functioning as a monitor, then, carries a formal role description as a Researcher or observer. The major expected behaviors involve developing an objective and independent set of data against which the authorizing body can judge the school system's level of compliance with its standards. But circumstances—and the monitoring organization's base and goals—often thrust the monitor into the other three roles noted.

First, the monitor—regardless of how neutral and objective the person may be in the exercise of his or her technical functions—is, by definition, an Advocate for the standards of the authorizing body. Most typically, this refers to the content of a given desegregation plan ordered or authorized by the courts. The monitor also is a process or procedural advocate, acting in behalf of certain established or to-be-established procedures in the system. While "neutrality" and "objectivity" are important elements of the ideology of monitoring, the monitor clearly is not neutral in base or impact on the system, and probably not in ideology regarding desegregation and the given plan.

The monitor functions as a Mediator in many contexts—between court and school officials, between school officials and citizens, and within the school system. With a mandate that permits the role occupant to range across normally restricted authority lines in the school system, the monitor quickly is identified as a message-carrier who can be used for clarification, buffering, intelligence-gathering, or problem-solving by the various parties. The monitor often is the first person outside the system to identify areas of trouble or noncompliance, and is in a position to quietly advocate internal remediation of the problem with the implied threat of utilizing the authorizing body's enforcement powers if compliance is not forthcoming.

It should be clear from this description of the monitor's base and functions than an occupant of this role also may carry implied powers as an Enforcer. While monitors themselves do not enforce the law or other standards, there are a number of ways they can influence or direct enforcement: by the problems they choose to highlight and study in the school system, by the ways they report observations to the authorizing body, and through their informal networks and relationships with the court, federal and state agencies, and various community power structures.

Of the variety of types of monitors and monitoring structures that have emerged and are emerging, the court-appointed citizens monitoring commission has gained the most attention. A national network of participants in such bodies has developed in the last few years, and the U.S. Congress has taken note of the growth of monitoring activities (*Congressional Record,* June 26, 1976). The first major national meeting on "Court-Appointed Monitoring Commissions" was held in Columbus, Ohio, in 1977, and attracted persons from 18 states and 26 cities. Significant features of these types of bodies now are summarized from the report of that meeting (Carol, 1977, pp. 2-13).

As part of their desegregation orders, some federal judges have named masters, experts, and/or citizen monitoring bodies to oversee implementation of the decree, to receive continuous input on citizens' perceptions, and to coordinate and manage the acquisition and reporting of data on compliance. Judges have appointed commissions ranging from 10 to 50 members, usually representing a broad spectrum of community leadership. Most court-ordered commissions are empowered on a year-to-year basis. Some of the better-known commissions have been established in Boston, Buffalo, Dallas, Dayton, Denver, Dekalb County

(Georgia), Detroit, Milwaukee, and Springfield (Illinois). Annual budgets vary from zero to $200,000. Staffing is non-existent in some commission (they rely on volunteers, university personnel, or state and federal agency staffs), while others have a full complement of professional and clerical staff.

The expected problems have arisen. Some monitoring commissions have been seen as competition by other citizens groups. Monitoring commissions commonly complain about a lack of clarity about their responsibilities. There are "communications" problems with judges (who may pay little attention to the commission after it is established) and with school officials (who may resent both the extra work often required by school personnel, as well as the appearance of another outside political interference in their governance and management of the schools).

The criteria for success of such commissions center around on-time implementation and broad community acceptance of the plan. Perceived success was found to depend on: (1) the clarity of the judge's charge and his or her commitment to follow-up; (2) the quality of legal counsel available to the commission; (3) the political and technical skills of the commission members and staff; (4) the attitudes and degree of cooperation from school officials; and (5) the degree of acceptance of the commission and its activities by the wider community.

The number of formal monitoring bodies—both court-appointed and with different bases—is expected to continue to grow. A framework for understanding these activities is developed in the next section.

MONITORING AS INTERVENTION: A TYPOLOGY AND DISCUSSION

Increasing intensity of monitoring activity and the progressive institutionalization of the role of monitor both seem to accompany the school desegregation process as it proceeds from the Decision stage to Planning and, finally, to the Implementation stage. In this section, the development of monitoring as a type of conflict intervention is traced from its place in the routine internal operations of the school system to the emphasis on external surveillance and accountability that emerges when school desegregation becomes an issue. The forms of monitoring that emerge then are cast in a typology in terms of their base and credibility, skills required, and typical activities.

Routine Monitoring in the School System

Monitoring routinely takes place in the schools. School districts monitor the academic progress of their students and the strength of their curricula through the use of standardized tests. Parents with school-age children and other persons interested in public education normally keep abreast of school programs and discuss the activities of school staff and administrators with one another. State and federal officials responsible for funding certain school programs or overseeing policies require reports from school administrators regarding educational matters under their jurisdiction.

School personnel are accustomed to the monitoring of educational programs, then, and to receiving and using the information about their problems and successes generated by monitoring.

These usual forms of monitoring generally do not present school officials with overwhelming or unanticipated problems, because the administrators can either determine what information is to be shared beyond the system or control the access of different parties to the information being requested. In each instance of monitoring, an implicit or explicit evaluation of school policies and personnel is being made, but the school district is largely in control of the evaluation process—either directly through the selection of consultants and the mode of evaluation, or indirectly through its ongoing relationship with public officials and limitations placed upon the evaluators by time and the law (Englert et al., 1977). The political implications of external monitoring and evaluation of school programs are clear to the school officials whose professional reputations may be at stake because of a negative evaluation which they, their program, or their staff may receive.

Desegregation and New Monitoring Activities

The established relations between school officials and the various parties who observe and report on educational practices often undergo change with the advent of desegregation. Not only are there demands for more information about the schools, but new questions are asked (often requiring officials to produce novel data) and new groups solicit information about school procedures and programs. The public schools' business becomes much more public and information control by the district becomes much more difficult. In this context, monitoring, regardless of the form it takes, can become an intervention strategy in its own right: the presence of non-school personnel reviewing the conduct of school staff on a daily basis, with the responsibility to report the progress of desegregation to powerful authorities like the courts, can influence the behavior of school employees. Thus, the issue of *who oversees the planning and implementation of desegregation programs* may be as important to school officials as what kind of desegregation policies are enacted. The importance of this issue is especially apparent when court-appointed monitoring commissions are present in the school district.

A Typology of Monitoring: Base and Credibility, Skills, Typical Activities

Table 1 summarizes important characteristics of the different types of monitoring bodies: the advantages and disadvantages of the base, skills, and typical activities of each type. This framework has been developed from the observation of monitoring activities reported in section IV and from a review of the growing literature on school desegregation monitoring (Stevens and Hunter, 1976; Na-

Table 1. Monitoring as Intervention

Type of Monitor: *School System Personnel or Party Paid by School System*

	Advantages	Disadvantages
Base:	Generally have the trust of school employees and are controlled by district officials. Can better mobilize the school system's resources in behalf of or against desegregation efforts.	Can be too closely identified with school policies and officials to be credible with the community. May be reticent to call for fundamental changes in school policies, or to mobilize resources that might threaten their superiors.
Skills:	Working knowledge of the schools, political alliances, and educational policies.	May be too close to school practices to recognize incipient problems. Their approach to conflict resolution is limited by their base as advocates for the system.
Typical Activities:	Collect data on racial percentages, achievement scores, distribution of staff, and fiscal resources. Issue reports on programs mandated by the courts.	Information about district problems may be guarded. Data requested by the courts or federal agencies can be selectively gathered and reported.

Type of Monitor: *Citizens' Groups, Either Appointed or Elected*

	Advantages	Disadvantages
Base:	Can enjoy strong community support. Can be identified as credible representatives by the authorities. Their grassroots network can mobilize efforts for or against desegregation programs.	May be composed of hand-picked supporters of the school system, or people with little support among critics of school practices. May not have or even seek grassroots support for their actions. Generally dependent on school officials to enact their suggestions.
Skills:	Can be essential in securing federal funds for school programs. Can obtain excellent information on how schools are meeting the educational needs of children and obligations imposed by desegregation. Can funnel complaints and information about desegregation from the community to the district.	May not exercise their ability to influence the access of schools to government funds. Can act as a buffer, protecting school officials from criticism. May not inform citizens of school policies. Do not have the technical skills to manage schools or the support of school personnel to carry out their ideas.
Typical Activities:	Oversee desegregation activities and report to the public and	May not have complete access to information needed to complete

(continued)

Table 1.—*Continued*

	Advantages	Disadvantages
	authorities. Hold community meetings. Can conduct some types of training related to monitoring school programs.	their monitoring activities. May avoid public meetings and training functions to keep access to schools.

Type of Monitor: *Federal and State Agencies*

	Advantages	Disadvantages
Base:	Have the authority to intervene in school programs as plaintiffs, technical assistants, or funding agents for desegregation-related activities.	Have a variety of tasks to perform in many communities, and cannot devote extensive intervention to any one community. Usually are not located in the community where their efforts are being felt.
Skills:	Can bring a variety of legal, monetary, and technical resources to bear upon desegregation-related problems.	Their information generally is not up-to-date or independently collected. Their influence is subject to court rulings and the vagaries of federal politics.
Typical Activities:	Solicit reports on school programs. Can make site visits, or withhold funds.	The information they receive often is not verified. Are not likely to withhold or withdraw funds, even when violations are proven, because of political considerations.

Type of Monitor: *Independent Organizations*

	Advantages	Disadvantages
Base:	Identified as experts in their fields. Can be independent of all parties and, thus, not viewed as biased for or against the school system or community.	Unless appointed by the judge, they have only their status as experts in some aspect of desegregation to enhance their influence. Have no power or natural constituency in the district. May be identified as an advocate by either the school system or community.
Skills:	May have a variety of technical skills and resources at their disposal. May be useful as observers and analysts of school problems. May have practical experience in conflict resolution and mediation.	May get no assistance from school officials to help remedy identified problems. May be distrusted because of their expertise and outside base.

Table 1.—*Continued*

	Advantages	Disadvantages
Typical Activities:	Collect sophisticated research data. Can speak with staff, students, and community to identify problems. Can train all parties on problem identification and prevention. Can provide information and requests to intervene to federal and state officials.	Access to school staff and other sources of information about the schools may be limited. Data collected for academic purposes may not be useful in the immediate situation.

tional Conference of Christians and Jews, 1976; Carol, 1977; Dayton Citizens Advisory Board, 1977; Racism and Sexism Resource Center for Educators, 1977; Sussman, 1977). The description of monitoring activities in section IV is built around this typology.

At this early stage in the development of monitoring as a special field, the issues and problems surrounding *effective* monitoring of school desegregation are numerous and complex. No single party has a complete view of the desegregation process, nor a monopoly on the truth. Each has its own peculiar strengths and weaknesses, and their skills can complement one another.

Our preliminary analysis leads to the conclusion that a comprehensive and accurate monitoring effort would require all four types of monitors—school, citizen, public agency, and independently-based—to work together in a district. But given their varying interests and constituencies, the problems of coordination are great, and they may work at cross-purposes, or against one another. One result, as the next section of this paper reveals, can be a fragmentary and heavily contested view of desegregation.

AN ANALYSIS OF MONITORING ACTIVITIES IN TWO SCHOOL DISTRICTS

These perspectives now are applied to monitoring activities in two school districts in the St. Louis area—the City of St. Louis Public Schools and the Ferguson-Florissant Reorganized School District in St. Louis County. The period of the analysis roughly corresponds to the three-year National Institute of Education contract under which the authors and their staff worked in the two districts from mid-1976 to mid-1979.

Background on School Desegregation in St. Louis and Ferguson-Florissant
The public schools in the City of St. Louis had a 1979–80 enrollment of approximately 66,000 students—down from a peak of 116,000 in 1961. Like the public schools in most older northern and border cities, the percentage of non-

white students has steadily increased from 37 percent in 1953, to approximately 50 percent in 1960, and nearly 75 percent in 1979.

The Ferguson-Florissant Reorganized (R-2) District encompasses parts of a number of municipalities in north St. Louis County. In a comparable time period, the predominantly white, former Ferguson-Florissant District grew rapidly to its peak student census of 20,000 in 1968, then had declined to 15,000 in 1975 before the merger, which encompassed two new districts, including the all-black Kinloch District, and brought the total back to more than 19,000 students. In 1979, the still declining total enrollment of the new R-2 District stood again at approximately 15,000.

The two school systems—one, a central city district in an old city rapidly losing population (from 780,000 in 1950 to an estimated 500,000 or less in 1980) and the other, a recently-merged district in an older area of the surrounding county—have been at different stages of the desegregation process during the study period.

A desegregation suit against the Board of Education in the City of St. Louis has been in the courts since 1972. In April, 1979, the District court ruled that the school system had not intentionally caused segregation. The ruling was appealed, and overturned by the Circuit court. The U.S. Supreme Court let the Circuit court ruling of intentional segregation stand, and the court-ordered plan developed by the school system for Fall 1980 classroom desegregation was still under appeal in July 1980 while the schools were making extensive preparation for its implementation. The case involves eight different parties, ranging from black and white parents groups, to the city, the state, the U.S. Department of Justice, and the NAACP (both the local branch and the national organization).

A consent decree signed late in 1975 failed to contribute significantly to the desegregation of the system. The same was true for a small magnet school program that resulted from that decree, a program which has enrolled only several thousand students and has been constantly embroiled in disputes about a permissive transfer policy that enables children to attend schools—including the magnet schools—outside of their appointed area.

As the legal complexion of the case has changed, so has 'ie political situation in the city. A number of efforts have been made to draw cc munity leaders into the desegregation process and to help citizens articulate their concerns regarding school desegregation. Predominantly white groups have taken a public stance of support for the general idea of non-discriminatory school programs, while opposing compulsory busing in order to achieve them. The black Concerned Parents of North St. Louis group (which filed the original suit in 1972) has been involved in conversations with predominantely white Southside groups. The St. Louis-based Danforth Foundation and the regional office of the National Conference of Christians and Jews have led efforts to build a community-wide coalition for peaceful and orderly school desegregation. Since the development of the A plan in May 1980, the city-wide Inter-Faith Clergy Council has engaged in heavy preparation to smooth the transition, and anticipates undertaking some monitoring-type activities.

In September, 1976 the Ferguson-Florissant R-2 District began its first year of classroom desegregation. The administrations and staffs of the formerly independent Ferguson-Florissant, Berkeley, and Kinloch districts had been merged on July 1, 1975. The school district of Kinloch, consisting of a small and entirely black community, had been gerrymandered into existence earlier in this century. While both the merger and initial year of desegregation met with some resistance, there were no major outbreaks of violence as had been feared. New busing and pupil assignment plans were approved by the court in the second and third years to help reduce some of the black enrollment in Berkeley schools. The same judge sitting in the St. Louis case plans to end the court's jurisdiction over the district soon, despite complaints from some Berkeley and Kinloch residents.

The judge's desire to withdraw from the suburban case and his record of inviting additional parties into the city case who might extend any legal ruling for years through appeals, revealed readiness on his part to submit future decisions regarding desegregation to the political vagaries of both districts. It also may reflect his recognition that no court is capable of resolving the thorny political problems generated by school desegregation. In any case, it is evident that political considerations will continue to play a large role in the desegregation process in these two districts.

School Desegregation and Monitoring in the City of St. Louis[6]

The City's magnet school program and the continued debate about desegregation in the courts and in the press have received more scrutiny by all segments of the community and the federal government than the smaller suburban district's desegregation order and plan. The greater attention paid to the City's schools since the raising of the desegregation issue in the courts in 1972 has not yet produced a clear and widely-accepted picture of the system's situation and problems. Observers of the school system would agree only in the broadest terms that the district: (1) is losing enrollment; (2) has an inadequate tax base; (3) has approximately a 75–25 non-white to white pupil ratio; (4) has a teaching staff that has shown resistance to attempts to improve racial balance among staffs at the individual school level; (5) is self-conscious about its image and desires to improve; and (6) is having serious problems in producing "basic academic achievement" (the major stated priority of the Board of Education) at levels acceptable to its patrons.

Each of the four types of monitoring described in section III was present in the St. Louis situation up to mid-1980; none of the monitoring was court-ordered. With the court order came a court-appointejd monitoring committee, which has only begun to function as this issue goes to press. Among the monitors functioning up to that time—and in some instances, to the present—are the following:

The School System. An evaluation department is responsible for collecting various types of data described below. In the summer of 1979, the district hired an "Advisory Specialist on Desegregation" to collect data and report problems to the superintendent, utilizing funds obtained under Title IV of the Emergency School Assistance Act (ESAA).

Government Agencies. The Office of Civil Rights (OCR) of the U.S. Department of Health, Education, and Welfare has continuously monitored the racial composition and distribution of students and teaching staffs, as well as the operation of certain HEW-funded programs.

Citizens Groups. Three types of citizens' groups of varying composition and influence have been involved in monitoring the St. Louis system: the Citizens Education Task Force (CETF), the ESAA Citywide Advisory Committee, and Parent Advisory Committees (PACs) related to each of the magnet locations and some additional schools.

Independent Organizations. Researchers from St. Louis area colleges and universities have been peripherally involved in monitoring, as have some of the staff members of the Danforth Foundation and the National Conference of Christians and Jews.

The role of each of these types of monitors in the St. Louis system now is examined.

School System. The City of St. Louis public school system has its own small evaluation department, which is responsible for collecting and analyzing information about educational offerings in city schools. Among its other tasks, departmental staff have acquired data on the progress of students in the magnet school program and the satisfaction of persons with that program. Senior magnet school staff were concerned from the inception of the program that data gathered by the evaluation team could be used against them. Throughout the entire first year of the Magnet School program in 1976–77, there were many charges leveled from within the school system at the staff, its specialized curriculum, and recruitment practices. Magnet schools were charged with causing shortages in supplies (magnet schools also were short of supplies), taking the best students (some magnet school staff felt they had received many of the system's problem students), and depleting non-magnet schools of some of their best teachers (staff for the first year were selected from a pool of volunteers from across the district—mainly teachers at magnet sites who did not want to leave their schools). Magnet school staff members were upset about these charges, but could do little to stop the persistent rumors regarding their program.

The magnet schools (several thousand students in ten special-emphasis schools such as mathematics and performing arts) were supported during their first school year, 1976–77, largely by federal HEW funds—some 85 percent of the cost. Notification of funding for the first year came in August, only weeks before the magnet schools were to open their doors for the first time. From the beginning, their operation has been under close scrutiny from the Office of Civil

Rights in HEW because of their inability to attract and hold enough white students to make up the minimum 30 percent of the student bodies as mandated by HEW. The external funding situation has remained on this same uncertain basis for each year of the program, although federal funds now comprise only about one-third of the cost of operating the magnet schools.

The discussions continue within the school system—about the viability of the magnet school concept, about the prospective "drain" of good students from neighborhood schools, and about the small number of students involved (approximately 4,000 in the 1979–80 school year). The incidence of missed communications and mistrust between the magnet schools and the evaluation department staff reflect the ultimately political nature of monitoring, even when it is conducted strictly within the school system.

Federal Agencies. The federal government also is involved in the monitoring of the magnet school program, but its interest differs from that of the school system's own evaluators. The Office of Civil Rights of HEW has paid special attention to the system's permissive transfer policy which has enabled students to attend schools outside of their assigned areas. The policy was criticized before the first year of the magnet school program, but the school system won a one-year delay in altering the guidelines for student transfers. The issue was raised again before the second year of the program, but this time funds for the magnet schools were withheld until modifications in the permissive transfer policy were enacted. As a result of these changes, some students had to return to their regularly assigned schools and others, who only recently had applied for admission into a magnet school, had to be turned away.

OCR's monitoring effort, while marked by insistence that the permissive transfer policy facilitated the maintenance of a dual school system in St. Louis and had to be changed, has recognized some important political realities in St. Louis. Foremost in the minds of local school officials and federal representatives was the need to attract and hold white students in the public school system. Thus, when the parents of several white children scheduled to return to their regular schools complained and received considerable attention from the media, both OCR and school officials permitted them to stay in their magnet school. In addition, neither federal nor local officials have been quick to point out that the magnet schools are not a radical departure from the old system of neighborhood schools which was so heavily contested in the courts.

Magnet schools are designed to provide an alternative to compulsory busing by attracting students of all races to an excellent program. But the majority of black children attending magnet schools have been bused in.

All in all, many white and black parents whose children attend magnet schools have been pleased with the program, although some children have been withdrawn because of bus transportation problems. The school system continues to balance such crucial local considerations as client satisfaction with the challenges of federal monitors who carry enforcement power to promote or end this and other programs.

Citizens Groups.   Desegregation also creates new opportunities for parental and citizen involvement in the schools. In St. Louis, there have been three different types of groups overseeing the desegregation process and trying to serve as liaisons between the school system and community: the Citizens Education Task Force (CETF, an umbrella group of citizens including members from St. Louis County as well as the City); the Parent Advisory Committees of individual schools in the system (PACs); and the ESAA Citywide Advisory Committee (CAC).

The Citizens Education Task Force, created jointly by the St. Louis Board of Education and the St. Louis Board of Aldermen, began operation in 1976 and has entered a period of reassessment in the fall of 1979 due to declining fiscal support, but with hopes expressed for new funding. Funded predominantly by the Danforth Foundation (up to two-thirds in one year) and corporate contributions from 1976 to 1979, the CETF was charged with achieving eight objectives related to improving: (1) student learning outcomes; (2) management; (3) school/community and public/private education linkages; (4) financing; (5) citizen participation; (6) community support for the schools; (7) intergroup relations (cited specifically in the charge were "tensions" which exist in the community as a result of differences in religious, cultural, racial, and economic backgrounds); and (8) staff relations. The Task Force synthesized these eight objectives in "two primary goals": "increasing public confidence in the schools" and "seeking ways to improve educational outcomes" (Wright et al., 1979, pp. 3, 14).

While none of these goals calls for monitoring per se, the 38 members of the CETF and their small executive staff (a director, associate director, and clerical staff, with an annual budget ranging between $100,000 and $200,000) immediately began organizing and collecting data required to develop strategies and recommendations. In the course of these activities, the CETF played the expected Researcher's role, but also appeared to many as a strong Advocate—for citizen influence in the school system, for a more open process of governance and broader sharing of information by the school system, and for broader community support of the public schools.

The CETF conducted a wide range of advocacy activities, despite the fact that its members never fully resolved a number of internal issues regarding their appropriate role. The major unresolved question during its three years of heavily-funded activities is a typical problem for all monitoring and quasi-monitoring bodies: what shall be the relationship to the school system? Many members felt that the fiscal sponsors of the Task Force wanted it to supply community support for the new superintendent and two of his major goals for the system—administrative reorganization (in a top-heavy structure with a decreasing student census) and a greater focus on site management. The CETF's executive director for 1977–79 described the split on the Task Force as between those who wanted to "talk out" their differences with the system and those who wanted to "confront" the system. Especially those in the second group said they "could not trust the school system," and persons in both factions used words like "watchdog" and "oversee" in describing the Task Force's role.

There have been other significant cleavages in the organization that have persisted since its inception: City versus County, upper versus lower social class, old/young persons with children in the system versus those without, pro-desegregation versus anti-desegregation, etc. The Task Force has been interracial, but race per se seldom became a primary basis of internal cleavages. In a statement which illustrates the built-in structural problems of such a broad-based organization, a young, blue-collar mother with children in the system said of an older, upper middle-class woman who resides in the County (with much feeling and just enough humor), "If she calls me 'My dear' once more, I'll punch her in the mouth." Both were white.

The CETF's activities have covered the entire range of what monitors generally do:

- Conducted intensive studies of the system and produced a series of recommendations to the school system on issues ranging from the impact of redevelopment on public schools, to better public information, to creation of a special city-wide vocational education district. (The recommendations are in varying stages of study and/or implementation by the school system.)
- Formally petitioned the school system to begin a community-based process, involving the CETF, to develop plans for quality integrated education before final legal appeals are resolved, as suggested by the Court. (The system has not done so.)
- Published a monthly newsletter, *The Monitor*, which covered court proceedings, test scores, legal rights of parents, etc.
- Formally petitioned the judge in the school desegregation case to designate the CETF to serve as the monitoring body during the Planning and Implementation stages. (The judge responded that he would make no such designation until and unless violation were determined.)
- Sponsored television programs on school desegregation, including a three-hour expert panel/audience participation/call-in format which drew the largest Nielsen rating of viewers in the 25-year history of public television in St. Louis.
- Sponsored a series of city-wide and neighborhood community forums on "Understanding Desegregation Processes," with a grant from the Missouri Committee for the Humanities, which varied in attendance from 15 to 600.
- Sponsored a series of bus tours of the entire district for PAC presidents and a number of informal meetings for parents across racial and geographical

lines—both of which were well-attended and positively evaluated by the participants.

- Petitioned the judge to enter a teacher/school board contract dispute in 1979 as a mediator; CETF officials believe their proposed intervention helped shorten the strike by promoting the joint negotiations of the parties.

In summary, the CETF had many of the characteristics of a citizens' monitoring group. It was, in our judgment, successful in the specific public education programs it undertook, in raising to the school system and the community-at-large a number of problems and recommendations which must be addressed by both the system and the city if the schools are to thrive, and in advancing the legitimacy of citizen/parent participation in all facets of school system operations. It has been less successful in determining a focus for its role, in gaining community support for its efforts and for the school system, in gaining support for its recommendations with the school board or any direct influence on the court, and in its various monitoring activities.

The Parent Advisory Committees could provide some needed support for monitoring activities. The PACs of magnet schools already were conducting unsystematic monitoring of the desegregation effort represented by each of their schools. The degree to which they have become involved depends almost exclusively upon the parents, because while magnet school officials have made a strong public commitment to consulting parents, principals have used or ignored these groups at will. Some groups of parents have assisted in the drawing-up of behavioral and dress codes for their children, and others have offered advice on a wide range of issues to their children's principals. A large share of parents have assumed the more traditional role of receiving information rather than collecting and acting on it.

There are many areas where participation could be increased. Some of the most involved parents are those whose children already were attending that particular school before it became a magnet school, and there remains a problem of how to include in PAC activities parents who live long distances from their children's magnet school. Many black parents find it especially difficult to go to evening meetings far from their homes. This problem will have to be overcome if black parents are to contribute to a monitoring effort in their children's schools.[7]

A final source of citizen influence in the city's desegregation process had been through the ESAA Citywide Advisory Committee. It was established so the school system could qualify for Emergency School Aid Act funds which support much of the magnet school program. The ESAA Citywide Advisory Committee is composed of persons from throughout the city, but they have not been as closely identified with the city's educational and political leadership as are those on the CETF. Members of the ESAA committee have been more willing to challenge district policies.

One notable example came during the planning for the magnet schools' first year. A good deal of money had been proposed for "environmental stress" retreats, where students could work on common problems and crises in an outdoor setting and, presumably, begin to overcome any prejudicial tendencies on their part. Parents reviewing the proposal objected strongly to the expense of the program and argued that white and black children already had opportunities to go on field trips together and could go on more of them for far less money than was being proposed. They wrote a letter to HEW and were able to deny funding to that portion of the grant proposal.

The entire ESAA committee was able to review only the initial draft of the proposal to HEW for the second year of funds for the magnet schools. Subsequent drafts never were approved by the committee as a whole. A similar situation has arisen in relation to the selection of staff for the magnet schools. The ESAA committee participated in the hiring process prior to the first year of the program, but was not consulted on staff selection before the second year. This led to some disenchantment among parents who had helped screening of applicants the first year.

So, lack of district-wide organization, skills, and training hampered the effectiveness of the ESAA Committee in its para-monitoring activities.

Independent Organizations. All of the problems in monitoring a desegregation process cited above are magnified when considering the role of the independent researcher as a potential monitor. Without a natural constituency except their fellow professional educators and without any formal power, independent researchers probably cannot be of substantial help to harried school officials and committed parent groups unless they are willing to bend their research interests to the advocacy goals these interest groups represent. Further, researchers may embarrass officials in technical reports and articles. Some school officials thus may try to ignore researchers if they can, and work with them when they must.

In the City school district, the political loyalties of the field staff involved in the UMSL project were suspected by magnet school officials until the project staff issued a confidential report which highlighted many of the political problems the magnet schools were experiencing. After that, relations grew more cordial. During the second year of the magnet school program, the project staff worked much more closely with several of the schools in the program and tried to make known the lessons that could be learned from the magnet school experience and applied throughout the district should a comprehenseive desegregation plan be enacted.

Project staff also have spent a good deal of time observing the maneuvering in and outside of the court which may lead to such a desegregation plan, and in producing two major reports summarizing the proceedings and making recommendations on a procedure for achieving a mediated desegregation plan. This activity has gained legitimacy for the project as a source of credible information—and, therefore, some degree of influence. In addition, the senior author was selected by the administration to serve as facilitator for the ongoing staff seminar for the superintendent and his top 25 staff.[8]

Foundation officials and researchers from other area universities also represent this category of monitoring. The activities of the Danforth Foundation and the National Conference of Christians and Jews have been described, with their sponsorship of the Interrim Citizens Steering Committee and the Interfaith Clergy Council both laying the groundwork for potential citizen monitoring in the future.

Researchers from other universities have been involved: as consultants to the various parties (two from the same department at Washington University have gone different routes, one in drawing up the desegregation plan presented to the court by the black parents group, and the other as a full-time consultant to the superintendent to develop closer linkages between the schools and other institutions), as providers of demographic data to all parties (St. Louis University), as "academic humanists" on the various programs sponsored by the CETF and other groups with Missouri Humanities money, and as evaluators of various school and community programs (including the CETF's workshops and forums). Of all this involvement, the most sustained has been that of the University of Missouri-St. Louis project staff in monitoring court proceedings and developing reports which summarize the situation and make recommendations.

Together, the foundation representatives and academic researchers in St. Louis form an extensive network both within and outside of the schools, and their information—if pooled and systematized—would afford a comprehensive picture of desegregation which no single party has available to it.

In summary, an examination of various monitoring and monitoring-related activities regarding the St. Louis public schools yields a picture of involvement of all four types of monitors, no court support for monitoring at this point while the desegregation case still is in the appeals stage, relatively little coordination among the various bodies conducting monitoring, and little demonstrated success in relating information discovered and strategies recommended to action on the part of the school system.

It may be concluded, however, that important organizational and technical groundwork has been laid for effective monitoring under the court-ordered desegregation plan and monitoring committee that began functioning in the summer of 1980.

School Desegregation and Monitoring in the Ferguson-Florissant School District

Unlike the City's school system, the Ferguson-Florissant Reorganized School District has no formal evaluation department. But like the City, the suburban district has been the site of activity of a court-ordered "monitoring" committee—the Bi-Racial Advisory Council established by the judge when the districts were ordered merged and desegregated in 1975. Also like the City, monitoring activities in the Ferguson-Florissant district have been fragmented and have made virtually no visible impact on the operations of the school system.

School System.   Monitoring of school programs, academic achievement, and student/teacher relations by the district is conducted under the auspices of one or more of the several assistant superintendents in the district. The merger and desegregation process have expanded the types and amount of information collected, but apparently not the process through which it is gathered. Nor does it seem that information about problems occurring in the schools has been systematically analyzed and acted upon. Funds had been designated to hire an evaluator for programs introduced into the schools because of the desegregation process, but that position was deleted from the budget shortly before classroom desegregation began in the fall of 1976, reportedly following a discussion with U.S. Justice Department officials.

The absence of a complete monitoring of each program's successes and failures is reflected in the required report submitted by the district to the federal agencies and the court. The formal reports describe the goals and types of activities called for under different parts of the desegregation program, but there is no assessment of their effectiveness. There has been a wide range of discretion exercised by school officials in the expenditure of desegregation-related funds. Community meetings to facilitate the desegregation process are listed in the reports without indications of the issues raised, recommendations made, or actions taken.

Such reports were prepared by the administration and transmitted to the judge and the Civil Rights Division of the U.S. Department of Justice twice a year for the first few years following the desegregation and merger order of 1975. Now, the reports are filed once a year, and the district is asking the court to be released from its jurisdiction. School officials have contended in the reports, in meetings of citizens and colleagues, and in the media, that desegregation in the district is proceeding smoothly. The court and the federal agencies have accepted this interpretation, although groups of black parents (and on at least one occasion a group of black students) have presented problems regarding the treatment of minority students to the district administrators, the school board, and the judge. In each case, no action has been forthcoming, and in some cases the complainants have been citicized for complaining.

Government Agencies.   The Civil Rights Division of the U.S. Department of Justice was a plaintiff in the suit against the district that resulted in the merger and desegregation order. The Community Relations Service (CRS)—a racial conciliation agency also in the Department of Justice, but without litigative or enforcement powers—helped draw up the desegregation order and develop plans for its implementation. The Missori State Commission on Education also was instrumental in the final plan which emerged and in preparations for implementation.

None of these agencies has engaged in systematic monitoring activities during implementation of the desegregation plan, even though substantial changes have been made from the original plan, including the closing of two relatively new all-black schools and the elimination of virtually all cross-busing (leaving the major impact of busing on black children).

The Civil Rights Division—faced with dozens of open desegregation cases at all times—has never formally monitored or even systematically investigated the implementation of the plan it won in legal proceedings. The attorney in charge has maintained liaison with the assistant to the superintendent in the district, generally on the telephone and in informal meetings in Washington, but only infrequently on site in the district. In the second year of classroom desegregation, the Civil Rights Division was reported to have conducted an informal telephone survey of 100 black families in Kinloch regarding their opinions of the desegregation process to date. Investigations by the UMSL project staff, public officials in Kinloch, the Community Relations Service, and a black district administrator yielded no one who had been part of the sample. The results—which were said to give the district a "clean bill of health"—were never released.

A CRS staff person inquiring about alleged problems in the district was told by the district that the survey indicated there were no basic problems. Both the CRS official and the Civil Rights Division lawyer alleged to have conducted the survey agreed that desegregation implementation had not been monitored thoroughly, adding that they are powerless to conduct adequate monitoring in the absence of a dramatic indication (mass protests or disorders, it is to be assumed) that the process is not working.

A further complication in many districts desegregating under court order is present in this case. Public agencies with special skills in monitoring and community relations—like the CRS and state and local human relations commissions—may be unable to establish a base for monitoring if the court or the Civil Rights Division continues to claim authority over the district. Here, as with a number of issues, the owners of the litigation process often prevent incursions into their presumed jurisdictions by bodies better prepared for the myriad of nonlitigative activities which contribute to the formation and implementation of social policy.

Citizen Groups. As in other desegregating districts, some citizens who are concerned about the problems their children have faced in the schools report a sense of powerlessness. Reported difficulties often are treated by school administrators as unusual incidents or aberrant behavior, rather than representing a pattern of problems to which systemic solutions can be addressed. This is especially clear in the case of black parents and students with problems, but also applies to some white parents and children.

In Ferguson-Florissant, complaints from black parents and students during the first few years of desegregation were referred to a black staff member who is a long-time Kinloch resident and former employee of the old Kinloch school system. Very few complaints moved beyond her office, although alleged problems continue to accumulate. She recently has been retired.

Complaints continue to emerge. In the fall of 1979, a group of Kinloch citizens is charging physical abuse of black students, the continuation of differential rates of suspension and explusion by race[9], differential placement of students in nonacademic courses by race, and discriminatory treatment of black staff. There appears to be no body or process in the district capable of receiving, investigating, analyzing, and recommending (or actually delivering) a response. The citizens have written to the judge regarding many of these issues, and two former Kinloch administrators have filed suit against the district regarding the discrimination changes.[10]

The court-ordered Bi-Racial Advisory Council, mentioned at the beginning of this section, was intended to be such a body—by the CRS and the State Department of Education, if not by the judge. The court created the Council from the board members of the old Berkeley and Kinloch districts who did not become members of the new R-2 board (only one board member from each district was added to the old Ferguson-Florissant board after the merger). According to a district official, there was no direct communication with the judge, no budget, no staff, and a vague mandate. Questions and problems were submitted by the Council to the district administration, but there was no mechanism for follow-up. Sometimes only three or four of the 18 members of the Council attended meetings, and it was discontinued in the fall of 1977, one year after classroom desegregation began.

A major reason for the ineffectiveness of the Bi-Racial Advisory Council as a monitor is by now familiar: it had no way of developing information independent of the district administration. Without independent information, staff, budget, specific mandate, or a close relationship with the judge (or a federal enforcement agency), citizens groups had no power base from which to negotiate their interests vis-à-vis district officials. Lack of daily access to decision-making channels is another problem. A case in point involves the time the Council voted against the administration's recommendation to close several schools, but the schools were closed based on the system's view that certain technical problems (such as the condition of the heating equipment) made it financially impossible to keep them open.[11]

Independent Organizations. The independent researcher in such a setting is without a firm base. Staff of the UMSL project learned this almost immediately after completing a needs assessment in several schools during the fall of 1976 when classroom desegregation began. Many administrators expressed surprise that problems had been identified and that their policies were seen as contributing to those problems, and each incident tended to be defined as isolated and unusual. Access to the schools has been difficult since then, but project staff have maintained a network and an interest in the situation in the district, including contacts with top administrators, staff, parents, and agency personnel concerned with the district. Lacking a mandate or a base for formal monitoring, any impact will be the result of informal influence networks.

The picture of monitoring that emerges in these two desegregating school districts, then, is one of fragmentation, problems of base and role-definition, and continued maintenance of control of the process by school district officials. Without active and accurate monitoring, it is difficult for desegregation plans to be intelligently amended as problems arise during implementation—or, as in the case of the St. Louis public schools, for interest groups outside the school system to gain sufficient input into the formulation and planning processes for any plan to receive wide community acceptance.

In these two school districts, attempts at outside influence, oversight, and/or formal monitoring have not been very effective (Monti, 1979b). This continuation of unilateral control by school administrators and board (whose major responsibilities include organizational maintenance of the school system) suggests that the chances for success of educational reforms like desegregation will continue to be low.

IMPLICATIONS FOR SOCIAL POLICY AND INTERVENTION STRATEGIES

The activities of the school desegregation monitor have been analyzed in this paper as an emerging social role and as a form of community conflict intervention. Four basic types of monitoring were identified in the light of the base of the activity: within the school system, citizen groups, government agencies, and independent organizations. An examination of monitoring activities in two St. Louis-area school districts at different stages of the desegregation process revealed the existence of all four types of monitors in at least a latent form, and indicated that monitoring efforts had not been very effective in reaching the goals (1) of gaining access to the school system as well as to independent sources of data on which to base recommendations, (2) of providing a systematic reporting and evaluation of the degree to which school system actions are meeting standards established by the court or other authorizing body, or (3) of facilitating changes in the actions of the system to conform more closely with those standards.

There are many implications of this analysis for both school desegregation policies and monitoring intervention strategies, which can be understood only in the light of certain assumptions noted below.

1. Conflict regarding school desegregation will continue at a high level throughout the United States for some years to come—in the courts, across racial and class lines, between professional groups (teachers vis-à-vis administrators, for example), and among parents and other patrons of the public schools.

2. As with all public service delivery systems, the operation of the public schools is first and always a political activity, involving the struggle of the various interest groups involved (board, administration, teachers, staff, parents, students, public agencies, community leaders, the courts, etc.) for control of the process of allocating scarce educational resources.

3. Monitoring is essential if the desegregation effort is to be orderly and produce outcomes acceptable to the courts as well as to the community and the school system.

4. As with every other social role, the monitor represents an interest group in the process of desegregation, so it is inappropriate to regard monitoring as a "neutral" activity. In terms of the intervention role typology presented, monitoring is a mix of Research, Advocacy, Mediation—and sometimes Enforcement.

Among the most important implications for social policy and social intervention are the following:

1. *If quality integrated education with a high degree of citizen involvement is a desired outcome of the desegregation process, then the operation of a combination of monitors is essential at all stages—Decision, Planning, and Implementation.* A broadly representative citizens' monitoring group, authorized and empowered by the court, should be at the heart of the activities in those situations where a desegregation plan has been ordered by the court. Experience in St. Louis and in other cities indicates that, to be able to effectively fulfil its role obligations, such a committee or commission should meet the following criteria, in addition to broad representation:

- Have a clear mandate and specific authority from the court.
- Have complete access to the school system, guaranteed by the court if necessary.
- Have a professional staff and adequate operating budget, with periodic training for staff.
- Conduct its operations openly and share information readily.
- Report often—in clear, direct language—to the court, the school system, and the community.
- Concentrate on follow-up and implementation of the recommendations it offers.

2. *Monitoring of school desegregation should be conducted from a variety of bases in addition to the broad-based citizens' group described above*. If accountability for actions and expenditures is to be forthcoming, it is imperative that each of the interest groups have the ability to look after its own interests. The involvement of the school system, government agencies invested in the schools, and independent organizations can all contribute the variety of bases and interests which insure that no one group will capture the process solely for its own purposes.

3. Increasingly, the courts are intervening in the programs of public service agencies on behalf of clients, citizens, patients, and students. Desegregation suits in the public schools and legal actions focusing on the conditions of confinement and inmate/patient rights in prisons and mental hospitals are the most typical examples. Administrators, board members, and commissioners frequently have complained that their authority to fulfill their obligations in running the system is being usurped by the courts. *Monitoring—especially citizen monitoring—can provide a method for helping shift the locus of control of school systems and other agencies back toward the local community, client groups, and institutions.* Courts have intervened because of allegations of unfair or inadequate service; administrators and professional staffs in schools (and other institutions) need the continuous input and overseeing of their patrons and clients if they are to meet the expressed needs sufficiently to avoid such court action. Returning accountability of local service institutions from the courts to local constituencies is possible with effective monitoring. Without it, school districts may be called back into court for nonperformance of the duties established in a court-ordered desegregation plan (Wright, 1979; Monti, 1980).

4. Like administrators in most institutions, school administrators tend to view problems or conflicts within their jurisdication as isolated incidents, aberrant behavior, or "accidents," rather than as part of a *pattern of behavior*. In fact, conflicts and problem-presentation are highly patterned. As long as officials continue to view them as unpatterned and essentially random, no action will be taken toward policy changes that could be responsive to the problems. *Monitoring, properly performed, can demonstrate beyond reasonable doubt that expulsion ratios, incidents between students and teachers, parental complaints, and teacher assignments, for example, represent a pattern which can be discovered and, if not addressed, can lead to the problems administrators fear most— instability and organized noncompliant behavior on the part of the clients and patrons.* The major aim of monitoring, in the words of one observer, is "to prevent 'accidents'."

5. The foregoing analysis also holds implications for social scientists and other researchers who operate from an organizational base independent of the school system, the courts, the community, or governmental agencies. *The major implication is that independent researchers should recognize that they, too, represent interest groups, and that their activity is not neutral.* The various parties-at-

interest will try to use academic monitors for their own interests. From a perspective of fairness and "evening up the odds," academic monitors could be urged to contribute their skills and the credibility of their organizational base to the parties in the process with the greatest stake and the least formal power—the parents and students. Most of the other interest groups have the resources to look after their own interests—the school system, the courts, the governmental agencies, and the corporate community, for example. Academic researchers who choose to assist parents and students in monitoring or conflict resolution should be prepared to accept the likely consequences of being perceived by the school system as parent and student advocates (Crain, 1976).

Within these parameters, one may predict that the role of the school desegregation monitor will continue to expand and become more clearly defined. One may also predict that as the role becomes more legitimated, the conflict surrounding its articulation will escalate. Social scientists as intervenors can play important roles in constructively dealing with conflicts in school desegregation and other current issues only if they are aware that any such work is a form of intervention, and recognize both the limited potential and the political limits placed on them by their structural base.

ACKNOWLEDGMENTS

The research on which this paper is based was supported in part by the National Institute of Education (NIE 400-76-0103). The opinions expressed herein are the authors' and do not necessarily reflect those of the NIE.

NOTES

1. Laue was principal investigator and Monti project director for a National Institute of Education contract (NIE 400-76-0103) from July 1, 1976 to June 30, 1979, entitled "Strategies and Techniques for Crisis Prevention in Local School Systems." In connection with this contract and ongoing work of the Center for Metropolitan Studies at the University of Missouri-St. Louis, they conducted research, engaged in workshops and training activities, and worked with private and public agencies (national as well as local) toward the development of constructive approaches to resolving desegregation-related conflicts in two St. Louis area school districts—the City of St. Louis and the Ferguson-Florissant R-2 school district. Three senior research analysts made important contributions to development of the data on which this paper is based. They are: Richard Patton, who monitored all court proceedings in the desegregation case in St. Louis and is the primary author of two major policy papers based on that work (see Patton and Laue, *Resolving the Desegregation Issue in the St. Louis Public Schools,* Parts I and II); Frances Thomas, who did extensive field work, especially in the Ferguson-Florissant District, during the first two years of the project; and Gena Scott, whose field work during the first year of the project was concentrated in the City of St. Louis.

2. The legal issues usually center on the question of whether school officials have deliberately or intentionally caused racial segregation in the system's schools in violation of the equal protection clause of the 14th Amendment to the U.S. Constitution.

3. Sixteen years of litigation were required in Los Angeles before the legal issues finally were settled.

4. Organizations currently involved in the practice of community disputes intervention include the Community Relations Service of the U.S. Department of Justice, the Federal Mediation and Conciliation Service, the Community Dispute Services section of the American Arbitration Association (Washington), the Institute for Mediation and Conflict Resolution (New York), the Community Conflict Resolution Program (University of Missouri-St. Louis), the Center for Teaching and Research in Disputes Settlement (University of Wisconsin), the Department of Law, Justice and Community Relations of the United Methodist Church (Washington), the Office of Environmental Mediation (University of Washington, Seattle), the Center for Community Justice (Washington—which works predominantly in the development of grievance procedures in prisons and schools), the Neighborhood Justice Centers in Atlanta, Kansas City, and Los Angeles, and hundreds of recently-formed neighborhood dispute resolution centers based in churches, synagogues, and various public and private service agencies. Three independently-sponsored conferences on community dispute resolution in 1979 in New York, New Jersey, and Kansas City attracted a total of more than 500 persons representing approximately 200 organizations.

5. This definition draws on Carol, 1977 (p. 3) and the authors' field research.

6. The data in this section and the following section are drawn from field work in the district conducted under the auspices of Monti, on Laue's interviews with system officials, and on an interview with John Wright, executive director of the Citizens Education Task Force from Summer 1977 to Summer 1979.

7. The former CETF director, who worked closely with the PACs and helped support their work across school and racial lines, concluded that they "did not have much of a role in monitoring." "Many people didn't know they were even on the Parent Advisory Committee," he said, "and some PACs never met. It depended very much on the principals, and some of them did not call the meetings, even though it was mandated by Title I for the magnet schools." In his view, the PACs "had no effectiveness at all as monitors" (Wright, 1979).

8. It is important to note that a consulting fee is offered to facilitators in this as well as in other staff seminars conducted concurrently, but the senior author has rejected such payment in an effort to maintain greater independence of base.

9. Suspension rates among black students in at least one school in the district were well over 50 percent in a recent year.

10. The allegations of discrimination became widely-known late in October, 1979, when one of St. Louis' major black newspapers carried as its lead story a description of a wide range of charges by the Concerned Parents of Kinloch against the Ferguson-Florissant district ("Ferguson-Florissant Accused of Bias: 'I Will Go To Jail If They Hurt My Children Again' Parent Says," St. Louis American 51, 33 [October 25, 1979] pp. 1, 14).

11. Another form of citizen monitoring which offers a variant on the typology involves the mass media. Media representatives have begun to become sensitive to the charges that they sensationalize reporting of actual or potential conflicts such as school desegregation. Yet if they were to extend ongoing in-depth coverage to the entire desegregation process, they could serve a valuable function in providing the background against which more specific monitoring activities can be conducted. In Ferguson-Florissant, it appears that the media tacitly decided to give very little coverage to the district once initial classroom desegregation was accomplished—both to avoid sensationalism and because the district is not as central to the life of the metropolitan areas as is the St. Louis public school district. As a result, a potentially useful source of monitoring was lost, and problems it might have revealed may not be addressed.

REFERENCES

Bartunek, Jean, Benton, Alan and Keys, Christopher (1975) "Third Party Intervention and the Bargaining Behavior of Group Representatives." *Journal of Conflict Resolution,* 19, 3 (September), pp. 532–57.

Burton, John (1969) *Conflict and Communication*. New York: Oxford University Press.

Carol, Lila (1977) *Viewpoints and Guidelines on Court-Appointed Monitoring Commissions in School Desegregation*. Washington, D.C.: Community Relations Service, U.S. Department of Justice.

Chalmers, W. Ellison (1974) *Racial Negotiations: Potentials and Limitations*. Ann Arbor, Mich.: Institute of Labor and Industrial Relations, University of Michigan, Wayne State University.

Chalmers, W. Ellison and Cormick, Gerald (1971) *Racial Conflict and Negotiations*. Ann Arbor, Mich.: Institute of Labor and Industrial Relations, University of Michigan and Wayne State University.

Coleman, James, *et al.* (1966) *Equality of Educational Opportunity*. U.S. Department of Health, Education and Welfare. Washington, D.C.: U.S. Government Printing Office.

Congressional Record (1976) *Desegregation and the Cities* (Part XVIII 00, "The Facts on Violence") 122, 101, Washington, D.C.: U.S. Government Printing Office.

Crain, Robert, *et al.* (1968) *The Politics of School Desegregation*. Chicago, Ill.: Aldine; (1976) "Why Academic Research Fails to be Useful," pp. 31–46 in F. H. Levinson and B. D. Wright (eds.) *Desegregation: Shadow and Substance*. Chicago, Ill.: University of Chicago Press.

Crain, Robert and Mahard, Rita (1979) "Research on School Desegregation and Achievement: How to Combine Scholarship and Policy Relevance." *Educational Evaluation and Policy Analysis*, 1, 1 (July-August): 5–16.

Dayton Citizens Advisory Board (1977) *Report of 1976–77 School Year in Dayton Schools*. Dayton, Ohio.

Deutsch, Morton (1973) *The Resolution of Conflict: Constructive and Destructive Processes*. New Haven, Ct.: Yale.

Englert, Richard, Kean, Michael and Scribner, Jay (1977) "Politics of Program Evaluation in Large Cities." *Education and Urban Society* 9, 4 (August): 429–50.

Ford Foundation (1978a) *Mediating Social Conflict*. New York.

Ford Foundation (1978b) *New Approaches to Conflict Resolution*. New York.

Foster, Gordon, Jr. (1973) "Desegregating Urban Schools, *Harvard Educational Review*, No. 43, pp. 5–36.

Gant, Herbert (1974) *Intervening in Community Crisis: An Introduction for Psychiatrists*. Washington, D.C.: American Psychiatric Association.

Goldaber, Irving and Porter, Holley (1974) "'The Laboratory Confrontation': An Approach to Conflict Management and Social Change," pp. 122–33 in *Putting Sociology to Work*. Arthur Shostak (ed.), New York: David McKay Co., Inc.

Kelman, Herbert (1972) "The Problem-Solving Workshop in Conflict Resolution," pp. 168–204 in *Communication in International Politics*. Richard L. Merritt (ed.), Chicago, Ill.: University of Illinois Press.

Kirby, David, Harris, T. Robert and Crain, Robert, *et al.* (1973) *Political Strategies in Northern School Desegregation*. Lexington, Mass.: Heath.

Kirp, David (1977) "School Desegregation and the Limits of Legalism." *Harvard Educational Review* 47, 2 (May): 117–137.

Laue, James (1970) *Third Men in New Arenas of Conflict: An Assessment of the National Center for Dispute Settlement and the Racial Negotiations Project*. New York: Ford Foundation.

———(1978a) "Community Peacemaking: Its Role in a United States Academy of Peace and Conflict Resolution." *National Academy of Peace and Conflict Resolution* (Hearings before Subcommittee on International Operations, Committee on International Relations, U.S. House of Representatives, 95th Congress, January 24-25, 1979). Washington, D.C.: U.S. Government Printing Office.

———(1978b) "Advocacy and Sociology", pp. 167–99 in George H. Weber and George J. McCall (ed.), *Social Scientists as Advocates: Views from the Applied Disciplines*, Beverly Hills, Ca.: Sage.

Laue, James and Cormick, Gerald (1978) "The Ethics of Intervention in Community Disputes," pp.

205-32 in Gordon Bermant, Herbert Kelman and Donald Warwick (ed.), *The Ethics of Social Intervention*. Washington, D.C.: Halsted.

Likert, Rensis and Likert, Jane Gibson (1976) *New Ways of Managing Conflict*. New York: McGraw Hill.

Monti, Daniel (1979a) "Some Consequences of Federal and Judicial Non-enforcement of Desegregation Policies." *Integrated Education* (in press).

———(1979b) "Administrative Discrimination in the Implementation of Desegregation Policies." *Evaluation and Policy Analysis* 1, 1 (July–August): 17–26.

———(1980) "Administrative Foxes in Educational Chicken Coops: An Examination of the Critique of Judicial Activism in School Desegregation Cases." *Law and Policy Quarterly* (in press).

Monti, Daniel and Laue, James (1977) "Implementing Desegregation Plans: The Social Scientist as Intervenor." *Education and Urban Society* 9, 3 (May): 369–84.

National Conference of Christians and Jews (1976) *Desegregation Without Turmoil: The Role of the Multi-Racial Community Coalition in Preparing for Smooth Transition*. New York.

Nicolau, Gerald and Cormick, Gerald (1972) "Community Disputes and the Resolution of Conflict: Another View." *Arbitration Journal* 27 (June): pp. 98–112.

Orfield, Gary (1978) *Must We Bus?* Washington, D.C.: The Brookings Institution.

Patton, Richard and Laue, James (1978) With Daniel J. Monti and Frances Thomas. *Resolving the Desegregation Issue in the St. Louis Public Schools*, Part I. St. Louis, Mo.: Center for Metropolitan Studies, University of Missouri-St. Louis; ———(1979) *Resolving the Desegregation Issue in the St. Louis Public Schools*, Part II. St. Louis, Mo.: Center for Metropolitan Studies, University of Missouri-St. Louis.

Pettigrew, Thomas and Green, Robert (1976) "School Desegregation in Large Cities: A Critique of the Coleman 'White Flight' Thesis." *Harvard Educational Review* 46 (February), pp. 1–53.

Racism and Sexism Resource Center for Educators (1977) *Checklist: Rate Your School for Racism and Sexism*. New York.

Ross, J. Michael and Berg, William (1978) *The Social Construction of a School Desegregation Controversy: A Crisis of Law in Society*. (Final Report, Grant No. NIE G-76-0038). Boston: Boston University.

St. John, Nancy (1975) *School Desegregation: Outcomes for Children*. New York: Wiley.

St. Louis American (1979) "Ferguson-Florissant Accused of Bias: 'I Will Go To Jail If They Hurt My Children Again' Parent Says." 51, 33, p. 1. St. Louis, Mo.: October 25, 1979.

Spiegel, John (1973) The Social Role of Antagonists and Third Party Intervenors in Violent Confrontations." *International Journal of Group Tensions* 3, 1–2, pp. 142–59.

Stevens, Leonard and Hunter, Frances (1976) *A Checklist for Assessing School Desegregation Plans*. Cleveland, Oh.: Greater Cleveland Project.

Sussmann, Leila (1977) *Tales Out of School*. Philadelphia, Pa.: Temple University Press.

Wehr, Paul, *et al.* (1979) *Conflict Regulation*. Boulder, Co.: Westview.

Weinberg, Meyer (1975) "The Relationship Between School Desegregation and Academic Achievements: A Review of the Research." *Law and Contemporary Problems* 35, pp. 241–270.

Wilkinson, J. H. (1979) *From Brown to Bakke*. New York: Oxford.

Wright, John (1979) Interview. St. Louis: October 14, 1979.

Wright, John, *et al. Citizens Education Task Force Report to the Community, 1977–1979*. St. Louis, Mo.: Citizens Education Task Force.

THE SLOWING OF MODERNIZATION IN MIDDLETOWN

Howard M. Bahr, Theodore Caplow
and Geoffrey K. Leigh

Although not specifically so described, the first *Middletown* report (Lynd and Lynd, 1929) was a study of modernization, in which Robert and Helen Lynd highlighted the contrast between a traditional society in 1890 and the "modern" attitudes and ways of the same mid-western community in 1924. Theoretical frameworks for studying modernization were still many decades in the future when the Lynds did their work, but they carefully recorded changes in ways of organizing and doing, which today would be identified as the institutional approach to modernization, and changes in ways of thinking and feeling, which would now be called the individual or socio-psychological approach to modernization.

The concept of modernity may be applied to social collectivities at any level of aggregation, from the individual through the community and the nation. At the

Research in Social Movements, Conflicts and Change, Vol. 3, pages 219-232
Copyright © 1980 by JAI Press Inc.
ISBN: 0-89232-182-2

individual level, modernity has two major components: ways of thinking and evaluating (attitudinal modernity) and ways of behaving (behavioral modernity). Doob's (1960) "psychological exploration" of the attitudes accompanying or preceding increase in "civilized" behavior established a clear distinction between the attitudes, motives, and goals of individuals and the behavior of these same persons, which might or might not be consistent with these psychological characteristics. Similarly, Portes (1973:16) distinguished between the structural-analytic level, on which modernization is a term denoting urbanization, literacy, industrialization, and economic development, and the cultural-analytic level on which "modernity is portrayed as a consistent set of values and general orientations permeating a society." Inkeles (1973:60–61) makes a similar division between modernization as reflected in patterns of social organization, or institutional modernization, and modernization as "a process of change in ways of perceiving, expressing, and valuing." Inkeles and his associates also separate individual attitudinal modernity from individual behavior (cf. 1973:82; Smith and Inkeles, 1966:373–376), although their indexes of individual modernity include informational and behavioral items as well as attitudes.

The Lynds used 1890 as a base period from which to measure the changes that had taken place in Middletown by the early 1920s. In 1890, Middletown had been in the earliest stage of industrial development. Before the discovery of natural gas in the vicinity, Middletown had been "a placid county-seat" which "still retained some of the simplicity of this earlier pioneer life." In the 1880s, "the thin edge of industry was beginning to appear," but the city was primarily an agricultural center. Even in 1890, after the surge of growth that accompanied the gas boom, the "developed industrial culture" of 1924 did not yet exist, for:

> The young Goliath, Industry, was still a neighborly sort of fellow. The agricultural predomi-
> nance in the county-seat was gone, but the diffusion of the new industrial type of culture was
> as yet largely superficial—only skin-deep (Lynd and Lynd, 1929:17).

Middletown showed how the industrial development—in our terms, the modernization—of Middletown had more effect on certain ways of thinking and doing than upon others. Some groups and institutions were modernized and others were not. Thus, the Lynds described Middletown as using "the psychology of the last century in training its children in the home and the psychology of the current century in persuading its citizens to buy articles from the stores," and the typical housewife as "living in one in the way she cleans her house or does her washing and in another in the care of her children or in her marital relations" (Lynd and Lynd, 1929:497–98).

They concluded that the rate of change had varied widely and the directions of change were "highly erratic." Many of the social problems of the community were perceived as "to no small extent traceable to the ragged, unsynchronized movement of social institutions." The Lynds identified "the process of secularization of Middletown's institutions" as a dominant trend and pointed out an accompanying "readiness to accede to the demands of a changing cultural environment," the "increased role of youth with its greater adaptability," the "shifting relative status of men and women," and the differences in normative restraints imposed upon identical activities by different groups in the community (Lynd and Lynd, 1929:499–501).

In other words, the Middletown of 1924 was undergoing modernization, but the effects of the process varied among individuals, groups, and institutions. More than half a century has since elapsed and it should now be possible to see whether the lags and leads observed by the Lynds have evened themselves out, or whether new disjunctures appeared as the process of modernization continued— perhaps even the condition of "future shock" so vividly described by Toffler (1970), with its social-psychological traumas and institutional incongruities.

This is a large problem, and we cannot hope to resolve it fully, either for Middletown or Middle America, but we do have some data that permit a modest, preliminary exploration. The Middletown III project is a general replication of the Lynds' two earlier surveys of the same city, carried out in 1924–25 and 1935 (Lynd and Lynd, 1929, 1937). The fieldwork for Middletown III was conducted in 1976–78; it included an updating of almost every time series mentioned by the Lynds in either *Middletown* or *Middletown in Transition,* as well as the replication, in one form or another, of the several surveys included in their study. Thus, in the Winter of 1977 the entire high school population of Middletown was asked to respond to a written questionnaire that included 20 attitude items from a questionnaire administered by the Lynds to high school students 53 years earlier. By a fortunate chance, some of these items may be used to describe individual modernity, and these two adolescent populations, approximately two generations apart, seem particularly appropriate for an inquiry into the rate of change of individual modernity. With respect to collective modernity, the Lynds' numerous time series, extended forward to the 1970s, enable us to measure parallel, or non-parallel, rates of change. Neither set of data is as good as we would like to have it, but both sets provide more reliable information about the base period than could be obtained by the customary method of reconstructing the attitudes and behaviors of the past from documents and reminiscences.

INDIVIDUAL MODERNIZATION: THE EMPIRICAL EVIDENCE

None of the attitude items used by the Lynds appears verbatim in the modernity scales used today, but several of them embody the same themes as indicators of modernity reported in the recent literature. For long-term comparisons, we are limited to the attitude items for which the Lynds published percentage distributions in *Middletown;* these consist of 20 items from the true-false questionnaire they administered to students in junior and senior social science classes, plus a few attitude items from the "life of the high school population" questionnaire administered to sophomore, junior, and senior students in English classes (Lynd and Lynd, 1929:509). Detailed comparisons between the 1924 and 1977 respondents for the entire "universe" of attitude items, and descriptions of the data collection process in 1977, are available elsewhere (Caplow and Bahr, 1979; Bahr, 1979).

The use of some of these items as indicators of modernity needs to be justified item-by-item:

One of the major dimensions of modern belief systems is empiricism, or belief in science (cf. Armer and Youtz, 1971:608, 623; Doob, 1960:31–33; Doob, 1967; Smith and Inkeles, 1966). The Lynds' item, "the theory of evolution offers a more accurate account of the origin and history of mankind than that offered by a literal interpretation of the first chapters of the Bible," clearly offers a choice between traditional and modern belief systems.

An attitude toward religion centered on its value in dealing with practical, human problems in contrast to other-worldly phenomena is also characteristic of modernized societies (cf. Cox, 1965). This attitude is (negatively) implied by the Lynds' item: "The purpose of religion is to prepare people for the hereafter."

The "growth of opinion" variable of modernity, as explained by Inkeles, includes the individual's willingness to form or hold opinions on a variety of problems and issues, and to tolerate or even enjoy a diversity of opinion. The modernized persons puts a positive value on variations in opinion (Inkeles, 1973:69). Armer and Youtz (1971:624) refer to the "value orientation" of "openness to ideas and experiences," and one of their items is "Persons should (always/sometimes/never) be allowed to express minority ideas." The Lynds' item on free speech is a close variation on this theme: "A citizen of the United States should be allowed to say anything he pleases, even to advocate violent revolution, if he does no violent act himself."

Although some students of modernization include the decline of religious commitment and observance as a characteristic of modernization, this viewpoint involves some inconsistencies. Inkeles (1977:162), for example, notes that although the United States is one of the most modernized of nations, its rates of church membership are among the highest in the world. Whether religiosity is compatible with, or antithetical to modernization, seems to depend on the nature of the religious beliefs and required observances, as even the most cursory acquaintance with Weber's (1930) *The Protestant Ethic* ought to suggest. On the other hand, the idea that the religious view of others, when different from one's own, may be worthy of respect is clearly part of the "openness to ideas" that is central to modernity. The item used by the Lynds to assess Middletown students' commitment to missionary Christianity, "Christianity is the one true religion and all peoples should be converted to it," may be interpreted (inversely) as a measure of "openness to ideas" in matters of personal faith.

Most of the currently-used scales of individual modernity include some reference to the mass media. Inkeles stresses that while modernized people may continue to rely on both modern and traditional sources of information, they "would have greater confidence in and rely most heavily on the newer mass media" (Inkeles, 1973:85), and Schnaiberg (1970:402) explicitly mentions passive participation in media consumption in substitution for personal interaction as an attribute of the modern individual. Consequently, two items used by the Lynds to gauge respondents' confidence in the mass media, one referring to Middletown's local newspaper and the other to national magazines, may be taken as indicators of individual modernity.

Whether modernization is more likely to strengthen or dissolve relationships in the nuclear family remains an unsettled question. Inkeles' (1977:162) review of the research evidence on this matter from the Harvard six-nation study indicates that even with respect to the extended family, the experience of modernization often strengthens rather than weakens the family. However, one of the Lynds' family-related items, namely students' identification of homemaking skills as a most desirable quality in a mother, touches upon the equalization of women that figures so prominently in most discussions of modernization (Inkeles, 1970:66; Schnaiberg, 1970:401; Sack, 1973:254; Armer and Youtz, 1971:624). If we argue that *not* to identify "being a good cook and housekeeper" as one of the two qualities most desirable in a mother reflects the more modern attitude, then that item can also be used as an indicator of modernism.

These then are the seven indicators of individual modernity, for which we have responses from a large proportion of Middletown's high school population in 1924, and again in 1977. The two distributions are summarized and compared in Table 1.

The percentages in Table 1 support the notion that Middletown students of 1977 are considerably more modern than were their grandparents at the same age in 1924.[1] They are much more likely to look to science rather than to the Bible in accounting for the origin of mankind, much more favorable to freedom of speech and much less sure of the universal applicability of the Christian religion. They have slightly more confidence in the local newspaper, and are significantly less likely than their 1924 predecessors to associate housekeeping with ideal motherhood. In other words, on five of the seven items, the 1977 adolescents were significantly more modern. The two items on which there was not clear evidence of increased modernity were the view of religion as other-worldly (the 1977 students were about as likely as the 1924 students to agree with the statement that the purpose of religion is to prepare people for the hereafter), and the degree of confidence in the veracity of national magazines (not too much should be made of this finding, because the 1977 item necessarily mentioned as examples other magazines than those used in 1924).

Despite the statistically significant differences displayed in Table 1, we were startled by the persistence and prevalence of non-modern attitudes among Middletown's adolescents. For example, despite the rise from 1924 to 1977 in the

Table 1. Indicators of Psychological Modernism, Middletown High School Students, 1924 and 1977

Item	Modernization Variable	Percent Agreeing			
		Males		Females	
		1924[a]	1977	1924[a]	1977
The theory of evolution offers a more accurate account of the origin and history of mankind than that offered by a literal interpretation of the first chapters of the Bible.	Belief in science	28%[b] (372) *	55% (253)	28%[b] (372) *	45% (275)
The purpose of religion is to prepare people for the hereafter.	Secularization	57 (203)	54 (271)	62 (290)	53 (310)
A citizen of the United States should be allowed to say anything he pleases, even to advocate violent revolution, if he does no violent act himself.	Openness to ideas	22 (217) *	53 (266)	18 (287) *	42 (293)
Christianity is the one true religion and all peoples should be converted to it.	Openness to ideas	90 (222) *	38 (411)	97 (299) *	39 (475)

Item	Confidence in mass media / Equality of women					
The Middletown newspaper presented a fair and complete picture of the issues in the recent election (1977: . . . picture in covering the issues and the candidates in the recent presidential election).	51 (142)	*	69 (147)		64 (176)	72 (162)
It is safe to assume that a statement appearing in an article in a reputable magazine like the *Saturday Evening Post* or the *American Magazine* is correct (1977: . . . like *Time* or *Newsweek* is correct).	45 (193)	*	41 (150)		54 (248)	* 41 (169)
Being a good cook and housekeeper is one of the two qualities most desirable in a mother.	57 (369)	*	41 (462)		52 (423)	* 24 (506)

*Percentage differences between adjoining columns are statistically significant at the .01 level.

a Sources for the published figures for 1924 used to compute the percentages and N's in this table are the following pages in Middletown (Lynd and Lynd, 1929): 200–201, 204–205, 316, 319, 477, and 524. The Lynds' format included the option of "Uncertain" as well as "True" and "False." Because of the ambiguity of the "Uncertain" response, we have recalculated the Lynds' published percentages to show the number of respondents who agreed with the item as a proportion of the total who indicated either agreement or disagreement. Thus, the percentages and percentage bases in Tables 1 and 2 do not agree exactly with those published in *Middletown*. The 1977 questionnaire allowed four responses, "strongly agree," "agree," "disagree," "strongly disagree," which were regrouped into "agree" and "disagree" for the present analysis.

b The Lynds did not publish breakdowns by sex for this item.

225

proportion of respondents affirming a belief in evolutionary theory over the literal Biblical interpretation of mankind's origin, about half of them still cling to a literal interpretation of the Biblical account of creation. The continuing secularization of religion between 1925 and 1937 noted by the Lynds in their second study (1937:304–307), and illustrated by various quotations (such as this one from a 1934 newspaper editorial: "So far as youth is concerned, we may as well admit that any formalism in religion is out of the picture"), might have been expected to proceed much farther than it has in the ensuing 40 years. The difference between the proportion of 1924 and 1977 respondents who affirmed the purpose of religion as preparation for the hereafter does not even reach statistical significance.

Thus, although the Muncie adolescents of 1977 are more modern than their predecessors of 1924, the proportion of them who continue to hold "nonmodern" attitudes with respect to science, religion, the mass media, and the role of women, suggest that the rapid rate of attitudinal change ascribed by the Lynds to the periods between 1890 and 1924 and between 1924 and 1935 must have slowed down after 1935.

The Lynds, although they were highly aware of Middletown's propensity to look to the past for the solution of present problems, seemed to prophesy—in their original study and again in its sequel, when they spoke eloquently of the "mounting restlessness of the young" (1937:486)—that there would be much more change in Middletown's values and activities in the ensuing decades than we now find to have occurred. Viewed against the concluding chapters of *Middletown in Transition* or against current pronouncements about "future shock," the recent effects of modernization upon individual attitudes in Middletown seem curiously modest.

To interpret this unexpected finding, we need to know more about the concurrent rate of institutional modernization in Middletown, and to this we now turn our attention.

INSTITUTIONAL MODERNIZATION: QUANTITATIVE INDICATORS

Institutional modernization may be defined as the process whereby a contemporary society improves its control of the environment by means of an increasingly competent technology applied by increasingly complex institutions. Note that the process is held to occur only in contemporary (19th and 20th century) societies and is assumed to be continuous and unidirectional, leaving no room for the possibility that an increasingly competent technology might be applied by decreasingly complex institutions, or the possibility that control of the environment might deteriorate in the presence of increasingly complex institutions. (These regressive possibilities used to appear much more remote than they do now).

If we want to measure the rate of institutional modernization in Middletown from 1925 to 1975, we must devise quantitative measures for the implied variable "control of the environment." To do this is to abandon the broad concept of "control of the environment" in favor of specific indicators that report particular kinds of controlling activity, but that probably do not tell the whole story about the relationship of man and environment and how that relationship evolves in a high-energy social system.

In studies of modernization at the Columbia Bureau of Applied Social Research in the 1960's Caplow and Finsterbusch (1964; 1967) experimented with many indicators, combined them into a variety of indexes, and finally settled—for methodological convenience—on telephones per capita (Caplow, 1971). This measure is obtainable from nearly all countries in reasonably reliable form and tends to put centralized and uncentralized economies on a more even footing than measures of consumer goods, like automobiles or housing. Moreover, its correlations with other quantitative indicators of modernization—more than 100 plausible ones were evaluated—are extremely high; Spearman r's often exceed .95.

Among the most meaningful of these other indicators are energy consumption per capita, industrial productivity per man-hour, life-expectancy at birth, all measures of formal education, the intensity of occupational specialization, calories consumed per capita, durable goods consumed per capita, per capita exposure to mass media, passenger miles traveled per capita, the ratio of vacation to work time, the proportion of the population urbanized, and the proportion of the labor force in white-collar occupations.

Although most of these indicators come in handy quantified form, they suffer from all sorts of Weber-Fechner, diminishing return and marginal utility effects, so that it can never be safely assumed that an increase of n units from T_1 to T_2 has the same social or psychological influence as an increase of n units in the same indicator from T_2 to T_3. It may have less, or more, or be incommensurate, depending on the overall shape of the curve and a variety of qualitative factors. To take two examples at random: an increase of one or two percent in literacy when a society's literacy rate stands close to 100 percent is much more significant than the same percentage increase would have been at an earlier point in that society's history when illiteracy was rampant; and a *decrease* in energy consumption per capita may signal more technological progress than an increase once the supply of energy has begun to run short.

Our preference for a ratio of telephones to population as the best single indicator of modernization rests upon the fact that, of all the available indicators, it is perhaps the least subject to the foregoing effects. For Middletown in the selected period, it is nearly free of the distortions that might be expected close to the start-up point of a telephone system when rates of increase tend to be exceptionally high or close to the saturation point when they tend to be exceptionally low. By 1925, Middletown already had a mature telephone system; the number of telephones per capita (.216) being about the same as the number of telephones per capita in France in 1973 (.217) (Statistical Yearbook, 1975). On the other hand, the 1975 telephone frequency of .448 was well below the level attained by some other American and European communities. A further advantage of the telephone series is that, being drawn from the list of subscribers that every telephone system requires in order to operate, the annual entries in this series are more reliable than those in other series obtained by *ad hoc* enumeration.

The available information on number of telephones in Middletown at five-year intervals between 1925 and 1975 is presented in Table 2. There are some minor difficulties in the comparison of the post-1950 data with the Lynds' figures for 1925–35. The latter were said to include "all extensions from business and factory switchboards and in private residences." Such totals are not available for the 1950–60 period, for which we have only the number of customers. For 1965–75, both number of customers and number of additional extensions are available, but residential extensions became much more common in the 1965–75 decade than they had been previously.

The unavailability of information about extensions for the 1950–60 era, coupled with the presumption that the presence of a telephone in a residential unit is a more significant indicator of modernization than the presence of multiple extensions, led us to a hybrid series, based on the Lynds' "total telephones" for 1925–35 (the only figures available) and on "number of customers" from 1950 to 1975. Also, since the median household size in Middletown declined from 3.13 in 1930 to 2.40 in 1970, and the mean size of family fluctuated from 3.13 in

Table 2.   Number of Telephones in Use in Middletown: 1925–1975

Year	Middletown Population[a]	Occupied Housing Units	Number of Customers	Residential Customers	Extensions	Total	Customers[b] per Household	Customers[b] per Capita
1925	36,500	—	—	—	—	7,871[c]	—	.216
1930	46,548	12,292	—	—	—	8,931[c]	.727	.192
1935	47,000	—	—	—	—	7,130[c]	—	.152
1950	58,479	18,007	21,005	—	—	—	1.166	.359
1955	63,400	—	23,784	—	—	—	—	.375
1960	68,603	20,930	26,813	—	—	—	1.281	.391
1965	71,100	—	30,610	24,741	20,922[d]	51,532[d]	—	.431
1970	69,082	21,590	34,157	28,338	30,042	64,204	1.582	.494
1975	79,932	—	35,776	30,163	37,148	72,924	—	.448

[a] Figures for 1925 and 1935 are from Lynd and Lynd (1937:517); all other intercensal figures are estimates from the Middletown III project. Details are available in a project memorandum by Geoffrey Leigh, "Population of Middletown."

[b] 1935 and earlier are total telephones per household or per capita.

[c] The Lynds (1937:564) reported the number of telephone instruments as including "all extensions from business and factory switchboards and in private residences."

[d] 1965 figures for extensions and total are estimates from percentages based on available figures for growth rates 1966–70.

Sources: Annual Report of Indiana Bell Telephone Company, Business Office, Indianapolis (1950–65); Annual Report of Indiana Bell Telephone Company, Managers Office, Middletown (1966–75). No figures were available for Middletown prior to 1950 except for the Lynds' tables in *Middletown in Transition*

1930 to a high of 3.52 in 1960 and then down again to 3.37 in 1970, it seems to us that the ratio of telephones (or telephone customers) to the number of households is a better indicator of access to telephones than the per capita ratio.
be.

As can be seen in Table 2, the number of telephones in Middletown increased between 1925 and 1930, then decreased quite sharply between 1930 and 1935 as a consequence of the Depression. There was a very rapid increase between 1935 and 1950, but data are not available to follow that increase in detail. However, from 1950 to 1975 we have increasingly complete information and it is evident that the rate of increase in telephones per household for the 20-year period, 1950–1970, was much slower than that for the preceding 20-year period, 1930–1950. In 1930, the ratio of telephones to households was .727; by 1950, there were 1.166 telephone customers per household, an increase of more than 60 percent. In 1970, the ratio of telephone customers to households was 1.582, an increase over 1950 of 36 percent. If this ratio is taken as an indicator of modernization, the rate of modernization from 1950–1970 was only about half the rate that prevailed from 1930–1950.

For reference purposes, we also include in Table 2 a column on number of telephone customers per capita; this series shows an even more marked deceleration from the earlier period to the later period. The .216 telephones per capita of the Middletown population in 1925 had increased to .359 by the midpoint of the period, 1950, equivalent to an uncompounded annual increase of 2.6 percent for the first 25 years. From 1950 to 1975, the further increase was from .359 to .448, an average annual rate of just under 1 percent.

Although we placed our principal reliance upon telephones per capita, other available series show parallel trends. Hospital admissions per capita—another good indicator of modernization—rose from .033 in Middletown in 1925, to .156 in 1950, and to .292 in 1975. The average uncompounded annual increase was 15 percent during the first period and a little over 3 percent during the second, notwithstanding that in the latter period there was a great expansion of hospital insurance and federally-supported medical care. The number of passenger automobiles per capita in Middletown's county increased from .173 in 1925, to .316 in 1950, and to .462 in 1975, at a nearly constant average increment of .068 per year but an average annual rate declining from 4 percent in the first period to 2 percent in the second. Another good indictor of modernization is the number of adolescents (aged 14 to 19) in school compared to those gainfully employed. In the decade 1920 to 1930, this ratio for Middletown increased from 0.158 to 0.365 at an average annual rate of 23 percent, while in the decade 1960 to 1970, it increased from 1.710 to 2.470 at an average rate of only 4 percent.

There may be an objection that these data do not take account of some entirely new technologies that were introduced during the half-century 1925–75—especially television, space travel, and computer science. This objection might have been well-founded with respect to television at some intermediate time, but by 1975 the growth of television—measured either by television sets per capita or hours of viewing per set—had approached saturation and leveled off, while space travel was too remote from the experience of local residents to have much effect on their attitudes or behavior. The case of the computer is a little more complex. Its use in Middletown businesses and homes was still accelerating sharply in 1975 without, as yet, having affected any social or psychological transformations. The potential of such transformation was there, however, and this must be marked down as a major area of uncertainty in our analysis.

SUMMARY

We set out first to determine whether Middletown adolescents were more modernized in 1977 than the adolescents of their grandparents' generation in 1924, and the answer based upon the several key indicators of individual modernization provided by our replication in 1977 of the Lynds' 1924 attitude survey, is clearly affirmative. However, on most of these indicators, the attitudes of the 1977 respondents were much closer to those of their 1924 counterparts than we had expected. Non-modern attitudes are still very prevalent among Middletown's young people and their eventual disappearance cannot be predicted with any confidence from the available evidence.

Needless to say, we have no way of telling, from measurements made at two widely-separated points of time, what the intervening trend may have been. It is conceivable, and not even very unlikely, that the Middletown adolescents of 1957 or 1967 may have had more secularized attitudes toward religion than those of 1977. In other words, we may inadvertently be recording a reaction back to traditional values rather than the result of a slow, steady drift away from them. But if this were the case, it would be another facet of the slowing down of modernization; such oscillations between the poles of traditionalism and modernity are uncommon under conditions of rapid modernization.

When we looked at some indicators of institutional modernization, the findings were essentially parallel. On the one hand, the process of modernization has indubitably continued. There are more facilities for communication, transportation, medical care, and education in Middletown now than there were half a century ago and the average citizen makes more use of these facilities now than then, but these quantitative changes have not been accompanied by any fundamental transformation. The industrial Middletown of 1924 was a different kind of community than the agricultural trade center of 1880 or the gas boom town of 1890, but today's Middletown—despite the quantitative changes and the many variations of detail—displays the same institutional patterns the Lynds described so painstakingly. It is still stratified the same way (Caplow, 1978). The same varieties of denominational Christianity are practiced now as then, with the same leaning toward extreme evangelism; the same two parties alternate control of the local government, with about the same degree of corruption. When we look at a particular institutional sector such as the relationships of the nuclear family

(Bahr, 1979) or the distribution of income and occupational status (Caplow and Chadwick, 1979), the persistence of old patterns is unmistakable. Even in trivial details, the new Middletown is like the old Middletown. High school basketball still engages the interest of the entire community. Adolescent social life still depends on access to the family car. Saturday night is still the best night for a dance or party. The Chamber of Commerce still preaches civic loyalty. The same local newspaper still preaches the ideology of small business to unheeding factory workers. The only conspicuous new elements in the local pattern are the massive intrusion of the television network into Middletown's homes and of federal agencies into its offices and factories, but for reasons that we do not completely understand, these outside influences have remained peripheral to local institutions.

The explanation of this peculiar and unanticipated stability is found, we think, in the slowing of modernization, revealed by the telephone data and other series. The forces of change have been winding down in Middletown and will probably continue to do so for some time to come. Middletown adolescents of today have so far experienced less social change than their parents or grandparents, and much less than their great-grandparents, who lived through the cataclysmic transition from a predominantly rural to a predominantly urban society and from an economy based on muscular effort to one drawing on vast supplies of mechanical power.

As its population has stabilized and as the rate of modernization has decelerated, Middletown has become, for the first time in its history, a place where the present resembles the past and prefigures the probable future. If nothing more, the contemplation of this specimen community may help to quiet some of the apprehensions aroused by futurists whose images of the past are as arbitrary and speculative as their images of the future.

ACKNOWLEDGEMENTS

This is Paper No. 14 of the MIDDLETOWN III PROJECT, Supported by the National Science Foundation, grant #SOC 75-13580. The investigators are Theodore Caplow, Howard M. Bahr, and Bruce A. Chadwick. Preparation of this paper was also supported in part by the Family Research Institute of Brigham Young University.

NOTES

1. This is a metaphor, but we estimate from other data that about 30 percent of our 1977 respondents *did* have one or more grandparents in the 1924 student sample.

REFERENCES

Armer, Michael and Robert Youtz (1971) "Formal Education and Individual Modernity in an African Society," *American Journal of Sociology* 76 (January):604-26.
Bahr, Howard M. (1979) "Changes in Family Life in Middletown, 1924-77," *Public Opinion Quarterly,* 44 (Fall):35-52.

Caplow, Theodore (1971) "Are the Rich Countries Getting Richer and the Poor Countries Poorer?'',
   Foreign Policy 1 (Summer).
Caplow, Theodore and Howard M. Bahr (1979) "Half a Century of Change in Adolescent Attitudes:
   Replication of a Middletown Survey by the Lynds,'' Public Opinion Quarterly, Vol. 43 #1,
   (Spring 1979):1–17.
Caplow, Theodore and Bruce A. Chadwick (1979) "Inequality and Life-styles in Middletown,
   1920–1978,'' Social Science Quarterly, Vol. 60, No. 3 (Dec.):367–386.
Caplow, Theodore and Kurt Finsterbusch (1964) A Matrix of Modernization. New York: Columbia
   University, Bureau of Applied Social Research.
———(1967) Development Rank: A New Method of Rating National Development. New York:
   Columbia University, Bureau of Applied Social Research.
Cox, Harvey (1965) The Secular City. New York: Macmillan.
Doob, Leonard W. (1960) Becoming More Civilized. New Haven, Ct.: Yale University Press.
   ———1967 "Scales for Assaying Psychological Modernization in Africa,'' Public Opinion
   Quarterly 31 (Fall):414–21.
Inkeles, Alex (1970) "Becoming Modern,'' et al. 2 (No. 3):58–73.
———(1973) "A Model of Modern Man: Theoretical and Methodological Issues,'' pp. 59–92 in
   Nancy Hammon, (Ed.), Social Science and the New Societies. East Lansing, Mich.: Social
   Science Research Bureau, Michigan State University.
———(1977) "Understanding and Misunderstanding Individual Modernity,'' Journal of Cross-
   Cultural Psychology 8 (June):135–76.
Lynd, Robert S. and Helen Merrell Lynd (1929) Middletown. New York: Harcourt, Brace & World.
———(1937) Middletown in Transition. New York: Harcourt, Brace & World.
Portes, Alejandro (1973) "The Factorial Structure of Modernity: Empirical Replications and a
   Critique,'' American Journal of Sociology 79 (July:15–44.)
Sack, Richard (1973) "The Impact of Education of Individual Modernity in Tunisia,'' International
   Journal of Comparative Sociology 14 (September):245–72.
Schnaiberg, Allan (1970) "Measuring Modernism: Theoretical and Empirical Explorations,''
   American Journal of Sociology 76 (December):399–425.
Smith, David Horton and Alex Inkeles (1966) "The OM Scale: A Comparative Socio-Psychological
   Measure of Individual Modernity,'' Sociometry 29 (December:353–77).
Statistical Yearbook of the United Nations (1975) Table 167.
Toffler, Alvin (1970) Future Shock. New York: Random House.
Weber, Max (1930) The Protestant Ethic and the Spirit of Capitalism, trans. Talcott Parsons. New
   York: Charles Scribner's Sons.

AUTHOR INDEX

INDEX PREPARED BY REX OLSON

SUBJECT INDEX

Bonaparte, Napolean, 122
  Also see Theory of press influence
Bond, Julian, 61

Carmichael, Stokley, 57
Carter, Jimmy, 114
  Also see Conflict, Egyptian-Israeli
Chavez, Cesar, 15
China, 11
Citizens Education Task Force, 204–
    206, 208
  Also see Conflict, community inter-
    vention
Clark, Ramsey, 12
Coalition for Human Rights in South
    Africa, 55, 62
  Also see Social Movement Organi-
    zation
Common cause, 13
Communications, 172, 175, 176, 179,
    181–188
  Also see Social Movement Organi-
    zation and Modernity
Communist party, 57
Community relations service, 209–211
Conflict, 29–39, 69–117, 169–184
  American-Soviet, 100, 101, 107,
    112, 113
  Cold War, 104
  community intervention, 191, 193
  Cuban missile crisis, 104
  de-escalation of, 99, 102, 103, 105,
    108–111, 113–115
  Egyptian-Israeli, 99, 102, 65–117
  escalation of (see: de-escalation)
  generational, 29–31 (see: Activists,
    socialization of)
  interlocking, xi, xii, 12, 13, 99,
    100, 106–111, 115
  objective conditions of, ix, x
  realism of, x–xiii, 76, 116
  Sinai, 110

Spanish American War of, 1898,
    123
subjective autonomy (see: objective
    conditions)
unrealism (see: realism)
Vietnam War, 7, 35, 36, 38, 39,
    101, 126, 146
World War II, 108, 170
Congress of Industrial Organizations,
    15
Consciousness
  radical, political, 24, 26, 27, 30
  of parents, 25, 30
  of students, 25, 30
  working class, 143–146, 161, 163,
    165
  Also see Ideology
Collective action, xi, 45–47, 51, 52,
    58, 61, 63–65
  collective good in, 48
  definition of, 45
  diffusion of, 51, 52, 54, 65–67
  goals of, 46, 59
  rationalism in, 46, 47, 49, 67 (see:
    Conflict, realism and objective
    conditions)
  selective incentives in, 48, 49, 51,
    53, 58, 64
  Also see Social movements
CORE, 11, 13
Cyprus, 102

Davis Cup Protests, 54–56, 62–67
Demonstrations, 57, 59, 60, 62, 65
  Also see Activism student
Department of Defense, 149
Desegregation, 189–191, 195, 199,
    209–212
Durkheim, Emile, 91

Engels, F., 144

INDEX PREPARED BY REX OLSON

Research in Social Movements, Conflicts and Change

A Research Annual

Series Editor: **Louis Kriesberg**
Department of Sociology
Syracuse University.

REVIEWS: ". . .recommended for graduate libraries." — *Choice*

". . .The papers are generally of excellent quality. . .a useful series of annual volumes. . ."
— *Social Forces*

". . .an excellent series of original articles. . .the papers are broad in scope and methodologically diverse. . .a welcome departure from the traditional 'social roots' approach and offers new insights into 'feedback effects' of social movements. . .useful anthologies that are theoretically informed and timely." —*Political Sociology*

Volume 1.   **Published 1978**   **Cloth**   **Institutions $ 32.50**
ISBN 0-89232-027-3   **350 pages**   **Individuals $ 16.25**

Volume 2.   **Published 1979**   **Cloth**   **Institutions: $ 32.50**
ISBN 0-89232-108-3   **293 pages**   **Individuals: $ 16.25**

Contents for Volume 2 continued

Belmont Abbey College. **Group Size and Contributions to Collective Action: An Examination of Olson's Theory Using Data from Zero Population Growth, Inc.,** *Harriet Tillock, Saginaw Valley State College and Denton E. Morrison, Michigan State University.* **"Just a Few Years Seem Like a Lifetime": A Role Theory Approach to Participation in Religious Movements,** *David G. Bromley and Anson D. Shupe, Jr., University of Texas-Arlington.* **Strains and Facilities in the Interpretation of an African Prophet Movement,** *Robert Cameron Mitchell, Pennsylvania State University.* **Ethnic Environment and Modernity: Reexamining the Role of Tradition in Development,** *Chava Nachmias, University of Wisconsin-Madison and Ezra Sadan, Hebrew University.* **Power-Dependence Relations in the World System,** *Larry Diamond, Stanford University.* **Ethnic Separatism and World Development,** *Elise Boulding, University of Colorado.* **Author/Subject Index.**

Volume 4.   Fall 1981   Cloth   Institutions: $ 32.50
ISBN 0-89232-201-2   Ca. 350 pages   Individuals: $ 16.25

CONTENTS: Introduction, *Louis Kriesberg.* **Collective Behavior and Resource Mobilization as Approaches to Social Movements: Issues and Continuities,** *Ralph Turner.* **Understanding Opposition to the Environmental Movement: The Importance of Dominant American Values,** *Riley E. Dunlap.* **Repression of Religious Cults,** *David G. Bromley and Anson D. Shupe, Jr.* **Comparative Perspectives on Industrial Conflict,** *Lillian J. Christman, William R. Kelly and Omer R. Galle.* **Capitalists vs. the Unions: An Analysis of Business Contributions to a "Right-to-Work" Election Campaign,** *Richard E. Ratcliff.* **Class Struggle, State Policy and the Rationalization of Production,** *Rhonda Levine and James A. Geschwender.* **The Miami Riots of 1980,** *Robert A. Ladner and Loretta S. Titterud.* **Welsh Nationalism in Context,** *Charles Ragin and Ted Davies.* **Social Change,** *J.W. Freiberg.* **Sponsorship in Refugee Resettlement,** *William T. Liu.* **Imperialism: Theoretical Questions on Transnationals, Technology, Culture and the State,** *James Cockcroft.* **Social Movements and Social Movements and Social Change: Reflexivity and Openness,** *Joseph R. Gusfield.*

(Ai) JAI PRESS INC., P.O. Box 1678, 165 West Putnam Avenue, Greenwich, Connecticut 06830.

Telephone: 203-661-7602   Cable Address: JAIPUBL

Research in Race and Ethnic Relations

A Research Annual

Series Editors: **Cora Bagley Marrett**
University of Wisconsin — Madison
Cheryl B. Leggon
University of Chicago

The contributions to this series consist of original research papers from an international community of specialists on race and ethnic relations. The purpose of the series is to explore recent theoretical and empirical developments in the field. Each volume will be organized around a particular theme. The first volume is focused on efforts to link specific empirical questions with broader theoretical issues. Specifically, the contributors present theoretical perspectives they have found useful in their own work, discuss the state of their work using such perspectives, and outline the kinds of additional research they deem essential for building the given theories or frameworks.

> **INSTITUTIONAL STANDING ORDERS** *will be granted a 10% discount and be filled automatically upon publication. Please indicate initial volume of standing order*
> **INDIVIDUAL ORDERS** *must be prepaid by personal check or credit card. Please include $1.50 per volume for postage and handling.*
> **Please encourage your library to subscribe to this series.**

JAI PRESS INC., P.O. Box 1678, 165 West Putnam Avenue, Greenwich, Connecticut 06830.

Telephone: 203-661-7602   **Cable Address: JAIPUBL**

Research in Social Problems and Public Policy

A Research Annual

Series Editor: **Michael Lewis**
Department of Sociology
University of Massachusetts
— Amherst

Volume 1.	Published 1979	Institutions: $ 30.00
ISBN 0-89232-068-0	224 pages	Individuals: $ 15.00

CONTENTS: **Preface,** Michael Lewis. **The Limits of Deinstitutionalization,** Bernard Beck, Northwestern University. **Small Winnings: Blue Collar Students in College and at Work,** Eve Spangler, American Bar Foundation. **Controlling Ourselves: Deviant Behavior in Social Science Research,** Myron Glazer, Smith College. **Models of the Decision to Conserve,** Robert K. Leik and Anita Sue Kolman, University of Minnesota. **Adoption in America: An Examination of Traditional and Innovative Schemes,** Howard Altstein, University of Maryland-Baltimore and Rita Simon, University of Illinois. **'The Race Relations Industry' as a Sensitizing Concept,** Lewis M. Killian, University of Massachusetts. **Affluence, Contentment and Resistance to Feminism: The Case of the Corporate Gypsies,** Margaret L. Andersen, University of Delaware. **Drift and Definitional Expansion: Toward the Hypothesis of Race-Specific Etiologies in the Theory of Criminal Deviance,** Michael Lewis and Anthony Harris, University of Massachusetts. **Crowding and Slums: A Statistical Exploration,** Harvey M. Choldin, University of Illinois. **Issues in Combining Social Action with Planning: The Case of Advocacy Planning,** Rosalie G. Genovese, Brockport-Cornell Management Studies Program and St. John Fisher College, Rochester.

Volume 2.	April 1981	Cloth	Institution: $ 30.00
ISBN 0-89232-195-4	Ca. 250 pages		Individuals: $ 15.00

CONTENTS: **The Emergence of Problem-Solving Professions: The Case of the Alcoholism Industry,** Joseph R. Gusfield, University of California-San Diego. **Normative Boundaries and Abortion Policy: The Politics of Morality,** Stephen L. Markson, University of Hartford. **Selection Processes in State Mental Hospitalization: Policy Issues and Research Directions,** Joseph P. Morrisey, State University of New York-Albany and Richard C. Tessler, University of Massachusetts-Amherst. **Other Things are Not Equal: Redirecting Equity Research on Deviance Processing,** Gary D. Hill, Southwestern University. **Women, Ecology and Social Policy,** Sylvia F. Fava, City University of New York. **Fan Violence: An American Social Problem,** Jerry M. Lewis, Kent State University. **The Political Economy of International Health: Focus on the Capitalist World System,** Ray H. Elling, University of Connecticut Medical Center. **Work: A Field Report from the Construction Industry,** Robert M. Cook, United Iron Workers Union. **Community Mental Health: A Perspective on the Role of Psychiatry,** Stanford Bloomberg. **The Welfare Response to Black Americans: History and Projection,** Michael Lewis, University of Massachusetts-Amherst.

INSTITUTIONAL STANDING ORDERS will be granted a 10% discount and be filled automatically upon publication. Please indicate initial volume of standing order
INDIVIDUAL ORDERS must be prepaid by personal check or credit card. Please include $1.50 per volume for postage and handling.
Please encourage your library to subscribe to this series.

JAI PRESS INC., P.O. Box 1678, 165 West Putnam Avenue, Greenwich, Connecticut 06830.

Telephone: 203-661-7602   Cable Address: JAIPUBL